THE
BACK STAGE®
GUIDE TO

THE
BACK STAGE GUIDE TO

ROBERT VIAGAS

Back Stage Books

New York

Senior Editor: Mark Glubke
Project Editor: Ross Plotkin
Design: Jay Anning, Thumb Print
Production Manager: Hector Campbell

First published in 2004 by Back Stage Books, an imprint of
Watson-Guptill Publications, a division of VNU Business Media, Inc.,
770 Broadway, New York, NY 10003
www.wgpub.com

Library of Congress Control Number: 2004108940

ISBN: 0-8230-8809-X

All photos courtesy of Ray Venezia

Manufactured in the United States of America

First printing 2004

1 2 3 4 5 6 7 8 9 / 11 10 09 08 07 06 05 04

For my sons, Benjamin and Nicholas

Acknowledgements

Special thanks to Louis Botto, Peter Filichia, Poppy Holmes, Andrew McGibbon, Ben Pesner, Ross Plotkin, Ray Romano, Catherine Ryan, Ray Venezia, Keith Viagas, Lillian Viagas, and Mark Glubke in the preparation, researching, and editing of this book.

CONTENTS

HOW TO USE THIS BOOK

Did you ever wish you had a friend who worked on Broadway who could tell you all the best shows, all the ways to save money (especially on tickets), how to get into insider events, great places to eat and great places to stay?

Well, now you do.

Consider this book your friend in the biz.

Anything you want to know about, or are unsure about, just crack this baby open, and you'll find it. The chapters are arranged more or less in the order of the process of planning a trip to the theatre, from picking the show and buying the tickets, to planning a meal and making sightseeing side trips. There's a map to help you get around, walking tours to see all the most significant sights, and even a glossary of terms so you can understand what insiders are talking about . . . and maybe sound like one yourself!

I have been fielding theatregoers' questions about Broadway since I began writing a column for my local newspaper when I was a teenager in the 1970s. Things really got busy for me when the old Prodigy online service appointed me Theatre Expert (my favorite official title ever) in 1989, and after I started Playbill On-Line in 1994. I've saved the hundreds of questions received and answers given since that time, and used them as the inspiration for this book.

I'm still gathering them. Send your questions to me at rviagas@backstage.com. I'll answer as many as I can.

CHAPTER ONE

A LITTLE HISTORY

Broadway has had a long and glorious history, filled with great art, great artists and a tremendous amount of drama, both on stage and off. Here's brief history of Broadway and a thumbnail guide to the most important shows, names and trends.

BEFORE 1866

There were theatres in New York almost from its founding. Maps show a theatre on John Street near Broadway in the first decades of the 18th century. The city soon attracted visiting performers from Europe, mainly England.

It was the era of the great actor/managers—directors were a future development—and the city saw visits from the likes of David Garrick and Edmund Forrest and, later, the American-born performers like the Booth brothers. Today's Booth Theatre is named for Edmund Booth, brother of Lincoln's assassin John Wilkes Booth, who also had a career as an actor.

Very popular at this time were the great touring minstrel shows, performed mainly by white actors in blackface, pretending to show-case the humor, music, and dancing styles of the plantation.

Barnum founded his circus in these days, catering to the public taste for the amazing and exotic. The legitimate stage survived on a diet of Shakespeare, who enjoyed a vogue in this period, often in doctored productions with the naughty bits left out and happy endings grafted onto the tragedies. Audiences nevertheless loved melodrama, often bloody and sensationalistic, and "toe-dancing" or ballet, the latter usually imported from Europe. People appreciated the artistic value of the dance. The fact that the ballet costumes revealed hitherto hidden details of the female form was not overlooked.

It was melodrama and ballet that collided to transform Broadway into what we know it today.

1866–1900

In 1866 the producers of a French ballet company lost their booking, and approached theatrical manager William Wheatley to see if its roomy Niblo's Garden theatre, at Broadway and Prince Street was available. Wheatley had already booked Niblo's with Charles M. Barras' melodrama, *The Black Crook*, about a fiend who delivers souls to the devil. The show employed several songs popular at the time.

Both shows were potential money-makers, so Wheatley got one of those bright 19th century ideas that went down in American legend. In this pre-Equity, pre-Dramatists Guild era, he simply decided to incorporate the ballet dancers into the story of *The Black Crook*. The melodrama would proceed normally, then, wherever he could find an excuse to bring in a dancing chorus, on came the ballerinas—nearly a hundred of them, memorably attired in skin-colored tights, playing the inhabitants of Fairyland. The opening night, Sept. 12, 1866, ran more than five hours. Tickets ranged in price from five cents to a stunning $1.50.

Was it a patchwork that really made no sense? Yes. Did the public love it anyway and flock to various incarnations of it for years and did it inspire numerous imitators? Yes, yes, and oh yes.

The Broadway musical was born. Sort of. But a lot had to happen to musicals before they were ready to produce *Oklahoma!*, *A Chorus Line*, and *The Producers*.

In England, the team of W.S. Gilbert and Arthur Sullivan brought a verbal and musical wit to the form known as operetta, which was growing out of comic opera. Shows like *H.M.S. Pinafore*, *The Mikado*, and *Patience* were as popular in the U.S. as in London—often through pirated and abridged versions. Partly to help trump these stolen productions, Gilbert & Sullivan debuted their *Pirates of Penzance* in New York.

It was the age of spectacle with producers struggling to outdo one another with sensational stage effects like burning buildings, chariot races, animal stampedes, and the like. In one production an army was shown marching into a giant pool of water, apparently to drown. During these years the theatre district, which had clustered around the 14th Street Union Square area, began growing north along Broadway, to Madison Square (where the first Madison Square Garden was located), then up through the 20s to Herald Square at 34th Street. In 1884, the first Playbill was printed, to serve a theatre on 21st Street.

Downtown, Ned Harrigan and Tony Hart put on a series of musical plays using broad ethnic humor to illustrate the ordinary lives of fellow immigrants struggling to make their way in America. Their Mulligan Guards characters were hugely popular with working class audiences, showing that you didn't have to be kings and queens of faraway countries to be entertaining characters on the stage.

The sheer inventive virtuosity of American talent gave rise to a form of theatre known as variety or vaudeville: individual comedy, dancing, singing, animal and "specialty" acts presented together on a single bill that repeated several times a day. Audiences liked theatre to be big, colorful and simple. Tragedies were woeful, preferably with a lot of blood and wailing. They like their comedies hilarious, with lots of knockabout physical humor.

But changes were starting to arrive with the ships from Europe. Playwrights like Ibsen, Strindberg, Chekhov and Shaw were employing a new realism and subtlety in their drama. Oscar Wilde showed how witty and intelligent comedy could be. A generation of actresses including Elenora Duse and Ellen Terry found a new acting vocabulary to interpret these works, and there was even a new way to see them: electric light was gradually replacing the dangerous gaslight lamps and burning lime used to illuminate the stage. The reason there are so few theatres surviving from before this time is that so many of them burned to the ground. The oldest existing Broadway theatres today were built in 1903.

But the building of one theatre in 1895 was a harbinger of the future. Entrepreneur Oscar Hammerstein (grandfather of the lyricist of the same name) chose the blacksmith district of Long Acre Square as the spot to put up his no-expenses-spared Olympia Music Hall. It took up the entire east side of the block of Broadway between 44th and 45th Street, today the site of a huge Toys 'R' Us store. An immediate hit, the Olympia attracted other showmen to build theatres in the neighborhood and, in 1904, *The New York Times*, built its newsroom and printing plant at 43rd and Broadway, eventually giving the plaza a new name: Times Square.

It was the beginning of a new era in theatre.

1900–1929

Broadway experienced explosive growth during these years—the adolescence of American Theatre. All but a handful of the Broadway theatres operating today were built during this time, and a typically American theatre began to find its voice.

L. Frank Baum adapted his own *The Wizard of Oz* as an operetta within a year of its publication as a book, and it was a sensation, inspiring imitators like *Babes in Toyland*. It was the golden age of operettas, written by masters like Victor Herbert, Franz Lehar, Rudolf Friml and Sigmund Romberg. Long-running hits included *The Merry Widow, The Desert Song, Rose-Marie, The New Moon, The Red Mill*, and *Blossom Time*.

Jerome Kern, Irving Berlin and George M. Cohan preferred a lighter touch creating scores that were less operatic and drew more on American musical forms, particularly in a series of intimate musicals Kern co-wrote for the Princess Theatre, starting in the 1910s.

The best songwriters of both schools were drafted for a new project. Starting in 1907, producer Florenz Ziegfeld mounted an annual variety show, inspired by the Folies Bergere of Paris, but with the name anglicized as the *Follies*. Produced annually through the end of the 1920s, the *Ziegfeld Follies* became known for the best in music, comedy, sets, costumes—and pulchritude. Ziegfeld cherry-picked the best talent from Broadway and vaudeville, creating an artistic home for the likes of Eddie Cantor, Fanny Brice, W.C. Fields, Ed Wynn, Will Rogers, Bert Williams, and even the conjoined Hilton sisters, Daisy and Violet.

Often, these were acts that "played the Palace," that is, the Palace Theatre, crown jewel of the B.F. Keith Circuit, which competed with the Orpheum Circuit and other chains of vaudeville theatre that thrived for most of this period.

Ziegfeld brought together Kern and lyricist Oscar Hammerstein II to write *Show Boat* (1927), the earliest musical still revived regularly today.

But Ziegfeld wasn't the only presenter of talent. Follies imitators cropped up left and right, and many did a creditable job, including Earl Carroll's *Vanities*, George White's *Scandals*, plus *Artists and Models*, *The Littlest Revue*, and *Charlot's Revue*, not to mention the *Greenwich Village Follies*. Al Jolson, the Marx Brothers, the Ritz Brothers, Fred and Adele Astaire, Marilyn Miller, Mae West, and Ethel Merman also rose to stardom during these years.

Many songwriting teams later to gain fame began writing during this period: the Gershwin brothers started working together; Richard Rodgers hooked up with Lorenz Hart; DeSylva, Brown, and Henderson began their collaborations, Cole Porter arrived from Yale to begin a long and distinguished career, and Vincent Youmans launched a bright, short career.

All these songwriters competing, collaborating and listening to one another gave birth to what's thought of as the Broadway musical "sound" created by classically-trained writers trying to sound "pop," and pop-trained writers trying to sound classical. Broadway music is at its best when you can feel the tension between the two.

American drama came of age as well, with Eugene O'Neill leading the way with dramas with majestic titles like *Beyond the Horizon*, *Desire under the Elms*, *The Great God Brown* and *Strange Interlude*. Elmer Rice, Sidney Howard, Marc Connelly and Edna Ferber are just a few of the writers who moved playwriting to a new level. Many were helped by theatrical cooperatives like The Theatre Guild and, later, The Group Theatre. Actors began to unionize, too. A successful strike in 1919 established the authority of Actors' Equity Association as the actors' union.

All this activity was chronicled in 15 daily newspapers, plus many magazines like Theatre Arts and the brand-new New Yorker, many of whose wittiest writers found themselves dining with playwrights and actors at the Algonquin Hotel on 43rd Street, a group that came to be known as the Algonquin Round Table.

And Broadway also reached its high-tide of production activity. The year 1927 saw two hundred and sixty four shows open on Broadway (versus thirty to forty a year in recent seasons). Seven shows opened on Christmas Day alone.

But the economic bubble of the 1920s was about to burst, and take a big hunk of Broadway along with it.

1929–1942

The advent of the Great Depression affected every corner of the theatre. Production activity fell by half. This doomed many of the less commercial theatres. All but one of the Broadway theatres operating along the old Rialto (Broadway between 34th and 42nd streets) went out of business and were demolished, many to become parking lots. Nearly all the theatres along 42nd Street converted to showing films.

Vaudeville, which had been declining in the 20s since the advent of radio and movies, died in the early years of the Depression. The Keith and Orpheum vaudeville circuits ended their rivalry and joined to become Radio-Keith-Orpheum (RKO), running the very businesses that had killed vaudeville. They converted most of their old vaudeville theatres across America to cinemas, many of which survive today, though sliced up into multiplexes. Vaudeville performers also dispersed into Broadway and these media, enriching them for the next generation.

It was also a very political period. Many educated theatre folk thought the end of capitalism was near, and either joined the Communist Party, or socialized with those who did, paving the way for the anti-Communist McCarthy hearings of the 1950s. Many dramas and musicals of the era reflected this political sensibility, notably those by Clifford Odets and Marc Blitzstein.

For all the economic desperation, many careers flourished during this period, notably those of George S. Kaufman, Moss Hart, Harold

LONGEST AND SHORTEST RUNS

The longest-running show in Broadway history was *Cats*, which totaled 7,485 performances between October 7, 1982 and September 10, 2000.

Many shows have run just one performance, most recently *The Oldest Living Confederate Widow Tells All*, in fall 2003.

Runners-up for Broadway's longest-running shows are *The Phantom of the Opera*, *Les Misérables*, and *A Chorus Line*. *Phantom* is on track to overtake *Cats* in January 2006—if it's still running.

At 17,162 performances, *The Fantasticks* stands as the longest-running Off-Broadway show. It opened on May 3, 1960 at a cost of $13,500—less than some contemporary musicals spend on shoes. It closed January 13, 2002.

Arlen, E.Y. "Yip" Harburg, Lillian Hellman, Ethel Merman, William Gaxton, Robert E. Sherwood, Maxwell Anderson, Rodgers & Hart, Cole Porter, many of whom also defected for a time to Hollywood where work was plentiful and well-paid.

Few shows achieved long runs during the 1930s, but it was a very creative and vital time.

1942–1964

This was the era when giants strode down Broadway.

Commonly considered the golden age of American theatre, this twenty-two-year period began with the opening of Oklahoma!, the first collaboration between Richard Rodgers and Oscar Hammerstein. They inspired some of their older colleagues like Irving Berlin and Cole Porter to write more challenging and integrated work like *Annie Get Your Gun* and *Kiss Me, Kate*, respectively, and they continued to top themselves with *Carousel, South Pacific, The King and I, Flower Drum Song*, and *The Sound of Music*.

Other major writers and shows from this era included Lerner & Loewe (*My Fair Lady, Camelot, Brigadoon*); Frank Loesser (*Guys and Dolls, How To Succeed in Business Without Really Trying*); Jule Styne (*Funny Girl, Peter Pan, Gypsy*); Kurt Weill (*Lady in the Dark, Lost in the Stars*); Leonard Bernstein (*West Side Story, On the Town, Wonderful Town*); and Comden & Green, to name just a golden handful.

It was also a great era of choreographers like Agnes de Mille, Gower Champion, Michael Kidd, Onna White and the early Bob Fosse. And stars like Gwen Verdon, Julie Andrews, Mary Martin, Judy Holiday, Rex Harrison, Yul Brynner, Carol Channing and Alfred Drake.

And those are just from the musicals. These same years saw the germination and flower of the careers of Arthur Miller (*Death of a Salesman, The Crucible*), Tennessee Williams (*Streetcar Named Desire, The Glass Menagerie*), along with Thornton Wilder, William Inge, Lindsay & Crouse, and many more. The Actors Studio took up the teachings of Stanislavky as interpreted by Lee Strasberg, and a hyper-naturalistic new acting style was developed to give life to many of these plays, referred to as "The Method."

Shelves of books have been written on this period, and it's impossible to do it justice in a few paragraphs. Perhaps at no other time was the mind of American society and the concerns of the commercial theatre so acutely in tune.

Luckily, succeeding generations have acknowledged the power of the plays and musicals from this period, and they form a major portion of Broadway revivals to this day.

Most of these shows originated in un-miked and un-air conditioned theatres. But technology began to change during this period, too. With the advent of air conditioning, shows could attract an audience through the summer. Where once 300 performances was considered a long run, now shows began to survive through the summer to reach the year mark (416 performances), and continue even longer.

In addition to all the action on Broadway, a revolution began to brew in the theatres of Greenwich Village, a smaller and more personal, less commercial type of theatre, soon dubbed Off-Broadway. By the late 1950s Joe Cino had begun offering readings and then staged shows at his Café Cino. Circle in the Square began offering training to playwrights whose visions were too outré for Broadway. *The Fantasticks* opened at the Sullivan Street Playhouse using innovative techniques borrowed from an Italian experimental troupe, and settled in for a run of nearly forty-two years. It was also during this period that Joseph Papp's traveling theatre truck broke down in Central Park, prompting the first free Shakespeare performances there. Later ensconced in the Delacorte Theatre in the park, and the Public Theater in the Village, the New York Shakespeare Festival began to revolutionize American theatre.

A lot happened uptown and downtown, and restoring the power of that era remains Broadway's holy grail.

1964–1975

TV, political polarization and the rock revolution began to take their toll in the mid 1960s. Things began to dry up.

Cole Porter and Oscar Hammerstein passed away, Lerner & Loewe stopped working together, Irving Berlin retired, Arthur Miller and Tennessee Williams seemed to have their best years behind them. Moreover, with the boom in electronic media, live theatre began to seem passé. The city also saw many of its daily newspapers merge or fold, until finally only three were left: The *Times*, the *News*, and the *Post*. This concentrated power in the hands of ever fewer critics.

More and more, theatregoers would pass beneath marquees that said "See a Show Just for the Fun of It!," which became a depressing reminder that the theatre behind it was empty. The raffish Times Square area began to become downright seedy.

This was also an era when many of those empty theatres were demolished to make way for parking lots, skyscrapers and other anonymous uses. Even among those that survived as cinemas, especially those lining the onetime acropolis of Broadway, West 42nd Street, many were converted to pornographic film houses, and the image of the creepy man sitting down front in a raincoat began to replace the glamorous images of old.

Which is not to say that a lot of great shows didn't open during these years. There was *Fiddler on the Roof, Man of La Mancha, Cabaret, Company, Follies, A Little Night Music, Promises, Promises,*

OLDEST AND NEWEST THEATRES

The oldest Broadway theatre still in operation is Disney's New Amsterdam Theatre on West 42nd Street, which opened October 26, 1903, but was used for decades as a cinema. Portions of the Lyric Theatre, which opened right across the street from the New Amsterdam on October 12, 1903, were incorporated into the Ford Center for the Performing Arts when the new theatre was built in 1997–98. The Ford Center, which opened with *Ragtime* January 18, 1998, is also Broadway's newest theatre.

The Lyceum Theatre, which opened, November 2, 1903, just days after the previous two, is the oldest continuously used Broadway theatre.

and many productions shepherded by producer David Merrick. It was a golden age for Stephen Sondheim, Bob Fosse and Kander and Ebb.

But it was a tough time for drama on Broadway. From 1963 to 1969, the Pulitzer Prize committee decided in four of those seven years that no play was worthy of the award, so none was given.

By a sad coincidence, William Goldman's landmark book *The Season*, happened to chronicle one of the worst seasons Broadway ever had, 1967-68, which, while brilliantly written, further exposed Broadway's decline.

The news was far better just forty blocks south. Off-Broadway, which had been born in the 1950s, came to full flower in the 1960s. It was the golden age of The New York Shakespeare Festival (which helped Broadway with transfers of *Hair* and *Two Gentlemen of Verona*), La MaMa Experimental Theatre Company, Café Cino, and dozens of other companies that sprang up, offering the kind of bold and trailblazing fare that Broadway was too timid or slow-moving to accept.

The late 1960s saw the Stonewall riot and the opening of plays like *The Boys in the Band* and *The Staircase*, which brought the hitherto forbidden topic of homosexuality out of the closet.

Playwrights like Sam Shepard, Lanford Wilson, Edward Albee, Jack Gelber, Robert Wilson, Richard Foreman and many more began to get produced and noticed, and their success would send ripples out into the theatrical world, giving energy to regional theatres, many of which were founded in the 1960s, and eventually to Broadway as well.

But for the time being, Broadway began to look like it was going to go the way of vaudeville and burlesque, into the history books.

And then, in 1975, a show opened that began the process of rejuvenating Broadway: *A Chorus Line*, which originated at Joseph Papp's New York Shakespeare Festival. Directed and choreographed by Michael Bennett, this backstage story about a group of chorus dancers auditioning for an unnamed musical told a compelling story with interesting, youthful characters. The music by Marvin Hamlisch and lyrics by Ed Kleban, sounded anything but fusty and wandered unselfconsiously back and forth between a pop and Broadway sound.

It was a blazing hot ticket, put Broadway back on the front pages of newspapers and news magazines, eventually became the longest-running show in Broadway history (sixteen years; later exceeded by *Cats*), and provided employment to a whole generation of young dancers.

It also had the secondary effect of convincing producers, writers, investors and media folk that Broadway was still capable of producing hits. Producers began to take chances again, resulting in an era of recovery. These were boom times for Joseph Papp, founder of The New York Shakespeare Festival, which became a major producing force Off-Broadway.

People began to realize that Broadway was not, after all, going to fade away like vaudeville, but would remain a part of the entertainment landscape. In an era when electronic media became triumphant, people began to appreciate the uniqueness of the live entertainment experience.

The emblematic producer of the era was Brit Cameron Mackintosh, who became the most successful stage producer in history presenting a series of grand-scale operatic musicals by Andrew Lloyd Webber and the team of Alain Boublil and Claude-Michel Schonberg. During these years, Mackintosh presented four of the biggest hits ever: *Cats*, *Les Miserables*, *The Phantom of the Opera*, and *Miss Saigon*, all of which debuted in London, transplanted to Broadway, and toured worldwide. Mackintosh pioneered the branding of shows, making, for example, the *Cats* you saw in New York virtually identical to the one you saw in London or Toronto or Sydney. All had decade-plus runs, provided employment to thousands of actors, pleasure to millions of theatregoers, and the riches of Midas to Mackintosh.

His shows had the effect of revitalizing The Road, the chains of musical-sized theatres across North America that had been starved for saleable proven hits. They also returned every few years to take advantage of repeat business and word-of-mouth.

His success also negated the old conventional wisdom that the English could not write musicals as well as Americans. American musical writers were in something of an eclipse during this period. There was one exception: Stephen Sondheim, who delivered his masterpiece, *Sweeney Todd: The Demon Barber of Fleet Street* in 1979, and had varying degrees of financial success (though nearly always critical raves) for *Into the Woods, Pacific Overtures, Merrily We Roll Along, Assassins,* and *Passion.* Sondheim's contemporaries like Cy Coleman (*City of Angels, The Will Rogers Follies*) and Kander & Ebb (*Woman of the Year, Chicago, Kiss of the Spider Woman*) continued to produce interesting shows. But Sondheim was so admired by younger writers that they either tried (unsuccessfully) to imitate him or abandoned writing altogether.

Other important developments:

- The growth of technology. The use of microphones and computerized sound and light boards became widespread. Box offices began to accept credit cards and telephone sales.

- The regional theatre movement, which had been born in the 1960s, flowered, with major works coming from theatres like the Goodman and Steppenwolf in Chicago, the Mark Taper Forum in Los Angeles, Long Wharf and Yale Rep in New England, the Alliance in Atlanta, the Alley Theatre in Texas, the Actors Theatre of Louisville in Kentucky, and many more.

- Playwrights who had been nurtured Off-Broadway in the 1960s and early 1970s also became more mainstream in the 1980s, including David Mamet, Lanford Wilson, Beth Henley, Christopher Durang and Wendy Wasserstein. August Wilson also began his massive cycle of ten dramas about African-American life in the 20th century, winning Pulitzer Prizes for *Fences* and *The Piano Lesson.* After many years in the critical wilderness (at least in the U.S.), Edward Albee became popular again in the early 1990s, winning a Pulitzer for *Three Tall Women,* and, later, a Tony for *The Goat, Or Who Is Sylvia?*

- Revivals, which had been comparatively rare in previous years, became a big business. The pace of revivals came to challenge the creation of new work. There were two schools of though on this. It was bad, because it created a backward-looking mindset. It was good, because it introduced younger audiences to the great productions of the past that they otherwise wouldn't get to see.

1996–PRESENT

The latest chapter in Broadway history began in the year 1996, when two events signaled that things weren't going to be the same anymore. The year began with a terrible tragedy, but a dramatic one: the death of composer Jonathan Larson the night before his musical *Rent,* based on *La Bohéme,* began Off-Broadway previews.

Rent itself went on to win both the Tony as Best Musical and the Pulitzer Prize for Drama. But, more than that, it attracted a young and devoted following. Part of this was owing to the youth-related subject matter and alt-rock score, and part to the policy of offering the two front rows at a bargain-basement price at every performance. The audience cultivated by *Rent* stayed in touch via the show's website, www.siteforrent.com, and other online forums, and has continued to make its presence felt.

The second formative event of the year 1996 was *Bring in'da Noise, Bring in 'da Funk*, Savion Glover's vision of black history in America told entirely through dance. It didn't fit neatly into musical theatre categories, opening the door for theatrical experimentation on Broadway that had previously percolated only Off-Off-Broadway and in innovative resident and university theatres.

This younger, more experimental, more plugged-in theatre crowd hasn't yet taken over Broadway, but has continued to affect the kind of shows being created today. They are served by a younger crop of producers like Jeffrey Seller, younger directors like Susan Stroman, etc.

Other recent developments:

- The renaissance of 42nd Street. Through a coordinated effort by government (especially Mayor Rudolph Giuliani), private industry (especially Disney) and quasi-governmental organizations (especially New 42nd Street), drugs and pornography were driven from the block between Seventh and Eighth Avenues. Many of the old Broadway theatres were refurbished (most notably the New Amsterdam Theatre) and a new one built (the Ford Center). The opening of The New Victory Theatre for children and Disney's popular *The Lion King* within a few months of each other, signaled that 42nd Street had transformed from hardcore adult fare to a kids' oasis seemingly overnight. New laws, stricter enforcement, and a real estate boom in the Times Square area helped, though some miss the area's raffish personality.

- The growth of the internet as a support system for Broadway. Through website like Playbill.com, TalkinBroadway.com, and usegroups like rec.arts.musicals, the audience found a collective way to get and share information and opinions about shows. The Frank Wildhorn musical *Jekyll & Hyde* was sustained first during the show's long tryout tour, and then throughout its Broadway run by a group of fans calling themselves "Jekkies." By the turn of the century, nearly every actor of note had a personal website and a devoted coterie of electronic fans. Virtually unknown in 1997, when *Jekyll & Hyde* opened, online ticket sales accounted for 14.1 percent of all such sales by 2002-03.

- One remarkable sign of change was the complete absence during this period of any new Broadway musical by 1980s titans Stephen Sondheim, Andrew Lloyd Webber or Boublil and Schonberg.

Younger writers, directors, choreographers, producers and other creative talent came to the fore.

- In their absence, younger writers began to produce a postmodern sort of musical. Some of the writers had three names: Michael John La Chiusa (*Hello Again, The Wild Party*), Ricky Ian Gordon (*Dream True, My Life with Albertine*). Some had two: Adam Guettel (*Floyd Collins*), Jeanine Tesori (*Violet; Thoroughly Modern Millie; Caroline, or Change*), Andrew Lippa, and William Finn (*Falsettos, A New Brain*). But only Tesori and Finn were able to write Broadway hits.

- Younger playwrights came to the fore, including Tony Kushner (*Angels in America*, actually 1993 and '94), Richard Greenberg (*Take Me Out*), David Auburn (*Proof*), Margaret Edson (*Wit*), Nilo Cruz (*Anna in the Tropics*), Neil LaBute (*The Shape of Things, The Mercy Seat*).

- Actress and comedian Rosie O'Donnell started a syndicated talk show that regularly showcased Broadway shows and personalities, helping to make a mass audience aware of the theatre, especially musicals. She eventually hosted three Tony Awards shows before leaving television to become a Broadway producer.

- Experimentation with boundary-crossing new forms led to a new Tony Award, Best Special Theatrical Event, instituted in 2001.

CELEBRITY DEBUTS

Marlon Brando made his Broadway debut playing one of the children in *I Remember Mama* (1944).

William Shatner, later to play "Star Trek's" intrepid Captain Kirk, made his Broadway debut speaking verse in a 1956 production of Christopher Marlowe's 16th century epic *Tamburlaine*. He played "Usumcasane, A Follower of Tamburlaine."

Movie star Kirk Douglas was first seen on Broadway as an Orderly in Katharine Cornell's 1942 revival of Chekhov's *Three Sisters*.

Latin heartthrob Ricky Martin first saw legitimate theatre limelight as a replacement Marius in Broadway's *Les Misérables*.

Film actor Richard Gere made his Broadway debut in a three-performance flop rock musical *Soon* (1971), and understudied the lead role of Danny Zuko in the original Broadway run of *Grease*.

- At the same time, there's also been a strong trend away from big operatic musicals and back toward musical comedy, pushed mainly by the thumping success of *The Producers* and *Hairspray*, and, to a lesser extent, *The Full Monty* and *Avenue Q*.
- But the distinction between rock musicals and just plain musicals became fuzzier and soon ceased to exist. Marc Shaiman's score to *Hairspray* was almost all rock, but no one called it a rock musical.

THE FUTURE

Well, what about it?

Broadway will continue to explore the tension between art and commerce, will continue to present a unique challenge to writers and entertainers, will continue to trade on the high-wire act that is live performing, will continue to cross traditional boundaries, will continue to be altered in subtle ways by advances in technology, and will continue to absorb influences from the culture around it.

And since theatre, as always, actually occurs in the hearts and minds of the audience, the future of Broadway will be made by you, the person reading this, by the simple act of going to see a show.

PICKING A SHOW

Some love Paris
And some Purdue
But love is an archer with a low IQ
A bold, bad bowman and innocent of pity.
So I'm in love with
New York City.

—PHYLLIS MCGINLEY

The dreaded words: "That stunk."

Few things are as disappointing as paying a whole lot of money for the privilege of sitting through something you hate. But even fewer things are as sweet as the thrill of seeing a great show that lifts you, heart and soul, right out of your seat.

There are no guarantees in life, but here are some tips on how to have the best chance to achieve that thrill—and avoid the "dreaded words." Step one is picking the kind of show you want to see. There are lots of choices, and when you look at a newspaper listing (called the "ABCs" for their outsize first letter) or a magazine directory, everything may sound tempting. But how to tell what's really great—and what's really lousy?

First, you have to know what you're looking for.

BROADWAY

There are two things in New York called Broadway. One is a street, one is an industry.

Broadway is said to be laid along the track of an old Indian path from the southern tip of Manhattan Island to the northern end. This Broadway was considered important enough to leave in place when the grid of numbered streets and avenues were laid out in the 19th century. It wanders diagonally in a sinuous line through that grid, crisscrossing the wide avenues and narrow streets at odd angles, and leaving both little triangular blocks and bowtie-shaped plazas. The plazas were perfect places for newspapers to back in their flatbeds full of newsprint rolls, and to send trucks full of printed papers racing out to newsstands. That's why two of the widest, Herald Square and Times Square, are named after newspapers.

Times Square occurs where Broadway crosses Seventh Avenue between 43rd Street and 47th Street. And here's where we get to the second thing called Broadway. It is the biggest and most visible part of the professional theatre industry in New York. Broadway takes its name from the street because, from nearly its earliest days in the 1730s, New York's major theatres have tended to cluster on or near Broadway. The first known theatre was near the southern point of Manhattan near what's now Battery Park. The center of theatrical activity moved north along Broadway as the city developed, reaching its current center at Times Square in the 1910s and 20s, about the time the city became fully built-up.

More Broadway history can be found in Chapter One.

"Broadway" has come to mean large-scale professional live theatre, using the top writers, actors, designers and directors. Splashy musicals, witty comedies, and dramas grappling with major themes provided some of the finest entertainment of the twentieth century, and seeded all other areas of the performing arts, particularly film, television, and popular music. But the ability of film and TV to show photo-realism broke Broadway's monopoly on naturalistic settings and dialogue. In the past fifty years, Broadway has fallen back on strengths that film and TV can't match: Its special ability to stretch the audience imagination in unique ways. Its ability to make the audience an active participant in a collective experience. And, most importantly, the high-wire-act quality of being live, right there in front of the audience.

Dance seems to come across better on stage than film, so there has been a great focus on dancing. Shows also have learned to embrace classic stage techniques. For example, *The Lion King* uses masks and puppets to create a world of the African savannah in the center of 42nd Street. Seen live, it works in a way that would never be accepted on TV. People have become so used to high-quality computer graphics that magical effects in movies and video games have become humdrum. However, on stage, knowing that the image can't be doctored, such magic reclaims its thrill.

If an actor puts a chair down on a stage and says, "I'm sitting in the cockpit of an F-14 fighter jet," audiences will imagine him in a fighter jet. In a film they'd demand to see such a jet, or a reasonable simulacrum. This willingness among audiences to wipe the dust off the imagination button gives Broadway shows a huge advantage. A new generation of theatre artists has figured out how to use this advantage skillfully.

They are called "plays" for a reason. Actors are grownups at play, putting on costumes and pretending to be heroes and villains and phantoms. Those in the audience are friends invited to join in the game. This is what you will get when you go to see a live show.

BROADWAY VS. OFF-BROADWAY VS. OFF-OFF-BROADWAY

There are three levels of live professional theatre in New York. Without getting into too much legal mumbo-jumbo (of which there is, rest assured, plenty) the location of the theatre is less important than size. The thirty-nine Broadway theatres have 499 seats or more, Off-Broadway theatres have 100 to 498 seats. Off-Off-Broadway theatres have 99 seats or fewer.

Most of the big musicals and dramas in New York play in the largest theatres in New York, which are on or near Broadway, mainly in the Times Square area. Of no less quality, though often smaller and more experimental in nature are the Off-Broadway shows, which play in smaller theatres that can be found in almost every corner of Manhattan, though mainly in Greenwich Village and near Union Square.

There are only four Broadway theatres that actually front on Broadway: the Minskoff at 45th Street, the Marquis at 46th Street, the Winter Garden at 50th Street, and the Broadway Theatre at 53rd Street. The rest are on side streets within a block or two of Broadway. In addition, the Vivian Beaumont Theatre is part of the Lincoln Center complex on Columbus Avenue where it crosses Broadway at 65th Street.

For the purposes of this book, the Broadway Theatre District is defined as a rectangle of midtown Manhattan bounded by West 41st Street, Eighth Avenue, West 55th Street and the Avenue of the Americas (Sixth Avenue), plus the blocks of 45th and 46th Streets between Eighth and Ninth Avenues. See Map.

However, Off-Broadway and Off-Off-Broadway theatres can be anywhere in New York—including Times Square itself, which has several of both these categories.

Off-Broadway earned its name in the 1950s not only for its distance from the Times Square theatre district (OB could then be found mainly in Greenwich Village, some forty blocks to the south), but also for offering more adventurous and experimental plays and musicals. To a great degree that's still the case, though as Off-Broadway has become more like a scale model of Broadway, an even smaller and more experimental theatre sprang up to challenge it, called Off-Off-Broadway. A more detailed description of Off-Broadway and Off-Off-Broadway can be found in Chapter Six.

TYPES OF SHOWS

For many years there were four types of Broadway shows: dramas, comedies, musicals, and revues.

Dramas are serious, non-singing plays dealing with significant ideas, themes or characters. There may be moments of humor, but overall the effect is more thoughtful, spiritual, or moving than comic. The essence of drama is conflict, and many of the best dramas show man grappling with great villains and gut issues. Many of Broadway's most important plays have been dramas, from *Death of a Salesman* and *A Streetcar Named Desire* to *A Long Day's Journey Into Night* and the more recent *Angels in America*, *The Piano Lesson*, and *Take Me Out*.

Comedies are plays that are designed primarily to evoke laughter.

As developed by the ancient Greeks, comedy and tragedy were distinguished primarily by how the main character—the "protagonist"—made out. The protagonist generally wanted something—a woman, a throne, victory in battle. If he overcame the forces arrayed against him and won his objective, his story was considered a comedy. If the forces defeated him, usually through his own overreaching hubris, it was a tragedy.

So much for the Greeks. To us, "comedy" has come to mean funny stuff. There's high comedy, comedy of manners, low comedy, black comedy and farce, but all are classed as comedy. Some of the most successful in Broadway history have been *Gemini, Harvey, Arsenic and Old Lace, The Man Who Came To Dinner, You Can't Take It With You, The Front Page,* and several by Neil Simon, including *Brighton Beach Memoirs, The Odd Couple,* and Pulitzer Prize-winner *Lost in Yonkers.* People love to laugh. If you do too, consider seeing a comedy.

Musicals are plays with music. Sometimes they're sung all the way through, like operas, but they often have considerable stretches of dialogue, and their music generally is affected more by jazz, big band, rock, and other popular styles. Musicals have main characters and stories (usually romantic), and most have dialogue scenes punctuated by songs and dances. At one time musicals were nearly all are comedic, and were called Musical Comedies. Classics of this kind are *Guys and Dolls, Oklahoma! , My Fair Lady, Hello, Dolly!,* and, more recently, *The Producers* and *Hairspray.*

There were musical dramas as far back as Show Boat in the 1920s, but shows like *West Side Story, Cabaret, Les Misérables,* and *Rent* showed that musicals could be quite serious, and still be very entertaining.

Revues are like musicals, but don't tell a story. Classics like the *Ziegfeld Follies, Hellzapoppin',* and *New Faces* had a series of comedy sketches, songs and specialty acts (like juggling) sometimes on a theme, or built around the work of a single historical period or personality. Once considered passé, revues have continued to have a life. Successful revues of the past thirty years include *Smokey Joe's Café, Dancin', Ain't Misbehavin', Jerome Robbins' Broadway, Sugar Babies,* and *Fosse.*

Don't confuse the word "revue" with a "review," which is an opinion of a show published in a newspaper, magazine or on the web. They are pronounced the same, but spelled differently.

In the last decade, the trend has been to blur the lines between these categories. Shows like *Def Poetry Jam, Bring in 'da Noise, Bring in 'da Funk,* and *Contact* defy or expand old-fashioned categories. There also has been a proliferation of **Solo Shows**, like *Elaine Stritch: At Liberty* and John Leguizamo's *Sexaholix . . . A Love Story* in which a star takes the stage for the entire evening, singing or dancing or speaking comic monologues.

In recognition of this, Broadway's annual Tony Awards in 2001 instituted a Tony Award for Special Theatrical Event. These shows are becoming increasingly popular.

WHAT DO YOU LIKE? WHAT DON'T YOU LIKE?

How is it possible to tell what you are going to like?

Start with your likes and dislikes. Maybe you think comedies are silly. Go for a drama.

Find dramas dull? Stick to comedies.

Some people hate musicals. Either avoid musicals, or pick a musical that has some qualities you like. They're not all one thing.

On the other hand, some people crave novelty. They want a show to take them on a journey they never expected. These are actually the best theatregoers, not just because they try a variety of things, but because they have the most satisfying experiences. Mind open, they go in saying to themselves, "I like what's good. I don't care what kind of show it is, as long as it's a good example of its kind."

SECOND ACTS

Lyricist Oscar Hammerstein II made his name for himself writing words to the music of Jerome Kern and others in a series of 1920s operettas, including *Rose-Marie*, *New Moon*, *Desert Song*, *Sunny*, and the epic *Show Boat*. But by the early 1940s, he appeared to be old and washed up, having written four flops in a row. However, matched with Richard Rodgers for the 1942 megahit *Oklahoma!*, his career was reborn. At that point, wary of hubris, he took out an ad in the trade paper *Variety* listing all his flops with the headline: "I did it before and I can do it again." His subsequent career included *South Pacific*, *The King and I*, *Carousel*, and *The Sound of Music*.

Composer Stephen Schwartz is another songwriter who came in from the cold. He had hit after hit in the 1970s—*Godspell*, *Pippin*, *Mass*, *The Magic Show*—but then nothing but flops from 1976 to 1995, when he wrote the lyrics to Disney's animated film musical *Pocahontas*. He returned to Broadway in 2003 with a new hit, *Wicked*, twenty-nine years after his last Broadway success.

But to make that kind of analysis, you need information. The mass media carry relatively little about Broadway. But there are several steady and reliable sources of information. And here's where to look:

GETTING INFORMATION ON SHOWS

You need two things to pick a show: fact and opinion. Despite the millions spent to advertise and report on Broadway, the bottom line remains that the best source of information is word of mouth. Ask friends and relatives, coworkers, and anyone else. Pick someone who goes a lot—someone who actually coughs up hard-earned cash for a show.

Try that guy down in accounting who sees everything. Or your Aunt Esther who goes with her temple sisterhood. The woman at the library who collects Playbills. Your brother-in-law with the expense account who's always entertaining clients. Your college roommate who makes a pilgrimage every summer and see five shows in one weekend. Your boss' wife who can afford to see everything. Your hairdresser.

They know what you like, you know what they like. They'll tell you, not only what the shows are about, but if they are worth seeing. They may not have seen everything, but they will have a sense of what's out there, and what you may like. You can even get a useful opinion from someone you think is an idiot: If they recommend a show, you know you'll hate it. That's useful information.

PUBLICATIONS

One drawback to word-of-mouth: very few people outside the theatre industry itself see and know about *everything* that's available. And fewer still can tell you what's coming down the road. For that, you must depend on the print, broadcast and web media. Here's a guide on how to use them with care and get the most out of them.

Even as the mass media have paid less and less attention to legitimate theatre, the number of informational outlets has exploded, largely thanks to the growth of the internet. But let's back up for a moment. The traditional source of Broadway information has been its newspapers and magazines. At one time New York had no fewer than fifteen dailies, each with its own phalanx of theatre reporters, gossips and critics. A columnist like Walter Winchell could grow so powerful that careers rose and fell at the stroke of his typewriter keys. The film and musical *Sweet Smell of Success* were based his exploits.

The number of general-interest dailies has shrunk to three: *The New York Times*, *The Daily News*, and *The New York Post*. The importance of suburban papers has grown, especially *Newsday* on Long Island, *The Record* and the *Star-Ledger* in New Jersey, and *The Journal News* in Westchester. But with a few exceptions, their coverage of all but the biggest stories consists of advance features and reviews. Features are interviews or essays, usually in the Weekend or Sunday editions. Reviews appear in the arts section of the papers on the morning after the opening night. Some papers print in the evenings, so they are available on Times Square newsstands by 11 PM or midnight. Many papers post the interviews on their websites as well, where they are archived and available throughout the run. More on internet news later.

Beyond the New York metropolitan area, *USA Today* also does features and reviews on the major productions, especially if they are star-driven, or are attended by scandal. Can you remember the controversies surrounding Rosie O'Donnell's musical *Taboo*? Can you remember any other theatre news from that time that got national coverage?

The New York Times*: Nevertheless, the *Times* is the paper producers want to be in. They prefer to make announcements of opening nights, stars, etc. in the *Times'* Friday theatre column, "On Stage and Off," which appears in the Weekend section from September to June. It's also considered a coup if the *Times* publishes a thoughtful piece in the weekly Arts & Leisure section the Sunday before opening night. These generally are discussions of what the play is about, interviews with the creator(s), illustrations of how the show fits into some trend, etc. Overall, however, the *Times* devotes significantly less space to breaking theatre news than it once did.

The *Times* is also the first paper critics grab on opening night to see what chief critic Ben Brantley thought of their show. Brantley doesn't have the cult-like following of his predecessors. He no longer has the power to kill every show outright, which must be a relief to all involved. But it is very difficult to run a show and become a hit without the *Times*. That remains a fact of Broadway life in the 21st century.

The *Times* also is known for its daily ABC grid of ads for Broadway and some Off-Broadway shows, though these no longer include ticket prices, which substantially diminishes their usefulness. More detailed listings appear on Friday and Sunday. Available on newsstands and in honor boxes on city street corners. Cost: $1. Web: www.newyorktimes.com (free, but registration required).

The New York Post*: The New York Times* no longer has a death grip on theatre news and commentary, but it is still way out in front in perceived importance. The runner-up is *The New York Post*, a tabloid-style paper with a strongly conservative outlook and a merry way with lurid crime stories and malicious celebrity gossip. Their crown jewel, from a theatrical standpoint, is columnist Michael Riedel who is heartily hated in the theatre business but religiously read. He treats theatre like any other news beat, somehow getting behind the scenes to report on backstage battles among stars, producers, directors and critics.

Very entertaining, though scarcely comprehensive. He leaves the reporting of consumer news to others, including fellow *Post* columnists, the syndicated Liz Smith and Cindy Adams. Not much in the way of listings, though. Cost: 25 cents in Manhattan, 25 or 50 cents elsewhere. Available at newsstands and in honor boxes. Website: www.nypost.com.

Brief descriptions of the longest-running shows, along with full ticket-ordering information, can also be found in Chapter Thirteen of this book.

Many others publications cover theatre news from time to time, and have listings of various detail and usefulness. Here are some of the best. Per-copy prices are considerably lower for subscribers:

Back Stage: The newspaper for working actors and actors who are looking for work. It's the best place to find casting calls for all manner of union and non-union acting work. There's also a considerable industry news section, and a wonderful section of reviews, often of Off-Off-Broadway shows that rarely get reviewed by the mainstream press. Available at newsstands. Website: www.backstage.com. Cost: $2.95.

New York: A glossy, weekly magazine targeted at wealthy Manhattanites. Acidic critic John Simon is widely read. The listings are pretty bare-bones, but cover more of Off-Broadway and Off-Off-Broadway than most competitors. Available at newsstands. Web: www.newyork-metro.com. Cost: $2.99.

The New Yorker: This upscale and intellectual weekly magazine has edged a little more mass and downmarket in recent years, but still retains some of the stardust from the long-gone Dorothy Parker years. Reviews tend to turn into essays (though still very much worth reading, usually). Listings have gotten thinner, and now include only shows that have opened recently. These contain the bare minimum of consumer information. But the capsule reviews still crackle. Available on newsstands. Web: www.newyorker.com. Cost: $3.95.

Theatrical Index: Weekly newsletter for journalists, producers and other theatre insiders. Detailed information on each Broadway, Off-Broadway and some regional shows, including names, addresses and phone numbers of producers, agents, company managers, etc. Has lots of great information on shows still in development. Distributed mainly by mail subscription, but can also be purchased at Drama Book Shop in Manhattan. Not available on newsstands. No website. Cost: $10.

Time Out: Originally published in Britain, this weekly magazine is a fat, entertaining guide to all of New York's nightlife, with the theatre info mixed in with movies, comedy, nightclubs, dance, etc. The listings (including ticket prices) pack a lot of information into a brief space, including capsule reviews of each show that give a little bit of their flavor. Available on newsstands. Website: www.timeoutny.com. Cost: $2.99.

Variety: Touted as the showbiz bible, this venerable publication (published in both daily and weekly editions) is a classic trade paper, written by and for people in the entertainment industry. The "Legitimate" section near the back has box office figures for all the Broadway shows, plus other business-related facts, figures and stories. Reports breaking news on business deals for shows in development. Cost: $1. Available on newsstands. Website: www.variety.com (subscription required).

The Village Voice: A tabloid newsprint weekly targeted at liberal residents of Greenwich Village, and people who wish they were. Once the final word on Off-Broadway and Off-Off-Broadway, it's now merely pretty good on the subject, at least as far as listings go. But critic Michael Feingold and a stable of freelancers still write the most knowledgeably about artists who make their careers below 14th Street. Available in honor boxes. Web: www.villagevoice.com. Cost: free.

All of these publications can be found in abundance in New York itself, and are available at newsstands across the city. However, if you don't have a subscription or if you live outside New York, keeping up on theatre news through these media can be a challenge.

Fortunately, day-to-day coverage of the theatre has shifted over the past ten years to the internet. As indicated above, many of these post all or part of their contents on their websites. However, there are some web-only sources that go into even more detail and are even more useful for folks trying to pick a show.

NEWS ON THE WEB

A recent industry survey found that more than 94 percent of ticket buyers have internet access. That may be either the cause or effect of the presence of about a half dozen large websites, and dozens of small ones, devoted to breaking news about Broadway.

Add to them the official websites of the various shows (listed in Chapter Thirteen), which are fonts of news and information, plus the fan sites for individual stars, and you have a gold mine of high-quality information available twenty-four hours a day from anywhere.

Playbill On-Line (www.Playbill.com): The first and still best of the theatre news websites. A staff of full-time and freelance reporters and columnists gets the most theatre news from the most places on a daily basis—not just in New York, but across North America and Great Britain, too. It has the most detailed and complete listings, right down to running times, number of intermissions and handicapped-access data. The Playbill Club offers daily discounts of ten percent or more on many shows. Aside from the breaking news of shows, stars, books, recordings, weekly box office figures (revealing which are the most popular shows), TV appearances, audio clips of interviews, Today in History, etc.—not to mention the entire contents of every Playbill program. Column highlights include Andrew Gans' "Diva Talk," Michael Buckley's "Channeling," Eric Grode's "Stage to Screen," Stephen Suskin's "On the Record," and Robert Simonson's "Week in Review." Disclaimer: I founded the news service on Playbill On-Line and am still employed by that company. But if you check out this site, you'll find I haven't half described all that's there.

Talkin' Broadway (www.TalkinBroadway.com): For web-savvy theatregoers, running home from the first preview of a show and posting their personal review on this website has become an integral part of the theatregoing experience. Though other websites have message boards and chat rooms, the "All That Chat" area (actually an electronic bulletin board) has become *the* place for theatre fans to debate the issues of the day, review shows out of town and in previews, share gossip and opinions, ask one another for recommendations, and alert one another when an actor is out sick, etc. Lots of actors (and producers) from the various shows also visit here to sample the *vox populi*, and sometimes to join in the debates. The site also offers news, reviews and columns, but "All That Chat" (www.talkinbroadway.com/forum/) is the main reason to visit here. It's especially useful if you're going to see a show long after opening night, and want to hear from someone who's seen it recently. One caveat: Beware of wildly enthusiastic but lone reviews. People don't have to use their real names to post here, and it's scarcely unheard-of for members of a production or even their press agent to attempt to improve the buzz on this site.

BroadwayStars.com (www.BroadwayStars.com): James Marino's running weblog of links to theatre news and features everywhere on the net. Not only does it jump you to major stories on all the websites listed here, it also highlights the rare theatre story appearing in other media across the U.S.—and sometimes comes up with a scoop itself. A great gateway to all the theatre on the web.

Broadway.com (www.Broadway.com): A commercial website that offers theatre news as an inducement to buy tickets at a considerable markup. Its strongest points are casting news from columnist Ken Mandelbaum, photos from celebrity shutterbug Bruce Glikas, and breaking news from reporter Cara Joy David. Probably the most widely advertised theatre website.

Theatermania (www.Theatermania.com): Another theatre news site with excellent listings, wide-ranging reviews and the Gold Club, which offers discounts on tickets and theatre-related services. The site's crown jewel is "Peter Filichia's Diary," the thrice-weekly column by a man whose knowledge of theatre, especially musical theatre, would fill a shelf of CD-ROMS.

The Tony Awards Website (www.TonyAwards.com): A treasure chest of information on the Tony Awards and the people who have won them. Extensive multi-media offerings are a highlight of this site, which is engineered for the Tonys by IBM.

Live Broadway (www.LiveBroadway.com): The website run by the League of American Theatres and Producers, with details on current shows, and lots of consumer information.

Internet Broadway Database (www.IBDB.com): No consumer information, but lots of historical and archival material on people and shows, going back hundreds of years, but focusing on Broadway.

You're the Critic (www.yourethecritic.com): A relatively new site where you can read (and post) reviews, not only of theatre, but all the arts.

Yahoo (http://news.yahoo.com/news?tmpl=index&cid=789): This news megasite has an Arts & Stage section that picks up stories from Backstage, Playbill, Variety, the Associated Press and Reuters.

The American Theater Web (www.AmericanTheaterWeb.com): Theatre news and listings.

New York Theatre Wire (www.nytheatre-wire.com): Features and news, with an emphasis on Manhattan's downtown theatre scene.

NewYorkCity.com (www.Nyc.com): Broadway-related vacation and hotel packages, hotel packages, etc.

Discover Broadway (www.discoverbroadway.com): Hotel and restaurant packages.

These websites are sources for theatre news and information. Find more on places to buy tickets on the internet in Chapter Three.

ADS, COMMERCIALS, AND POSTERS

These are the least objective way to get consumer information, but they're also the most readily available. Marketing theses have been written on what makes an effective ad. Most theatre ads do little more than convey an image, usually the show's poster, or a picture of the star, plus some basic consumer information. Some ads are used to announce the advent of ticket sales (though rarely the prices), or the replacement of a leading character, but most print advertisements are simply there to remind you of the show's existence.

The poster itself does little more. Full-size posters on display in Shubert Alley and at commuter train stations are called "three-sheets" and are rarely seen or collected, mainly because of their size. Much more common are the 18-inch by 22-inch smaller posters, called "window cards," printed on heavy paper stock, which go in cases in front of the theatre, and are often displayed in the windows of theatre-area businesses. Some, like the designs of Paul Davis and James McMullen, are beautiful artworks, and grace the walls of theatre-lovers everywhere.

But they don't tell you much about what the show is going to be like, ticket prices, etc.

Neither do the ABC ad grids that appear in *The New York Times* and other papers. Named for the larger initial letter in each listing, the ads generally list the show's title, theatre address, performing times and phone number, and not much more.

A better bet is a handbill called a "herald." These can be found at hotels, at the TKTS booth in Times Square, and almost anyplace else you see a rack of tourist brochures. They are far more useful than either a poster or a print ad. Most includes performance dates and times, ticket information, and sometimes a little description of the plot. Some also include, or function as, coupons to be redeemed at the box office. They may also contain quotes (laudatory only) from critics.

But don't trust these quotes. They are often taken out of context, and many can be from less-respected critics.

Radio ads, especially for musicals, at least let you hear some of the music, which can be useful in letting you know what you're getting into. TV ads also let you see what the show looks like. But remember that both are very brief, as is the nature of broadcast media.

Worst of all are those man-on-the street television interview ads with people who've just come out of seeing the show, and seem to think it's the greatest thing since the opening night of *My Fair Lady*. Knowing the power of word-of-mouth, the producers use people with that neighbor-next-door look, and try to simulate real word-of-mouth,"

Naturally, the people who say "hated it" don't get in the ad.

Often they use the cast album from the show (if it's a musical), as background music. My advice: Tune out the encomiums and focus on the music. It will tell you what you need to know better than an empty quote. Better yet: get the cast album yourself and listen. It's as close as you can get to the actual in-theatre experience.

THE TONY AWARDS

The awards, given the first Sunday in June to the best of Broadway, also function as a great big annual commercial for Broadway, offering excerpts from most of the nominated musicals. The Tonys are a way to window-shop for shows, especially if you are planning to head to Broadway in summer time.

THEATRE INFORMATION IN TIMES SQUARE

Say you've agreed to meet a friend at a theatre and you know the name of the theatre, but not the address. Or say you remember the title of the show, but not the theatre. What can you do?

One of the least-known treasures of the Theatre District is the Times Square Visitors Center at 1560 Broadway on the east side of Times Square between 46th and 47th Streets, perhaps significantly, midway between the Times Square McDonalds and the legendary Palace Theatre. It's open 8 AM to 8 PM seven days a week.

It offers a place to buy tickets for any Broadway show and many Off-Broadway shows all under one roof. There is a cornucopia of information on each show, including on standing room and student discounts, plus clean rest rooms and a place to sit down in real theatre seats and take a load off while kids can play an arcade video game.

You can also make a beeline directly across Broadway for the TKTS booth in Duffy Square, that's the northern (uptown) half of the Times Square bow, the triangle formed by Broadway, 47th Street, and Seventh Avenue. It looks like a modern art confection of white canvas squares emblazoned with the red TKTS logo. More on that in Chapter Four. The booth attendants themselves will be busy helping paying customers and unable to help you. However, the wranglers who keep the line moving are often very knowledgeable, and in front of the booth itself, on the 47th Street frontage, there are usually tables piled with heralds for the various shows. You can find the theatre's address there.

Playbill also publishes the Broadway Theatre Guide with all pertinent information. It's free and designed to be distributed at hotels and other gathering spots, and a pile of copies can generally be found nestled among the heralds at TKTS. The color of the cover changes each month.

Most (but not all) Broadway shows display full-size posters in Shubert Alley, a promenade connecting the two busiest streets in the theatre district, 44th and 45th Streets between Broadway and Eighth Avenue, and considered the heart of the theatre district.

Doormen at the area's hotels are often knowledgeable as well. If worst comes to worst, newsstands on both sides of Times Square sell

LONG LIFE TO YOU TILL THEN

Irving Berlin, composer of *Annie Get Your Gun* and hundreds of hit songs, died in 1989 at age 101.

George Abbott, director, writer and performer in 112 Broadway productions, died in 1995 at age 107, averaging better than a Broadway show a year for his entire long life.

The New York Times, which runs addresses for Broadway and many Off-Broadway shows each day in the ABC grid in the Arts section.

INFORMATION AT YOUR HOTEL

Nearly every hotel in New York employs a concierge whose job it is to make your stay happy. Find out this person's name and alert him/her, even before you arrive, that you are a theatre fan and want to max your theatre fun. Treat this person right and they can steer you to great events and big discounts.

Most hotels also maintain racks of heralds, coupons, twofers, listing guides and other information. Don't depend on these alone; ask the concierge to cut through the clutter and let you know what's good. If you have special interests, or want to see only family shows, or only dramas, or shows with jazz, or shows with tap dancing, tell the concierge.

Some hotels now also make available the *Zagat Survey: New York City Theater Guide*. It operates much like Zagat's well-known restaurant-rating guides, and is based on the collated opinions of actual ticket-buyers. How useful are its polls? The highest-rated show in the spring 2003 guide was the Off-Broadway musical, *Hank Williams: Lost Highway*. Was that really the best show in New York at the same time *Hairspray*, *The Producers*, and *The Lion King* were running? Zagat's people apparently thought so.

GIVING TICKETS AS GIFTS

Tickets make great gifts, but picking them out can be a pain. Yes, the hot ticket du jour is always welcome, but what if it's beyond your budget or otherwise unobtainable?

Giving tickets is word-of-mouth in action. As with any present, the better you know the person, the easier it is to shop for them. This may be a challenge if you are taking, say, a first date and want to make a good impression.

You may wish to ask a friend of your gift recipient what shows they've seen and what they might like. You can also think back on TV shows or films they've liked. Did they like Oscar-winner *Chicago*? How about HBO's *Angels in America*? That certainly makes it easy. Many musicals and dramas pack a comparable emotional punch.

Fans of movie thrillers might like stage thrillers. Ditto fans of classic rock, many of whose practitioners have turned to the stage in recent years, like Billy Joel with *Movin' Out* and Elton John with *The Lion King* and *Aida*.

If they like watching the Olympics, they might like the acrobatic *Stomp*. If they like figure skating, they might like one of the bigger dance shows. Since the success of Frank Wildhorn's "This Is the

Moment" from *Jekyll & Hyde* as a figure-skating theme, it seems every other show comes with a rink-ready power ballad.

Seeing Stars—Stars are stars for a reason. People like to look at them and see what they do. This carries over to stars in all areas of endeavor. If the person on your gift list liked a performance by Nathan Lane, or a play by Richard Greenberg, or music by the team of Ahrens & Flaherty, or something choreographed by Susan Stroman, or directed by Joe Mantello, well then, check to see what their latest work is. They and their colleagues are all busy and prolific professionals and always have a new project in the pipeline.

If you save *Playbills*, as many people do, check the Who's Who section to see who created the shows you or your beneficiary have liked, and use that as a guide to what may work as a gift.

Kids—Taking a child to his or her first Broadway show is one of the great thrills of a lifetime—or can be.

How to tell when a child is old enough? If the child can't be still and quiet during a one-hour video at home, they won't make it through a Broadway show. Most theatres suggest that children under age four not come.

But if a child has heard from friends that *The Lion King* was cool . . . or wants to know why there is a commercial on TV that shows a live *Beauty and the Beast* . . . or if the child comes back from a class trip to a theatre complaining that the other kids were making too much noise, you have an opening to talk about live theatre and gauge the reaction.

If you know a child who loves to dress up, loves to sing for company, loves to be in school plays, or loves to put on music and "dance around the living room" as the song in *A Chorus Line* goes, you're looking at a prime candidate.

P.S.: With a blessed few exceptions (The Paper Bag Players, Theatreworks/USA notable among them) most of the touring theatre groups expressly for children are mediocre, at best. What is good can be found at a special theatre in Times Square that showcases the best children's theatre from across North America, and even overseas. It's the New Victory (www.NewVictory.org) on 42nd Street and offers many great opportunities for First Theatre Experience.

However, once most kids are ready for the theatre, I say they're ready for Broadway at full-strength.

See Chapter Twelve for tips on how to make that first experience more pleasant for everybody. See also Chapter Eleven for a once-a-year special event, Kids Night on Broadway, that offers a free child's ticket for every full-price adult ticket sold.

Teens and Older Folks—Teens often like shows with teens or young adults in them, such as *Rent*. They like shows with an off-kilter way of looking at the world, like shows with a young hero overcoming challenges, and like to see plenty of color and movement. Contemporary subjects work best, although a recent Broadway revival of Shakespeare's four hundred-year-old *Henry IV* proved popular with high schoolers because it had good jokes, lots of action and generally wasn't at all boring.

Older people often like musicals with period music, and intelligently-produced revivals, especially if they have some emotional connection to them, like a first date or a favorite song. Many older folks also have a keen appreciation for fine drama, especially if they are educated. However, many older people object to expletives.

Violence—For some reason, violence seems extra violent on stage. People who wouldn't flinch from seeing a graphic dismemberment in a movie or video game, get outraged at a highly stylized or choreographed or even implied killing on stage. Perhaps they know the only things getting hurt in a film are pixels in a special effects computer program. The aliveness of the stage makes such acts seem much more real. Keep that in mind when picking a show for a child or a sensitive adult.

Nudity—Nudity has gone through several phases. Nudity of both sexes in the 1960s gave way to an acceptance of female nudity or female toplessness. More recently a fad for male nudity has been running its course, with shows like *Take Me Out*, *The Full Monty*, and the actually rather innocent *Naked Boys Singing* gaining acceptance. The latter has been running for years. Originally appealing mainly to gay audiences, it's become a magnet for bachelorette parties. There will always be a basic voyeuristic appeal to the sight of a nude human standing there boldly before you. But not everyone appreciates this appeal, or wishes to appear to appreciate it.

Revivals—Revivals are previously-produced shows that are brought back, usually with a new cast, and often with an innovative idea on how they should be staged. Some revivals are hailed and enjoy long runs, like recent revivals of *Chicago* (made into an Oscar-winning film), *Cabaret* and *Kiss Me, Kate*. However, revivals as a group are often are mocked by critics and bemoaned by pundits. But audiences flock to them, if they're done well. Nostalgia? Partly. But critics and pundits tend to be older people and they forget that for younger audiences, these are the first time they've ever gotten to see these shows. Plays are not like DVDs. They're not forever preserved or forever the same. Once they close, they evaporate, like a dream. Revivals give new audiences a chance to enjoy pleasant dreams for the first time. A mixture of new shows and revivals is healthy.

Challenges—In general, audiences are surprisingly open to shows that push them slightly over a border. While some revel in the shock of the new, others prefer a more modest challenge—but a challenge nonetheless. Contrary to conventional wisdom, they don't like to be told only things they already know. The imagination is a muscle that likes exercise.

Generally, to paraphrase common wisdom, people like to see new things done in an old way, or old things done in a new way. Look at *Hairspray* (based on a film) or *Rent* (based on the same story as the opera *La Bohéme*).

People also like to learn something at the theatre. They like shows about far-off places or long-gone times, preferably if the costumes are colorful and the rules are different. They especially like to see made-up places. Look at the appeal of *Wicked* and *Alice in Wonderland*. Keep this in mind for the armchair traveler on your list.

Now that you've picked your show, it's time to buy tickets.

CHAPTER THREE

BUYING TICKETS–FULL PRICE

Once you've decided more or less what show, or at least what kind of show, you want to see, it's time to buy tickets.

This is the part of the theatergoing experience that can create the most stress. I'll get a bad seat! I'll pay too much! What do all those people who already have tickets for the sold out show know that I don't know?

This chapter will walk you through every step of the process, and offer tips on how to get what you want and avoid getting what you don't want. Many people wish they had a theatre friend who would know inside sources of information and secret outlets for tickets, and who could help steer them around pitfalls. Now, you do!

RESERVED SEATING

Your local cineplex sells tickets on a general seating basis. The earlier you come, the better a seat you will get. Broadway shows and virtually all Off-Broadway do it differently. Shows have what's called reserved seating. Your ticket entitles you to a specific seat, indicated by the number on the ticket. Ticket H10 entitles you to sit in row H, seat 10, and no other. When ordering tickets, keep this in mind. Ask what part of the theatre your seat is in, whether it's close to the front or the back, close to the center or the sides. If you have a preference, make it known.

PARTS OF A THEATRE

Most modern Broadway theatres are divided into the main floor, called the "Orchestra" because it's on the same level as the orchestra, and the second floor or "Mezzanine," which is Italian for "middle level," but in practice means the balcony.

Some theatres have a second, higher, balcony, which may indeed be called the "Balcony." Trained by movies and TV to expect to see actors' faces close-up, modern audiences hate to sit in balconies or at any great distance from the stage whatever. Nowadays, some shows in two-balcony theatres simple close off the second balcony.

Your tickets may say "Rear Mezzanine" also, which means the last two or three rows at the back of the balcony, the farthest seats from the stage, and generally the cheapest.

You may also encounter "Box" seats, which are at the farthest side of the Mezzanine, practically next to the stage frame, called the Proscenium. I've had friends buy Box seats thinking they're the best seats in the house, only to find they can barely see half the stage. "What's so great about Box seats?" they ask. The answer is, Box seats are left over from the days when theatregoing was a social event. People would dress up in their best finery, not so much to see the show, but to be seen by their social rivals in the rest of the audience. Bottom line: Don't buy box seats if you can help it—unless you're famous or planning to come dressed to kill and want to show off. Many boxes are now used for extra lighting equipment.

Another bargain that's no bargain is the first couple rows of the orchestra. These may be OK for dramas and comedies, especially for people whose hearing isn't what it used to be. But you will find yourself looking up a lot of nostrils.

The first few rows are no bargain at musicals especially, because you tend to hear the orchestra more than the singers. This is especially true if you're sitting in the front on right side, where the percussionist usually sits. I attended a flop rock musical version of *Hamlet*, called *Rockabye Hamlet*, in which I had the misfortune to sit in the front row on the right side. Not only were the lyrics drowned out by the pounding of the percussion, but when the bald and heavily perspiring actor playing Polonius would go into a spin, an unpleasant sprinkler effect set in. You get the picture. A little farther back is better.

Many musicals today offer the front two rows at a reduced price to students or people who are willing to go through a lottery process, but pay substantially less. See Chapter Four for details.

A few theatres also have a "Dress Circle," which is a fancy name for the Front Mezzanine.

What they *should* have is different names (and prices) for the different parts of the Orchestra. Most theatre Orchestra sections are laid out on the American plan, which consists of two aisles running down the left and right sides of the playhouse. This creates a wide, fan-shaped center section (usually with triple-digit ticket numbers, e.g. F101 to F121), and two comparatively narrow sections against the side walls, usually numbered in odd single digits on one side (F1, F3, F5, etc.) and even single digits on the other side (F2, F4, F6). More on seating in Chapter Five.

The front of the Mezzanine offers a much better view of the stage than the back of the Orchestra, but many people would rather pay a higher price and sit in the back of the Orchestra than a lower price to sit in the front of the Mezzanine. Somehow, going up a flight of stairs is considered an indignity, wounding to their status. Such people are silly. Trust Uncle Robert: Front Mezz, especially for big musicals, has the best seats in the house. It offers you, not only a clear view of the actors' facial expressions, but a panoramic view of the stage "picture," and the best mix of orchestra and voice sound.

A few theatres, like The New York State Theatre at Lincoln Center, are laid out in a modified European-style, also known as Continental seating, which consists of long rows of seats whose only access is aisles against the walls on both sides. The drawback with this is, if you have to get up to go to the bathroom, you may have squeeze past thirty or forty pairs of knees, instead of just eight or ten. The Minskoff Theatre in Times Square has a hybrid of the two, with an unusually wide center section and relatively narrow side sections.

Nevertheless, the reality is that the best part of the theatre is considered to be rows 4-10 of the Orchestra. In the industry, the fifth-row aisle seats (generally F101-102) are called the *Times* seats, because these supposedly are the best pair in the house—the place they seat *The New York Times*' critic on opening night. You know my opinion.

PERFORMANCE TIMES

Union rules generally allow no more than eight performances a week, but the arrangement of those performances is left more or less up to the individual producer. A standard week consists of six evening performances Monday through Saturday at 8 PM, a Wednesday matinee at 2 or 3 PM, and a Saturday matinee at 2 PM. Some shows swap out a Monday night in favor of a Sunday performance. Other combinations also crop up.

Kid-oriented shows like *The Lion King* and *Beauty and the Beast* may have earlier curtain times at some performances to accommodate early bedtimes.

In 2003, some shows moved Tuesday evening performances back to 7 PM. The move was popular and the experiment is still underway. But many people just assume an 8 PM curtain—and wind up missing much of the first hour. Read your tickets! Check curtain times!

BIGGEST BOX OFFICE

The Broadway revival of *The Producers* earned the most money ever for a Broadway show in a single week when it took in more than $1.6 million over New Year's weekend, 2003–04. It was thanks largely to the return of original stars Nathan Lane and Matthew Broderick that week.

The Producers also holds the record for attracting the most Tony Award nominations of any single show (fifteen) and also winning the most of any show (twelve). It might have won more, but the other three were in categories in which multiple *Producers* folk were nominated.

During holiday periods shows sometimes change their regular schedules. There's often a Christmas Day performance and a New Year's Eve show regardless of what day of the week these holiday fall on.

EACH THEATRE IS DIFFERENT

Each Broadway theatre has its own unique layout, size and feel. Before you buy tickets you may want to look over the seating chart (posted at the box office and on the Web), and get an opinionated sense of where the good and bad seats are.

BUYING AT THE BOX OFFICE

Even with all the technology at theatregoers' fingertips, tickets are still most commonly sold right at the theatre's box office—about a quarter of all tickets are sold there, with phone sales and internet sales close behind.

Here is some practical advice to make the experience of box office purchase easier, more efficient and more pleasant for everyone involved.

First and most important, have a clear idea of the date you want to come and the section of the theatre you want to sit in. You should have two or three backup dates in mind. However, if, for some reason you must have tickets for a certain date and no other—say, for example, you have a brother in the military and he's "On the Town" for only that one day—prepare to be flexible on the area of the theatre you want to sit in.

- The farther in advance you buy, the better chance you have of getting a good seat.
- Most box offices are open 10 AM to curtain time Monday through Saturday, and noon to curtain time Sunday.
- It's much easier to get tickets for weeknight performances than weekend performances. Weekend matinees are easier than evening shows. Friday is easier than Saturday. Saturday night is always the toughest ticket. Try to avoid it if you can. Next to every box office window on Broadway is a calendar and a seating chart. Use them!
- Everyone wants the first ten rows in the center, but these are not always available. Use the seating chart to consider where else might be acceptable. You may also wind up saving some money thereby.
- Have your money or travelers check or credit card in hand as you approach the window, especially if there is a line. Some theatres take personal checks, but you will need photo identification. Amex, MasterCard, and Visa credit cards are preferred, and cash is always welcome.

- Avoid using your cell phone at the box office window, especially if there is a line. Line up alternate dates in advance.

- The top price for a regular Broadway ticket is now about $100 for the Orchestra section of a musical on Saturday night. But keep in mind that tickets may be much cheaper for mezzanine and balcony, and for weeknights and matinees. Dramas and comedies also usually charge a lower price than musicals.

- You can avoid most telephone and internet processing fees by buying at the box office. But it is an increasingly common practice to tack on a $1 or $1.25 "project support payment" or "facility fee" or "New 42nd Street Surcharge" of fifty cents to as much as three dollars on some tickets, regardless of where they are sold. They seem like terrible p.r. for the theatre owners, when they could so easily be subsumed into the regular ticket price. But there you are. Some theatres will list your tickets as an odd $91.25. This is simply the facility fee sticking out like a bump under a rug.

- Double-check the ticket time if you have tickets to a child-oriented show (the curtains are usually earlier). Sunday performances for all types of shows are also often at odd times.

- Try not to buy tickets during the last thirty minutes before curtain time, especially if the show is a hit. Box office windows are used mainly for pickups of reservations at that time.

- Don't wait until the ticket has been printed and handed over to you to say, "Do you have anything else?"

- When you get the tickets in your hand, check the date and location on the tickets before you walk away from the window. Mistakes are sometimes made. It's your responsibility and in your interest to double check that you got what you asked for.

- If the ticket seller tells you the show is sold out, don't bother asking, "Don't you have just *one* seat left?" If they had it, they'd try to sell it to you. However there are ways beyond the box office to get tickets to sold-out shows. A guide appears later in this chapter.

BUYING BY PHONE

Many of the same principles apply to buying by phone, though phone sales involve a handling fee of several dollars per ticket.

Most Broadway show tickets are sold by two large companies, Telecharge and TicketMaster, which are used, respectively and mutually exclusively, by the two large theatre-owning companies, the Shubert Organization and the Nederlander Organization. Smaller theatre-owners like Jujamcyn, Disney, Roundabout and MTC generally have ticket-selling deals with one or the other of those two big ticket-sellers.

Here are the Broadway theatres, and the phone sales company that serves them:

Telecharge: 1-212-239-6200 in New York; 1-800-432-7250 elsewhere.

Al Hirschfeld	Lyceum
Ambassador	Majestic
Belasco	Music Box
Biltmore	Plymouth
Booth	Royale
Broadhurst	Shubert
Broadway	St. James (special NY
Cort	number: 1-212-239-5800)
Ethel Barrymore	Studio 54
Eugene O'Neill	Virginia
Golden	Vivian Beaumont
Imperial	Walter Kerr
Longacre	Winter Garden

TicketMaster: 1-212-307-4100 in New York; 1-800-755-4000 elsewhere.

Brooks Atkinson	Marquis
Circle in the Square	Minskoff
Ford Center for the	Nederlander
Performing Arts	Neil Simon
Gershwin	New Amsterdam (special
Helen Hayes	NY number: 1-212-307-4747)
Lunt-Fontanne (special NY	Palace
number: 1-212-307-4747)	Richard Rodgers

Independent

American Airlines Theatre 1-212-719-1300

HOW CAN I TELL WHAT THEATRE A SHOW IS AT?

If you're not sure which theatre your show is at, look it up in the ABC listings, or call the Broadway Line at 1-888-Broadway (1-888-276-2392) and a brief climb through a phone tree will eventually connect you to the correct phone sales company. Outside the USA, the Broadway Line can be reached by calling 1-212-302-4111.

You can also look up your theatre on one of the websites (Playbill.com. Broadway.com, etc.) that let you search by show title, and then tell you the theatre.

WHEN YOU CALL

Phone sales are strictly by credit card. Have your card ready, know which part of the theatre you wish to sit in, and have two or three alternate dates in mind.

Sample conversation:

> *Operator*: Hello, Telemaster. How can I help you?

> *You*: Hello, I'd like four tickets, preferably together, for *The Phantom of the Producers*, on the Saturday matinee performance, February 30. I'd like to sit in the center section of the orchestra, or in the first five rows of the mezzanine.

> *Operator*: I'll check. (Pause.) Those sections are sold out, I'm afraid. I do have two pairs in the side sections, but they're not together.

> *You*: How far over are they? On the aisle, or against the wall?

> *Operator*: Six seats in from the aisle.

> *You*: Can I do better the next day, Sunday Feb. 31?

> *Operator*: I'll check. (Pause) Matinee or evening?

> *You*: Matinee.

> *Operator*: I can get you four together in Row R.

> *You*: Sold!

The operator will ask for you name, credit card number and expiration date. You may also get a confirmation number, and the seat numbers of the tickets.

If there are several weeks before the date on the tickets, you'll have the option to get the tickets in the mail or have them waiting at the box office. The mail route gives you the peace of mind of having the tickets in your hand before you set out for the theatre, but you are subject to the vagaries of the mail system. Having them held at the box office produces a slight anxiety that something may go wrong with the ordering system, but if you write down your seat numbers and your confirmation number on a piece of paper, you can use that as a safety blanket. Certain venues use an electronic system called TicketFast that allows you to receive the tickets via email and print them from your home computer.

Otherwise, tickets are sent either by standard mail or an express mail system, though there is generally a higher fee for the latter.

Generally, tickets ordered less than ten days before the performance can not be sent by mail, but are held at the box office for you to pick up when you arrive.

Useful tip: Tickets go on sale via telephone and the internet sometimes weeks before they go on sale at the theatre's box office.

Useful tip: When you know a big hit is coming, check newspaper ads and websites for the date that tickets go on sale. Generally they are advertised to go on sale on a Sunday at 10 AM. HOWEVER, the dirty secret is that they often can be purchased earlier on Sunday morning, or sometimes even on Saturday, no matter what the ad says. It pays to check, especially if the tickets are for a special event or a limited run where being at the head of the virtual line is crucial.

Useful tip: Some shows strike deals with credit card companies to make their tickets available only to holders of that card, for a week or two before tickets go on sale to the general public. Amex, for example, does this most frequently, alerting its cardholders to the deal via mail, and sometimes in an ad. If you don't hold the right kind of card, find a friend who does, and work out a deal to reciprocate in the future.

One frustrating thing about calling the box office: you can't get the box office. If you call, say, the Majestic Theatre, you don't get the Majestic Theatre. You get a centralized ticket-selling office. This is fine for buying the ticket, but if you want to know something specific about the theatre, or want to get through with a message for someone, they generally aren't able to help you. However, if there is a real emergency, the operator will often agree to act as intermediary, and contact the real box office for you.

BUYING ONLINE

Buying tickets online is similar to buying by phone, but without the personal touch of the operator. As with phone sales, you must use a credit card, and you will pay a service fee.

Ordering online also is more complicated, especially for an internet neophyte. Both Telecharge and TicketMaster required that you set up an account that will allow the services to bill your credit card. Creating the account is free and not especially difficult, though it is more time-consuming than simply reading your credit card number to an operator.

Even once your account is set up, you will have to navigate a page full of pull-down menus to determine date, time, section of theatre and price. The upside of this is that you can search out multiple dates and sections at your leisure without the pressure of dealing with a busy operator.

And now for the fees:

TicketMaster charges a $6.25 "convenience charge" per ticket.

Telecharge adds a "service charge" of $6 and a "handling charge" of $2.50 per ticket, though what the difference might be is not explained.

Large commercial websites charge even more. Broadway.com, for instance, charges a 20 percent fee on all tickets, which also covers handling. They claim that for the money, the tickets will be especially good.

TICKET BROKERS

Brokers used to be kings of the ticket-selling business, but their business has largely been usurped by the big ticket agencies, and by online sales. Now, brokers handle less than two percent of the business. But they have carved themselves a niche.

Licensed or out-of-state brokers buy up desirable blocks of seats, and sell them at a markup sometimes greater than the face value of the ticket itself. What are you buying from a broker? Convenience and access. They hunt down the tickets for you, and get them for you when the box office and the high-tech selling services are sold out.

Here is a list of some of the more prominent brokers that handle Broadway tickets:

Broadway Inner Circle—www.broadwayinnercircle.com

The Ticket Company—www.tickco.com

Broadwayshows.org—www.broadwayshows.org

Concert Tickets Express—
www.concertticketsexpress.com/theatre.html

Go Tickets—www.GoTickets.com

Ticket Center—www.tickctcenter.com

Ticket Depot, Inc.—www.ticketdepot.com

Ticket Finder—www.ticketfinder.com

TicketsNow.com—www.tickets.com

StubHub—www.stubhub.com. Not technically a broker, but an exchange where people can buy and sell tickets like stock market shares.

Specializing in Group Sales

Best of Broadway—www.bestofbroadway.com

Prestige Entertainment—www.prestigeentertainment.com

Broadway.com—www.broadway.com/groups

FYI: If you have tickets you need to sell for some reason, many of these brokers also buy tickets from the public, especially if the show is in demand.

SCALPERS

Scalpers illegally sell you tickets at an inflated price—sometimes massively inflated—for a sold-out show, or at the last minute, or in a premium section of the theatre.

New York State law prohibits reselling of tickets more than 20 percent above their face value. Street scalpers can be seen loitering near or beneath the marquees of hits. These are easily spotted and risk arrest, and so appear appropriately furtive. Beware of rip-off artists.

These are not be confused with poor zhlubs who can't make that night's performance or who have a second ticket owing to illness of a partner. These folks can often be induced to sell for a discount. You can recognize them because they appear appropriately desperate.

Scalpers always sell for more than face value. You usually have to know someone who knows someone. Hotel concierges can sometimes be of help in this area, especially if asked with a note of pleading urgency in the voice, and a tip in the hand.

In a recent phenomenon, scalpers sometimes approach people online in chat rooms and message boards.

In any case, expect to pay a fat premium. Remember: they're called scalpers for a reason.

For example, in the early days of the *Producers* phenomenon, otherwise unobtainable orchestra seats on Saturday nights were going for thousands of dollars above the already (then-)breathtaking $100 face value.

Since none of this jackpot goes to the producer or the creators, those people have a special reason to detest scalpers. In an attempt to get in on the payday, *Producers* producers created the Broadway Inner Circle, a legal organization that sells the filet mignon seats for $480. Editorial writers gnashed their teeth over this, but the circle has since widened to include other red-hot hits.

When there is limited supply and unlimited demand, black markets will always spring up. If you have the gelt and want the ducats, the market will respond.

HOW TO USE BOX OFFICE CHARTS

Several outlets publish weekly accounting of the Broadway box office. Variety has been doing so for decades. It compiles its own figures, and even posts them online. Playbill On-Line also posts the figures, broken down in several useful ways, based on information from the trade organization, the League of American Theatre Owners and Producers.

The list is of interest, not just to accountants, but to ticket buyers. For instance, you can tell if a show is selling standing room by looking at the figure for percentage of capacity. If a show is listed as having sold 101.8 percent of its "capacity," you know that 1.8 percent represents standing room.

Though the TKTS booth does not announce in advance what tickets it will sell each day, you can get a pretty good idea by looking at the box office figures. If a show is doing less than 90 percent of capacity, there is a pretty good chance the ticket will appear at TKTS, at least for part of the day. If a show is doing less than 75 percent, it's almost guaranteed to be stocked at TKTS nearly all day.

If a show is selling less than 60 percent of capacity, it's a pretty solid guess that the show hasn't got long for this world. Get over to see it fast, and keep in mind that there are probably discounts galore. See Chapter Four for advice on how to find them.

The figure for "average ticket price" is useful, too. The top price for most musicals is now $100. The closer the average is to $100, the less likely you are to find discounts. But if that figure starts slipping down toward an average of $70, you know somebody is getting them at discount, and it might as well be you. The only time this doesn't hold true is the last week of previews, when a lot of the tickets are going out free to critics. The average price will generally plummet that week, but does not necessarily indicate discounting.

WHEN TO BUY OR PICK UP YOUR TICKETS

Box offices for most show open about 10 in the morning, and stay open until curtain time.

The best time of day to buy tickets is any time up until about an hour before the show. That last hour can be pandemonium, as people who have ordered online or by telephone arrive at the box office to pick them up. Most theatres will not sell tickets at all during the last half-hour before curtain.

I always thought shows should keep the box office open after the evening show is over—or at least until intermission. That way, people who liked the show could pick up tickets for friends. But it doesn't work that way. Box offices close within a half-hour or so after the curtain rises for the evening show, and the last stragglers rush up to claim their tickets. Box offices stay open during and after matinees.

BUSY SEASON AND SLOW SEASON

There are times of the week and year when it is harder to get tickets, and times when it's easier. If you target the slower times, you have a better chance of getting a good seat.

Saturday and Friday nights are the toughest tickets. You have a far better chance of Monday and Tuesday. It's not unusual for a show to be sold out Saturdays for months, but still have nice pairs for this coming Tuesday.

Most Mondays are so dead, some shows drop them in favor of Sunday matinees. Wednesday matinees tend to get school groups and senior women. Weekend matinees tend to attract families. Keep this in mind if these are factors in your ticket hunt, pro or con.

On a yearly basis, the busiest night on Broadway is New Year's Eve. The busiest week is the week between Christmas and New Year's Eve. If you want tickets for this week, plan well in advance. Thanksgiving week is also popular. Ticket prices are significantly higher on New Year's Eve.

Tickets are also tight in the spring, in the week following the annual Tony Awards each June, and throughout the month of December.

The slowest times of year are the winter doldrums of January and February, and the dog days of July, August, and early September. As detailed in Chapter Four, many appealing discounts are available at these times. They're also the easiest times to get good seats on short notice for almost any show.

THE HOTEL CONCIERGE

If you are staying at an upscale hotel, you can call upon your concierge to do the ticket hunting for you.

Some hotels, like the Marriott Marquis on Broadway at 46th Street, have a separate theatre office to book tickets for guests. Expect to pay a service charge of fifty to one hundred percent—but the tickets will be premium.

At other hotels you can deal directly with the concierge. Policies on service charges vary from hotel to hotel. The concierge at the budget Broadway Inn on 46th Street, a half block from the Marriott, will not only help you find full-price seats, but also can arrange discounts with many shows, with no service charge at all.

IF A SHOW IS COMPLETELY SOLD OUT, IS THERE ANY WAY I CAN STILL GET TICKETS?

Believe it or not, the answer is yes. One of the things that most drives people out of their minds with frustration is calling a hot show, hearing that it is clean sold out, but knowing, deep in your heart, that if you only knew someone, you could wangle a ticket somehow. But there's no magic to it—as long as you have money.

Brokers—See the section on Ticket Brokers for names, phone numbers and websites of these businesses, which buy and sell tickets to the most desirable shows. Their websites let you type in dates, and get back a list of tickets available for that night. Be forewarned: They are expensive. But you can get them, even last-minute, even for most of the toughest performances.

For example, in the second week of December 2003, the $100 face-value *The Lion King* front orchestra tickets for the Saturday after Christmas, Dec. 27, were selling for $425 at The Ticket Company (www.tickco.com).

On the same date, $480 face-value front orchestra tickets for the New Year's Eve performance at which Nathan Lane and Matthew Broderick were returning to the roles they created in *The Producers*, were going for $1140.

Ebay—This popular virtual garage-sale website has a separate section for Broadway tickets. It has two functions: One is for people who have extra tickets they don't want or can't use themselves, selling them at a steep discount, sometimes just five or ten dollars. The other function is quasi-legal scalping. People who have valuable tickets to sold-out performances of big hits sell them (singly, in pairs or sometimes in multiple pairs) for a steep markup, sometimes multiples of the printed price. The stock is spotty, however. And there is no way to know if the tickets you're getting are legit. Buyer beware! Website: www.ebay.com.

Broadway Inner Circle—To channel scalper money back to the creators (and investors), a group of producers got together in 2001 to create the Broadway Inner Circle, which sells the best tickets to the biggest hits at a fat markup. Ticket that usually cost an already-pricey $100 are sold for $120, $240 or $480, depending on the show, and on how hot its tickets currently are. The website is www.BroadwayInnerCircle.com, and the phone is 1-866-847-8587.

Charities

If you'd rather see your money go for a good cause, there are several theatre-related charities that control a limited number of great tickets for tough performances:

Actors' Fund—This organization, which helps elderly or disabled actors, also controls two pairs of Broadway tickets for each performance. These are also tax deductible and must be ordered at least 48 hours in advance by phone at 1-212-221-7300 x111 or 1-800-FUNDTIX (1-800-386-3849) x111, or through the web at www.actorsfund.org/tickets/FUNDTIX.html.

Broadway Cares/Equity Fights AIDS—Producers of the biggest hits withhold a limited number of "house seats" at sold-out shows on Broadway, Off-Broadway and around the U.S. to be sold at double face value through the CaresTix program to benefit BC/EFA's efforts to care for AIDS patients and support research to cure the disease. These are tax deductible and can be ordered by phone at the Care-Tix Hotline: 1-212-840-0770 ext. 229 or 230 or 263, and through the web at store.yahoo.com/broadwaycares/caretix.html.

The Damon Runyon Foundation—Named for the writer who created the characters in *Guys and Dolls*, this charity was founded by Rodgers and Hammerstein in the 1950s, and helps raise money for cancer research. The producers set aside four to six of the best seats for each performance, to be sold by this outfit. Those who refer friends to this service are eligible for discounts. Tickets can be ordered by phone at 1-212-455-0550. The website is www.cancerresearchfund.org/btHowItWorks.html.

WHAT IF MY SHOW CLOSES?

Commercial shows, such as most of the ones on Broadway, close for one main reason: they've stopped making money. Think of a show as a small business. It has fixed expenses every week, mainly salaries, but also insurance, theatre rent, etc. If a show sells enough tickets at the box office to cover those expenses, it can stay open. If it fails to cover those expenses, it must go out of business, or, in theatrical parlance, "close."

Some shows are open only for limited runs. Generally these are part of subscription series, and must close to make way for the next in the series. Or else they are commercial shows open for a limited number of weeks, after which, for instance, the star is scheduled to make a movie, or do something else that makes him/her unavailable to continue. Then, even if the show is sold out, it may still close.

If you are still holding tickets for a show that closes abruptly, you are entitled to a refund at your point of purchase. If you buy online or by telephone, the ticket service you used, Telecharge or TicketMaster, will arrange the refund. If you bought at the box office, the show is required to post an address on the front of the theatre where you can send for a refund. Usually, it's the producer's office or the box office of a nearby theatre. You can usually get this address over the phone even if you didn't order the tickets by phone.

REFUNDS AND EXCHANGES

Nearly every box office on Broadway has a sign warning, in strict tones, that people should look closely at their tickets because no refunds or exchanges are allowed.

And that is generally the case—nevertheless, there are exceptions that are not publicized, but available all the same.

It's true that you generally can't just change your mind about a show and, presto, get your money back. Producers do this so they don't have to worry about a tidal wave of refunds if, say, a show with a big advance sale opens up and gets bad reviews.

However, there are circumstances under which produces will cut ticket-holders some slack, and will either arrange an exchange for another show date or credit the cost back to a credit card.

In general, it's much easier to arrange an exchange than an out-right refund. It's also much easier to arrange to credit your credit card account, than to have the box office manager count out dollar bills. If you purchased your ticket with a credit card, an electronic refund may be the only kind offered. Telecharge has a separate customer service line, which is 1-800-543-4835. For TicketMaster, you must call their main line at 1-212-307-4100 and ask a service rep to switch you to customer service. See the section of this chapter on phone sales for a complete list of which theatre use which ticket service.

So let's look at the circumstances under which refunds and exchanges are made, from easiest to hardest:

The Performance Gets Cancelled: Producers hate to cancel shows, and do it only in extreme circumstances. Broadway, as an industry has shut down only a handful of times in the last decade, during a blizzard in 1996, in the 48 hours following the Sept. 11, 2001 attacks, and during a blackout in August 2003.

If a show gets cancelled, most shows will automatically credit your account, if you bought with plastic. Otherwise, you must bring or mail your tickets back to the theatre box office, and a refund will be made. If tickets were mailed, the mailing charge may not be refundable.

My Show Closed But I Still Have Tickets for an Upcoming Date: Ditto above. Most shows will automatically credit your account, if you bought with plastic. Otherwise, you must bring or mail your tickets back to the theatre box office.

The Star of the Show Is Out: One of the facts of life of live theatre is that actors sometimes get sick. Sometimes even the big star you've been waiting months to see.

Union rules require producers to notify the audience when an understudy or standby goes on. Notifications can be done in any two of the following ways: a sign in the lobby, an announcement on the theatre's public address system, or a slip of paper in the program.

Theatre news websites try to keep the public abreast of who's in and who's out. But sometimes the producers themselves usually don't know until hours before the show. They do not have the resources to call all ticket holders to warn them.

Can you get your money back if the star is sick? The short answer is: "Yes, usually." There is no industry-wide rule on this. Judgment calls are made on a show-by-show basis.

A general rule of thumb: If the star's name is above the title on posters and the marquee, the show will give refunds or exchanges for a future date. If the actor's name is below the title, refunds and exchanges are optional.

If you want a refund or exchange, you should make that determination within the first few minutes after you learn of the change. It's not fair to sit through the whole show, or even the whole first act, and then ask for a refund. If you want the refund, go to the box office or the house manager's office and say so emphatically, but not rudely. It's not the box office's fault, nor the producer's.

There is one other option: Stay to see the understudy. Understudies are trying to live out the *42nd Street* dream, and often give a hundred and fifty percent.

Inclement Weather: This is the one that causes the most headaches. Many ticket-holders feel that if the roads are dangerous and trains are delayed, shows should automatically make a refund. Most producers feel, however, that if the actors can get to the theatre, the audience can get to the theatre.

However, there is no industry rule on this, according to the League of American Theatres and Producers. The actual policy varies from show to show, and may depend on the severity of the weather. The best idea is to call Telecharge or Ticketmaster, ask to speak to Customer Service, and politely make your case. You're likely to be pleasantly surprised. Two out of three times that I have sought such refunds recently, I have been granted them. In one case they exchanged for another date; in the other case they credited my credit card account.

I'm Not Feeling Well or The Baby Sitter Cancels at the Last Minute: These are very tough refunds to get. But, again, if you make a good case, an operator may take pity on you.

I Hated the Show: Almost impossible. Sometimes the producer of a controversial show is prepared to handle offended walk-outs at the box office. But don't wait until the end of the show to ask for your money back. And your chances drop to zero if you try the next day. A ticket is a contract to do the show for you—not a guarantee that you will like it. This is why it pays to learn as much as you can about a show before you see it.

HANDICAPPED ACCESS

Broadway has made great strides in the past two decades in opening the theatre experience to audiences with many types of physical challenges. Though anyone reading this who has those challenges knows there's a lot more that could be done.

Some of the older theatres especially are largely inaccessible to those in wheelchairs, especially the balcony areas and rest rooms. But the newer theatres have been compelled to conform to accessibility standards. New York, both the city and the state, have passed laws requiring that theatres be both smoke-free and at least partially accessible to wheelchair-bound patrons.

Nearly all Broadway theatres have areas of the Orchestra designated for people in wheelchairs. In many cases, the seats in these locations can be easily removed to make a spot for a wheelchair. Management needs to be notified in advance when these tickets are purchased. Most theatres also have specially designed aisle seats, called "transfer seats," with armrests that fold back or come off so people can transfer easily from wheelchair to seat. Such seats are marked with a blue and white wheelchair symbol.

Shubert theatres offer seats at the regular Orchestra price (i.e. top price) and at the lowest price for the given show. Those in wheelchairs are also allowed to buy one additional ticket at the lowest price, for a companion. To arrange for these seats, call Access Services at 1-212-239-6222 or, outside the New York metropolitan area, 1-800-872-8997.

The number for Nederlander theatres is 1-212-869-0550.

Theatre Access Project (TAP): Theatre Development Fund, the same organization that runs the TKTS discount tickets booth, also sponsors the Theatre Access Project, which serves wheelchair-bound theatregoers and even those who have trouble climbing stairs for medical reasons. Also served by TAP: people who are hearing-impaired, blind or have low vision. TAP arranged discount tickets in parts of the theatre that best meet the person's needs. TAP also sponsors signed performances of Broadway shows—one each month—for the hearing-impaired. It also encourages "open captioned" shows—that is, shows with supertitles—for the same reason.

To inquire about TAP tickets, call 1-212-221-1103 (TTY: 1-212-719-4537, check the website at www.tdf.org, or send an email to tap@tdf.org.

CHAPTER FOUR

BUYING TICKETS—DISCOUNT

What's the biggest problem with live theatre? Let's all say it together: Tickets cost too much.

Producers aren't (always) gouging. It honestly does cost a lot to pay all those actors to show up and sing and dance live, not to mention the musicians, ushers, and so forth. But if you love theatre, you want to see as much as you can within your budget. Luckily for you, there is a surprising number of ways you can buy discount tickets. Not all are advertised, but they exist just the same.

Some are well known. A few will surprise you.

TKTS

The best-known Broadway ticket discounter is the TKTS booth at the north end of Times Square. Theatre folk also call it "The Half-Price Line." The booth—actually a fairly prosaic trailer swathed in red and white canvas panels that say "tkts"—has become a familiar icon of the Theatre District. Between eight and ten percent of all Broadway tickets are sold at TKTS each year.

People ask why the booth is outdoors and there are only two lines and only five ticket windows and you can buy tickets only for that day's performance. The answer is: Producers don't want to make it too easy for you to buy discount tickets because they don't want you to

The TKTS discount ticket booth in Duffy Square.

buy discounts. They want you to buy full price, naturally. But they accept the need and advantage of discounts grudgingly. Producers may hate to discount tickets, but most of them hate empty seats even more, and half (or three-quarters of) a loaf is better than none.

Discount tickets to many Broadway and Off-Broadway shows are sold each day at the TKTS booth in Times Square, along with certain dance and music events. There's a second TKTS booth in lower Manhattan with slightly different rules, but here's how Times Square works.

Where: TKTS is located in Duffy Square, the triangle formed by Broadway, Seventh Avenue, and West 47th Street at the north end of Times Square. There are two lines, one running down Seventh Avenue, the other down Broadway. On busy days lines double and triple back on themselves, but move fairly quickly once the ticket windows are open.

Price: Tickets are sold at fifty or twenty-five percent off, wth a three-dollar service charge. Tickets are for that day's performance *only*. No advance tickets are sold. All sales are final. No refunds or exchanges are allowed.

Type of Tickets: Tickets are usually the least desirable among the most expensive tickets—the sides and the back of the orchestra. Do not expect to find tickets to the biggest hits at the TKTS booth. The only tickets offered at TKTS are the ones the producers have decided will not sell at full price.

Payment Options: Cash or travelers checks only. No credit cards or personal checks are accepted. TKTS does offer gift certificates on its website: www.tdf.org.

Business Hours: Tickets for evening performances are sold 3 to 8 PM Monday through Saturday. Tickets for Wednesday and Saturday matinees are sold 10 AM to 2 PM on those days. Tickets for Sunday matinees 11 AM to 3 PM, and for evening performances, 3 PM to closing, which varies each week.

Arrival time: Generally, get to the booth as early as possible. People start lining up an hour or more before opening time. The booth has only a finite number of tickets, and the best ones go quickly. Some theatres send extra allocations of tickets from time to time later on, so availability is constantly changing throughout the day. Sometimes a batch of great seats lands at TKTS right around 6 PM, when producers decided they are not going to need their "house seats," but there is no guarantee. Electronic boards facing 47th Street tell what's available at a given moment. If you don't see a show listed there, there's no point in asking at the window. It won't be there.

As with all shows, the worst days to get tickets to the hits are Friday and Saturday evenings. The best are Monday and Tuesday evenings, especially in January and February.

Downsides of TKTS: You can't buy tickets for future dates. The lines are outdoors, neither heated in winter, nor cooled in summer nor sheltered on rainy days.

Useful tips: Both lines move at about the same pace and draw on the same pool of tickets. There is a wrangler at the front of the lines who keeps traffic flowing snappily. If there is more than one person in your party, have one person get in line and the other go up and peruse that day's offerings. Pick a first choice and then a second and third. Have your money ready.

The TKTS line draws street musicians and hucksters handing out all manner of discount coupons, ads, flyers, heralds, invitations to TV show tapings, etc. Most are harmless. You'll also encounter scalpers, or people who say they have an extra ticket to sell. Some of the latter people are legit, but many are ripoff artists who will sell you something that looks like a ticket, but later turns out to be a counterfeit. Don't give your money to anyone on the Half-Price Line unless they're TKTS ticket agents inside the booth windows.

TKTS Lower Manhattan Theatre Center at South Street Seaport: There is a second TKS booth at this visitor magnet near the southern tip of Manhattan. It's located at the corner of Front and John Streets, which is the rear of the Resnick/Prudential Building (199 Water Street). Tickets for evening performances Monday to Saturday are sold from 11 AM to 6 PM Tickets for Sunday evening shows are sold 11 AM to 3:30 PM There is one key difference to this TKTS booth: matinee tickets are sold the day previous. You can buy Saturday matinee tickets on Friday, Wednesday matinees on Tuesday, and Sunday matinees on Saturday.

TDF MAILING LIST

TKTS is run by an underappreciated organization called the Theatre Development Fund (TDF), who sole purpose is to promote live theatre. TKTS is only a part of its discounting activity. One of the best but least-known discounts is the TDF Mailing List, now 75,000 subscribers strong, which offers tickets at discounts of fifty to seventy-five percent off for many Broadway and Off-Broadway shows, as well as many other music and dance performances New York. Many big musicals that cost $100 full price are available for $26 from TDF. Non-musicals are a few dollars cheaper.

Not all shows are available all the time, but the list of discounted shows runs to several typewritten pages, and it arrives in your mailbox each month, like a sort of Treasure Chest of the Month Club. You can use none—or you can go out every night of the month and never pay full price. All you have to do is make the call.

The TDF Mailing List is restricted to one of the following eligible categories: students, teachers, union members, retirees, civil service employees, staff members of not-for-profit organizations, performing arts professionals, members of the armed forces and clergy. It's a pretty wide-ranging list. To get on it, send proof that you belong to one of those groups (i.e. photocopy of a student ID, union card, etc.) along with a stamped, self-addressed envelope to: Theatre Development Fund, 1501 Broadway, 21st Floor, New York, New York, 10036-5652, and they will send an application. There is an annual membership fee of $22.50, which you can make back in savings on the purchase of your first ticket. To save time, an application form can be downloaded from the TDF website at www.tdf.org.

There are special discount ticket programs for the disabled and for especially adventurous theatregoers as well.

STANDING ROOM

That big red sign "SRO"—Standing Room Only—was once posted proudly outside productions that were selling out. Reading the box office figures in Variety or one of the online services that post them, you may see that a given show is selling 101.4 percent of its seats. That's not a misprint; that's Standing Room.

Standees don't stand just anywhere. Fire regulations require that aisles be kept clear. Standees are generally arrayed at the back of the orchestra, often where they can rest their arms on the cushioned balustrade that runs along the back of the last row of orchestra seats. Once there, you are expected to stay there, standing, the entire show. Most ushers keep a gimlet eye on standees to make sure they don't succumb to the temptation to slip into an empty seat. Some ushers are more lenient. In either case, bring comfortable shoes.

You generally pay a very modest fee for Standing Room, something on the order of twenty dollars at a show that may cost one hundred to sit down, just a few inches away. A few shows have been known to sell standing room even when the show was not sold out, but nearly all today put these cheapest tickets on sale only after every seat is gone. Some, like The Producers, allow potential standees to wait on line outside the theatre, then put the Standing Room tickets on sale two hours before curtain time. Others, like Mamma Mia!, put them on sale at the box office as soon as all the seats sell out.

Policies vary from show to show. I've never seen Standing Room sold on a website. Sometimes Standing Room can be purchased by phone, but you must ask for it. In most cases, Standing Room is sold only at the theatre's box office. But if you are patient and have a good back, you can see otherwise sold-out shows for a fraction of its full price.

Some shows don't offer Standing Room for the simple reason that there is a wall at the rear of the orchestra that blocks the view.

And sometimes, on really big hits, even the Standing Room sells out.

PAPERING THE HOUSE

"Trading Spaces" never had as good a deal as this.

This kind of "Papering" is interior design of a very expensive sort. It's the giveaway of free tickets to a lucky group. It's something producers do when they are not selling out, but want to *look* like they are—a critics' preview, for instance.

Producers find a large group of people, generally at a company the producers own, know, or want to butter up. They tell employees, effectively, "Come and get it," and the employees score pairs of tickets for free. The downside, of course, is that shows that need to paper are generally in trouble of one sort or another. Recipients do, however, sometimes luck out if the show becomes a smash.

All the same, the recipients of "Paper" are asked to keep mum about the provenance of their ducats. The whole point is to make the show look plush and flush—not desperate.

How do you get your company on this list? Tell your boss to make friends with, or become, producers. If you know someone who works in a theatre-related industry, ask them to keep you in mind next time paper is offered. If you're in HR, seek out producers and see if there's anything your company can do in return for getting on the "Paper" list. This could be the beginning of a beautiful friendship.

HERE'S THE SKINNY

Two of Broadway's biggest hits were cast against physical type. Arthur Miller imagined *Death of a Salesman's* Willy Loman as a diminutive man. Instead, the original Broadway cast starred the tall and robust Lee J. Cobb. Dustin Hoffman fulfilled the original vision in a 1984 revival.

In "Tevye and His Daughters," author Sholom Aleicheim imagined his milkman as a skinny starveling. In *Fiddler on the Roof*, the musical adaptation of his story, he was played by the rotund Zero Mostel, though he was replaced by the comparatively willowy Herschel Bernardi.

RUSH TICKETS

For many years, Broadway and Off-Broadway shows offered what was known as "Student Rush" tickets. That is, tickets for half-price or less sold on the day of performance to people who could produce student I.D. The idea was to encourage a younger (and smarter) audience that couldn't afford full price. Students basically got whatever tickets hadn't sold at full price.

The whole concept of Student Rush was transformed in 1996 with the advent of *Rent*. Instead of handing the students rich people's leftovers, the producers set aside the closest seats in the house, the two entire front rows, to be sold to students at $20, then less than a third of the orchestra price.

Students embraced the opportunity and lines began forming at dawn. Waiting on the Rush line for *Rent* became a touchstone for young theatregoers of the late 1990s. They were hip and enthusiastic and, since they were down in front, they added a lot of energy to every show. The policy was quickly emulated by other shows hoping to attract the same young audiences. And, sadly, the process was quickly abused by scalpers.

Box office personnel have since devised several different ways to weed out most scalpers while keeping the Rush tickets. Be prepared for lines at each.

The Lottery: Shows with a lottery require that you show up at the theatre no later than three hours before curtain time. Most people start arriving much earlier. Upon showing a student ID, you are given an index card on which to write your name and whether you want one ticket or two. Tickets are put in a tumbler and drawn until the number of available seats is used up (generally two dozen or so). No credit cards are accepted. Students with ID, cash and winning index card in hand then proceed to the box office where the ID and card are checked one last time, and the tickets sold. Among shows with a lottery, some offer the front rows of the orchestras, some offer the last two rows of the mezzanine (balcony).

Traditional Student Rush: Go to the box office on the same day of performance, generally two to four hours before curtain time, show your student I.D. (sometimes a second photo ID is required as well) and get one or two tickets at a steep discount. Tickets are offered for as little as $20 for a $100 seat; $10 for a $50 seat. Policies differ at different theatres, and different shows make different parts of the theatre available for Student Rush.

Last-Minute Rush: Certain shows offer half-price tickets at the box office a half hour before curtain. These are called "Rush" for a reason!

No-Rush Student Rush: Some shows offer "Rush" tickets in advance for certain nights of the week.

Check with individual shows for their Rush policies. Many post them on their official websites.

TWO-FERS

Two-fers are ticket-shaped coupons that allow you to buy real tickets at a discount. These are rarer today than in years past, and are generally used by shows that have been running a long time. Originally they literally offered "two" tickets "fer" the price of one. Today they are more like regular coupons, and offer ten to fifty percent off single tickets.

You can always find two-fers at tourist centers, most hotels, the Times Square Visitor Center, and at the tourist information center in Grand Central Terminal, 42nd Street at Vanderbilt Avenue.

GROUP SALES AND THEATRE PARTIES

In unity there is thrift. If you can get together a group of ten or more (or fifteen or twenty, depending on the show) you can get a group discount of ten percent or more.

The telephone number for group discounts for specific shows are listed in the ABCs of *The New York Times*, and certain other places.

For Shubert theatres: 1-212-398-8363 in New York, 1-800-223-7565 elsewhere.

For Nederlander theatres and all Disney shows: 1-212-703-1040 in New York, 1-800-439-9000 elsewhere.

For Jujamcyn shows: 1-212-302-7000 in New York, 1-800-677-1164 elsewhere.

Groups can also be arranged online through Theatreparty.com (www.theatreparty.com) or by calling 1-212-889-4300, outside New York 1-800-331-0472.

You call these numbers (some group discounts are also offered online), and here you run into another one of the areas of ticket buying that cries out to be updated. Instead of telling you immediately whether the tickets are available, you are asked to leave the number of tickets requested and several alternate dates. Then you must wait for a week or longer before they get back to you and let you know if your tickets are available for any of those days. In the age of computerized box offices, there's really no excuse for this.

Just because you are a member of a group does not necessarily mean you will sit with or even near others in your group. Your cohorts may be scattered in knots of two, four or twelve here and there about the theatre, wherever seats are available. It's harder to put together a group for a hit show, but easier to put together a group two or more months ahead of time.

Is there an alternative? There is: a website, www.showtix.com, arranges groups and gets back to you much more quickly, twenty-four to forty-eight hours or so, but the discount is much less, sometimes just four or five percent or so.

Want to join a group? Many local community centers, churches, synagogues, adult education programs, social clubs, etc., in the New York area organize groups on a periodic basis. If you join the group or register your name with them, you will be notified of shows and dates. Some work on a subscription basis. You pay an annual fee with the understanding that you'll see, say, two musicals and a play, or five new plays, or three classics, etc. And then the shows are chosen depending what opens and sounds interesting or gets good reviews.

Groups from beyond New York are usually organized by travel companies. Call your travel agent, your corporate travel office, or an AAA agent, or check websites for package deals.

Theatre Parties are groups with a goal in mind. They are run to benefit charities of various kinds. The manager will buy a block of tickets at a group discount, then resell them at a higher price, keeping the difference as a donation for the given charity. These are also popular with religious groups, which operate them, like bingo, as a benefit for the house of worship. Check yours. Nothing like having fun while helping a good cause.

SECOND-ACTING

I hate even mentioning this. By definition, it's the practice of mingling with the intermission crowd and sneaking in to see the second act of a show for free. It's stealing and trespassing, and takes the salad out of actors' mouths. People who are discovered second-acting are generally given the boot. House managers at many theatres have been cracking down on this recently. I've never heard of a show prosecuting someone for this—but they could if they wanted to.

KIDS' NIGHT ON BROADWAY

For many children, that very first theatre experience is the beginning of a lifetime of pleasure. To help parents, kindly aunts and uncles, and other indulgent grownups give this gift, Broadway initiated "Kids' Night on Broadway," a one-night-a-year deal, traditionally the first Tuesday in February.

For this special night, every adult who purchases a full-price theatre ticket can obtain a second free seat for a child. Curtain time is moved back to 7 PM so kids can get home at a reasonable hour. The event has come to be embraced by all but the most solidly sold-out shows, and now includes related events throughout the evening to welcome the young theatregoers to Broadway (and Off-Broadway).

In 2003, for example, the evening began at three in the afternoon with a party at Madame Tussaud's wax museum on 42nd Street, hosted by former Backstreet Boy Kevin Richardson, then starring in *Chicago*. Dancers from that show taught the children some dance moves, followed by a sing-along with cast members from *Hairspray*.

However, you can't just walk up on "Kids' Night" and get the tickets. "Kids' Night" takes some planning. The date is announced each fall, and tickets go on sale in October, usually only for a few weeks. The sales window closes in mid November. To track these dates, visit the event's website at www.kidsnightonbroadway.com or call the Broadway Line at 1-888-BROADWAY.

OTHER STUDENT DISCOUNTS

Student ID Discount: In addition to the Student Rush tickets, some shows offer a flat discount of 10–25 percent for students, especially college students, who can show a current photo student ID. Ask the student center at your school if such discounts have been arranged. You may also try presenting your ID at the box office.

HipTix: To cultivate young audiences, Roundabout Theatre Company offers free membership and steep ticket discounts (about 50 percent) to subscribers under the age of 35. All you need to do is fill out an application form at www.hiptix.com. You don't have to be a student to take advantage of this discount.

Volunteer Ushering: Here's a way to see a show for free—over and over again. Several theatre companies, both Off-Broadway and on, have slots for volunteer ushers. They do require that you serve throughout the limited run of the show (four to six weeks), and there often is a waiting list. But if you are going to be in New York for an extended period, and want a cool volunteer job, it's worthwhile to call and ask that your name be put on the list:

> Roundabout Theatre Company—Signup at the box office, 277 West 42nd Street
>
> 45 Bleecker Theatre—1-212-253-7017
>
> Century Center for the Performing Arts—1-212-982-6782 ext. 11
>
> John Houseman Theatre—1-212-967-7079
>
> New York Theatre Workshop—Email elizabethl@nytw.org
>
> Primary Stages—1-212-333-4052
>
> Signature Theatre—1-212-244-7529

TRAVEL PACKAGE DISCOUNTS

If you are traveling to New York by air or Amtrak, make sure to ask for theatre ticket discounts. Many airlines offer plane/hotel/show packages that get you hefty discounts on all three if you buy them together, and in advance. Continental Airlines markets itself as the official airline of Broadway, and offers Broadway-related travel packages at certain times of year.

Beware of scams. If you buy through a travel agent you know, and the components have well-known names, you're probably all right. But if you get an offer in a spam email that offers a great ticket paired with a no-name airline and hotel you never heard of, you're taking a big chance. Ancient wisdom holds true here. If an offer looks too good to be true, it probably isn't true. Be very wary of strangers offering discount tickets.

But you don't have to be a tourist to take advantage of some travel discounts. New York's commuter system, the MTA, offers discounts to commuter rail travelers with the purchase of the same MetroCard that gets you a ride on MetroNorth, the Long Island Railroad or NJ Transit. For each full-price show ticket you buy, you can request a voucher, redeemable at any open commuter rail ticket office for a free round-trip rail ticket. You can also order them by phone, but you need a discount code, which can be requested by phone at 1-212-532-4900 (outside New York City, 1-800-638-7646) and can be found on the MTA website, www.mta.nyc.ny.us/mnr/html/inbound.htm.

ON-LINE DISCOUNTS

You can also get discounts every day, via email, from Playbill.com's Playbill Club. Membership in the Club is free and can be arranged by visiting the website and clicking on the "Playbill Club" icon. They ask for your email address, and you soon begin receiving daily offers for discounts of 10 percent or more on Broadway and Off-Broadway shows, plus some regional shows and special events. In the last year, at least one show offered a "fire sale" of 65 percent. The offers come in the form of a numerical code that you must use when you go to the box office, log on to a ticket-selling website like Telecharge, or telephone the box office. You must still pay any box office service charge. The Playbill Club also offers discounts on theatre-related merchandise such as books, calendars, mugs, collectible *Playbill*s, etc.

TheatreMania's Gold Club is a well-named discount feature. Once you've joined, you have access to a seat-filling service: great tickets for nothing more than a five-dollar service charge. There are limitations, however. You must wait in the Gold Club area of the website, repeatedly hitting "refresh" on your browser. This effort often will be rewarded with great tickets, usually for the same day's performance, for less than the cost of a movie ticket. But you must claim them there and then, and pay the service charge with a credit card on the spot. You also **must** show up once you have reserved the tickets. If you decide to blow them off, you can have your membership canceled. They want those seats filled!

Other websites have similar clubs that offer discount codes.

You can redeem these and other discount offers through www.BroadwayOffers.com.

One dirty secret of this situation is that once the discount code for a show is established, anyone can use it, not just the members of that particular club. A website called BroadwayBox.com (www.broadway-box.com) gathers these discount codes from all the websites that offer them, and lists them, free, to the public. It's a great resource.

Another website that acts as a directory to online discounts is www.entertainment-link.com/tkts.asp.

PAY-WHAT-YOU-CAN

This discount is rarely seen on Broadway. It's more the provenance of institutional theatres Off- and Off-Off-Broadway, which, as part of their mission (and public or private foundation funding) do a certain amount of community outreach to all economic strata.

As the name indicates, there is either no set fee or a minimal "suggested donation." In either case, the idea is for the theatregoer to decide what he or she can afford, and pay it, even if it's one thin dime. There is generally no paperwork; the honor system is in force here. If you are a regular theatre lover and you've been laid off or otherwise suffering a streak of hard times, this is the perfect way to stay in touch with the theatre world.

Generally a special "pay-what-you-can" performance is designated early in the run, or on certain nights (generally slow ones, naturally). These are usually announced on the company's website. You may also wish to call ahead and ask.

SUBSCRIPTIONS

One of the great money-savers requires an appreciable upfront outlay of cash, but can be well worth it: a subscription series.

Much of the most interesting theatre in New York is created by theatre companies—not-for-profit organizations that produce a series of plays each year, generally four to six, each for runs of four to six weeks each. When you subscribe to one of these theatre companies, you buy tickets for several shows at once—generally an entire season's worth, or a sampler of three or so.

By buying several shows at once, you can save ten percent or more off the price of each ticket.

For example, Broadway's Roundabout Theatre Company has a top regular price ticket of $66.25 for interesting productions like Patrick Stewart in Harold Pinter's *The Caretaker* or Nathan Lane in *The Man Who Came To Dinner*. If you buy a three-play package for $175, you save $23.75 overall. If you buy the entire five-play season for $275, you

PUT A LITTLE MORE MASCARA ON

Harvey Fierstein worked as a drag performer in downtown cabarets. He told his own life story in a series of short plays that came together as *Torch Song Trilogy*, which opened on Broadway, won the Tony Award as Best Play, and turned his life around. He wrote the libretto for the musical *La Cage aux Folles*, and returned to drag—though on a much higher level—as Edna Turnblad in *Hairspray*, which won him another Tony, his fourth.

save $56.25, almost the cost of one ticket. Effectively you're getting to see a Broadway show nearly for free. These prices are subject to change.

It's a win for you because you get to save money on a lot of theatre, and it's a win for the Roundabout, because they get a big chunk of their annual income in the bank before they even begin.

To reward subscribers, theatre companies offer tempting goodies as bonuses, including first choice at the best seats, the ability to exchange tickets at the last minute, and special privileges like discounts on parking and restaurants, snacks at intermission, a chance to meet the stars in person, cocktail parties, and sometimes even a special subscriber lounge.

The Roundabout's "Penthouse Lobby," for instance, offers a view of the rooftops of Broadway, and faces directly into part of *The New York Times'* newsroom. They have all sorts of social events, including singles get-togethers, that make the theatre into a kind of private club.

In buying a subscription, you also buy into the artistic vision of the artistic director, or by a board of directors, and here's the potential downside. If the season's shows do poorly, you're stuck. It's like a marriage: you're in it for better or worse.

There are dozens of non-profit subscription theatres in New York, most of which are Off-Broadway and will be dealt with in Chapter Six. There are three such troupes on Broadway, though all do some producing Off-Broadway as well:

- Roundabout Theatre Company, headquartered at the American Airlines Theatre on 42nd Street, which focuses on star-driven revivals of plays and musicals. Website: www.roundabouttheatre.org.

- The Manhattan Theatre Club, headquartered at the Biltmore Theatre on 47th Street, which emphasizes new plays, many by a stable of associated playwrights, including David Auburn (Pulitzer Prize for *Proof*), Charles Busch (*The Tale of the Allergist's Wife*) and David Greenberg (*The Violet Hour*). MTC sold out all its subscriptions in 2003-2004. It continues to produce Off-Broadway shows at its two additional stages at the New York City Center. Website: www.mtc-nyc.org.

- Lincoln Center Theater: It's a theatre company, not a building, though it's headquartered at the Lincoln Center complex on Broadway in the West 60s. LCT produces a mixture of revivals and interesting new plays, mainly at the Vivian Beaumont Theatre and the Mitzi Newhouse Theatre there, but also sometimes at the Cort Theatre on 48th Street, and elsewhere. Some recent productions included the 2000 Tony-winner for Best Musical, *Contact*, plus a *King Lear* with Christopher Plummer, *Parade*, and *The Sisters Rosensweig*. Website: www.lct.org. Instead of a subscription, LCT offers a membership system that functions in an analogous way.

WINTER SALES

As mentioned earlier, the slowest time of year for Broadway is January and February. It's cold, and people are sitting at home glumly contemplating their credit card bills. To help fill the seats and build up body warmth in the theatres, some Broadway producers periodically announce winter sales. These are seen especially on the longer-running shows that are confident sales will bounce back come spring, but need help a little push to get the box office over the frozen hump of winter. Oddly, such sales rarely take place in winter itself. Generally the sales are announced in the fall, when people are shopping for the holidays. Discounts are sometimes as steep as fifty percent, though such deals usually are couched as two-for-one sales. You buy in November or December; you see the show in January or February. These are advertised in *The New York Times*, and sometimes in other papers, as well as on the show's website. You can also look up season discounts at www.SeasonsofSavings.com and www.ILoveNYTheater.com.

CHAPTER FIVE

SEATING

Next to every box office is a seating chart, which shows where your seat is located in that theatre. All are now available online as well, though it can be a chore hunting for them, and many fail to show every seat

These little maps are pretty self-explanatory. But there are a few things to note.

They're generally laid out with the orchestra, mezzanine and/or balcony side by side. In a real theatre these sections often overlap, so balcony seats are still are far from the stage, but not as far as a seating chart makes them look. You have to imagine them in 3-D.

Similarly, box seat are often shown as a little group on either side, though they may actually overhang the lower end of the orchestra . . . yet are usually pretty bad anyway.

For most theatres with three orchestra sections (left, center and right), note that all the odd-numbered seats are on one side and the even numbers are on the other side. This creates a situation where seats G-2, G-4 and G-6 are side-by-side, while seats G-1, G-3 and G-5 are way over on the other side. In the center section they are consecutively numbered, G-101, G-102, G-103, et cetera.

Note that Row A is not always the front row. Some theatres have covered over part or—in the case of many non-musicals—all of the orchestra pit. The extra rows in front are numbered AA, BB, CC, et cetera.

The Gershwin Theatre, Broadway's largest, also has a ZZ at the back of the orchestra.

PLAYWRIGHT LAURELS

Alfred Uhry is the only playwright to have won the Tony Award, the Oscar, and the Pulitzer Prize. The Pulitzer (1988) and Oscar were for his play (and film) *Driving Miss Daisy*. He won the Tony Award twice: in 1997 for Best Play (*Last Night of Ballyhoo*) and in 1999 for Best Book of a Musical, for *Parade*. Things didn't start out so well for him. His Broadway debut, writing the lyrics to the musical, *Here's Where I Belong*, closed on opening night in 1968.

Seating can vary from show to show in other ways as well. The accompanying seating charts were accurate as of spring 2004.

THE BEST AND WORST SEATS IN EACH THEATRE

Broadway theatres were built one at a time, by hand, by craftsmen with unique knowledge and unique challenges relating to the size and shape of the piece of property they were building upon. Knowing some of these quirks will help you pick a good seat, and avoid a bad one.

And some whole theatres are better than others for various reasons. Some have multiple balconies. Some are very wide, like Winter Garden, which can be good or bad, depending on the show. Some are very narrow, like Lunt-Fontanne, some intimate like Music Box, some beautiful like the New Amsterdam and the Hirschfeld. Some are better for musicals than plays.

Al Hirschfeld—Known until 2003 as the Martin Beck, this beautiful theatre is ideal for musicals, though a little large for the dramas and comedies that sometimes get booked there.

Ambassador—Sitting diagonally on its plot, this theatre goes very wide in the middle of the orchestra and the front mezzanine. Think twice before buying the extreme sides. It is medium in size between a musical house and a play house, and therefore creates a nice intimate feeling at musicals—at least in the center of the house.

Marquee of the Al Hirschfeld Theatre, with a neon Al using his own head for an inkpot.

Marquee of the restored Biltmore Theatre.

American Airlines—Formerly the Selwyn, this is one of the 42nd Street playhouses rescued from porno and karate films. It was lushly restored as the headquarters of Roundabout Theatre Company, and renamed for a big donor. One of the few theatres where even the Rear Mezzanine seats are good. Great amenities like wide seats, extra leg room, a bar that sells actual food (as opposed to just candy) and espresso and such, plus an upstairs bar lounge.

Belasco—Magnificently arrayed in dark wood, the Belasco sports two balconies, which are sold as Mezzanine and Balcony. The Balcony is very steep, so watch out if your footing is unsure, and offers a panoramic view of actors' heads.

Biltmore—Recently refurbished at a cost of many millions as the new flagship of the Manhattan Theatre Club. All modern amenities, and a beautiful lower lounge with photos from famous MTC shows. But the décor is unspectacular. A very big plus: the orchestra has been reconfigured with modified stadium-style seating so you're much less likely to have a head in front of you. Lots of leg room.

Booth—With just about 800 seats, it's one of Broadway's best theatres for intimate shows, especially small-scale dramas and solo shows. Located at the uptown end of Shubert Alley.

Broadhurst—Broadway's most sought-after theatre for dance shows (it was one of Bob Fosse's favorites—*Dancin'* and *Fosse* both played there for years). Has a nice intimate feeling, even though it has about 1150 seats.

Broadway—Located near the uptown end of the theatre district, this 1,765-seat former cinema is the opposite of intimate, and best reserved for big musicals like *Evita* and *Les Misérables*, both of which opened here. A lot of the seats are in the Rear Mezzanine. Bring binoculars.

Brooks Atkinson—A medium-size playhouse with good sightlines, even on the sides of the Mezzanine.

Circle in the Square—A unique bullet-shaped playing area is surrounded on four sides by seats, though sometimes the flat end of the bullet is closed off to create a backdrop. Perfect for unusual shows like *The Rocky Horror Show* and *Metamorphoses*, which lend themselves to in-the-round staging. But expect to spend at least part of the evening looking at the back of the actors' heads.

Cort—Another theatre with a lot of seats in the Mezzanine and the upper Balcony. Lots of OK views from the Mezzanine, but sometimes the Balcony gets closed off. And just as well.

Ethel Barrymore—One of Broadway's most perfect theatres, especially for classical dramas and comedies. Excellent acoustics.

Eugene O'Neill—Another medium-size playhouse with good sightlines, sometimes also used for moderate-sized musicals.

Ford Center for the Performing Arts—Opened in 1998, but incorporating the architectural details (and site) of the 1903 Lyric Theatre, this is simultaneously Broadway's newest and oldest theatre. With 1,839 seats, it's also one of the biggest. It is spacious and the stage itself is colossal—perfect for epics like *Ragtime* and *42nd Street*. One oddity: the Mezzanine and Balcony are set unusually far back from the stage. The Mezz starts over Row S of the Orchestra. Balancing that, this theatre has perhaps the best legroom of any theatre on Broadway, and the seats are comfortably wide.

Gershwin—At 1,933 seats, Broadway's biggest theatre. Best for musical extravaganzas and concert shows. Huge Orchestra seating area with roomy seats. Built in the 1970s, and slightly resembles the spaceship in *2001: A Space Odyssey*, though the Theatre Hall of Fame in the upper lobby has helped humanize the space a bit.

Golden—At 928 seats, one of the smaller Broadway theatres. Narrow, but not long, it has excellent seats throughout the Orchestra. Not a bad place to sit in the Mezzanine, either. It has only twelve rows up there.

Helen Hayes—Formerly the Little Theatre, and well named at that. At 499 seats, it's Broadway's smallest theatre, and generally used for solo shows and small-scale plays, thought the occasional tiny musical has sneaked in as well. Small Mezzanine. Even the bad seats are OK.

Imperial—The auditorium itself is located on 46th Street, but the entrance and marquee are on busier 45th Street, leading down a long corridor to the seats. The Imperial is one of a half dozen of the most

Marquee of the Broadway Theatre, with displaying the logo for Bombay Dreams.

Marquees of the Ford Center (home of the musical 42nd Street) and the New Victory Theatre on 42nd Street.

in-demand musical theatres, home to *Fiddler on the Roof*, *Pippin*, most of Gwen Verdon's shows of the 1950s, and, for many years, *Les Misérables*, which moved here from the Broadway. This is the stage where Ethel Merman first belted "No Business Like Show Business" in *Annie Get Your Gun*. I sat in the last row of the Mezzanine for *Dreamgirls*, and could feel the power bouncing off the ceiling from Jennifer Holliday's "And I Am Telling You I'm Not Going."

Longacre—Two balconies and a comparatively small Orchestra mean the Longacre is one of the last-booked Broadway theatres—which is a shame, since its nearly 1,100 (roomy) seats puts it in a class with some of the smaller musical houses. Relatively few musicals wind up there, however, while it mainly gets booked by ambitious straight plays. Nevertheless, it has had its share of hits through the years, including *Ain't Misbehavin'* and *Children of a Lesser God*.

Lunt-Fontanne—A long, narrow auditorium and one of this writer's least favorite theatres. Avoid seats in the rear of the Orchestra and Mezzanine.

Lyceum—Old and beautiful, but not the most comfortable theatre you ever attended. Seats are narrow and there's not much leg room. Helps remind you how much more petite audiences were a century ago, when this theatre was built. Has a Mezzanine and a Balcony.

Majestic—One of Broadway's most sought-after theatres. As the name indicates, a grand dame of a theatre, with a vast Orchestra, perfect for shows like longtime tenant *The Phantom of the Opera*. Rodgers and Hammerstein liked it so much, they kept it occupied for the better part of a decade in the 1940s and 50s, with their *Carousel*, *Allegro*, *South Pacific*, and *Me and Juliet*. They were followed later in the decade by Meredith Willson's *The Music Man*. Musicians and audiences have always had a special love for the Majestic.

Marquis—Built in 1986, the Marquis is one of Broadway's newest musical houses, with comfortably spaced seats in a warm rose-and-tan interior. I watched Julie Andrews deliver her famous "egregiously overlooked" diatribe against the Tony Awards from the far side and back of the mezzanine, and caught every word and facial expression. Built as part of the Marriott Marquis Hotel, it has a unique configuration. The box office is at street level on Broadway near 46th Street, but the auditorium is located three stories above street level and accessed through a series of escalators and one of the hotel's upstairs lobbies. Make sure you leave extra time to get up there. Three classic old theatres were demolished to build the hotel, and designers seem to have made the Marquis extra appealing to compensate.

Minskoff—Built in the 1970s, this rather stark theatre has roomy seats arranged on a modified European design with long central rows. I spent many hours working on a book about a show here, and got a chance to observe the stage from every angle. The Rear Mezzanine affords a surprisingly good view of the stage, but the extreme sides of this wide theatre should be avoided, unless you get them on discount. The theatre entrance is located in a pedestrian breezeway that passes under One Astor Plaza. From the lower lobby there is a long escalator

SWEEPING SUCCESS

Super producer Cameron Mackintosh began his career in the theatre as a teenager, sweeping floors at London's Drury Lane Theatre. He went on to produce the four most monetarily successful shows in theatre history: *Cats*, *The Phantom of the Opera*, *Les Miserables*, and *Miss Saigon*. The last-named musical ran for more than a decade at, you guessed it, The Drury Lane Theatre—making him a millionaire many times over.

that takes you to the upper lobby where you enter the auditorium (and which overlooks the center of Times Square).

Music Box—Theatre built by and for Irving Berlin as the optimal space to present his musical revues. It's still one of the coziest and most audience-friendly theatres anywhere; perfect for dramas, comedies or small musicals. Especially warm acoustics.

Nederlander—The flagship of the Nederlander Organization, this theatre, the only Broadway house below 42nd Street, was traditionally tough to book. All that changed in 1996 when *Rent* found the frontier location between the Garment District, the Theatre District and the Port Authority Bus Terminal to be a reasonable analogue to the show's own East Village setting. It was a match made in theatrical heaven. The entire interior and exterior have been distressed to emphasize that similarity and create and "environmental theatre" experience. So, unless you are in on the joke, the place is going to look like a rundown mess that's been tricked up by grunge artists. The theatre itself is a bit wider than you'd perhaps like, but comfortable.

Neil Simon—Formerly the Alvin, this 1,350-seat theatre has such an expansive feeling, it regularly is sought by the biggest hits, which have included *Annie*, *A Funny Thing Happened on the Way to the Forum*, *Hairspray* and recent revivals of *The King and I* and *The Music Man*. Perfect for intelligent, non-epic musicals. A kid-friendly theatre.

New Amsterdam—After a multi-million-dollar restoration by Disney, the onetime home of the *Ziegfeld Follies* is Broadway's most beautiful theatre, an art nouveau masterpiece of flowing, intertwining lines on vividly colored floral themes. The Balcony is so high, you can sometimes see angels. Though, while we're on that subject, the upper

The marquee of the New Amsterdam Theatre, once the headquarters of the Ziegfeld Follies, now restored by Disney and the playground for the jungle creatures of The Lion King.

levels are supposedly haunted by the ghost of Olive Thomas, a one-time Ziegfeld girl who committed suicide, and who is said to greet the occasional lone visitor with a perky "Hello!"

Palace—The single most legendary theatre in America, this was the highest you could get back in Vaudeville days, when "playing the Palace" carried a magical cachet. There is a special electricity that performers feel when standing downstage center at the Palace, where Judy Garland, the Marx Brothers, Gwen Verdon, and a hundred other giants once held the spotlight. Long since converted to a Broadway musical house, the gold-and-crimson Palace has a few oddly arranged seats, like the raised sides of the orchestra separated by marble railings. And it's hard to imagine that vaudeville audiences could see much from the back of that Balcony, which obscures parts of the stage. Also said to be the most extensively haunted theatre on Broadway. Disney opened its *Beauty and the Beast* here, then moved it elsewhere so it could open *Aida* here.

Plymouth—Good medium-side theatre, one of the workhorses of Broadway, and nearly always booked. Good views from all angles.

Richard Rodgers—A sought-after smallish musical house, which serves as a showcase for the composer's memorabilia. The orchestra is steeply slanted—which is good, because you're less likely to have a head in front of you blocking your sight line. However, as a result, people have to go up a flight of stairs to get to the rear of the orchestra. They sometimes freak out and think they've got tickets in the Mezzanine or Balcony. It's actually a good layout though, unless you have standing room, in which case, you miss the top of the stage.

The marquee of the Palace Theatre (left) and the entrance of the Times Square Information Center, topped with billboards.

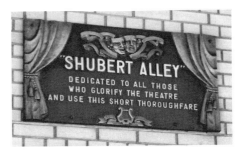

The plaque dedicating Shubert Alley on the Shubert Theatre.

Marquee of the St. James Theatre, home to Oklahoma!, Hello, Dolly! and, currently, The Producers.

Royale—Virtually identical to the Plymouth next door. Good views and acoustics, but narrow seats.

Shubert—The flagship of the Shubert Organization chain is one of Broadway's most perfect musical houses. Longtime home to *Chicago*, *Babes in Arms*, *A Little Night Music*, *Bells Are Ringing*, and, for sixteen years, *A Chorus Line*. Problems with sightlines from some Mezzanine seats have been fixed in recent years.

St. James—One of Rodgers and Hammerstein's favorite theatres, and home to their *Oklahoma!*, *The King and I*, and *Flower Drum Song*. Also the longtime home of *Hello, Dolly!*, and, more recently, *The Who's Tommy* and *The Producers*. It's as big and wide as these productions suggest. Something about the design seems to concentrate energy in the center of the space. There's little as thrilling as sitting in the middle of the St. James when a number goes over really well.

Studio 54—Originally opened as the Gallo Opera House, it achieved its greatest fame in the 1970s as a disco and den of iniquity. It was refurbished as a nightclub-type theatre for the long-running *Cabaret* revival, and at this writing is being rearranged once again as a legitimate theatre for use by Roundabout Theatre Company's larger productions. Needs a fix-up.

Virginia—One of the smaller musical theatres, it was built by the Theatre Guild in 1925 and lived through several incarnations and names (The Guild, ANTA) before being purchased by Jujamcyn. The audience enters a two-tiered lobby that is actually underneath the auditorium. Access is through two stairways to the right. Owing to its size, it has hosted musicals (*City of Angels*, *The Wild Party*, *Little Shop of Horrors*) as well as plays (*King Hedley II*, *Cat on a Hot Tin Roof*) and even solo shows (Bill Maher's *Victory Begins at Home*). It used to have an odd lopsided seat layout in the Orchestra and an odd line of seats dubbed the "Loge in the Mezzanine." But it now looks more like a standard theatre. The front Mezzanine feels especially close to the stage, and has extra wings of seats on both sides to capitalize on that.

Vivian Beaumont—A problem theatre since it was built in the 1960s as part of the Lincoln Center complex. The thrust stage arrangement meant that seats in the center were fine, but seats on the sides had you looking into actors' ears. Recent refurbishment has ameliorated, but not solved, this problem, along with some acoustical challenges.

Walter Kerr—Smallish theatre formerly known as the Ritz. Good for small, intense dramas and intimate comedies. Avoid the tiny (two rows!) but stratospheric second balcony.

Winter Garden—Headquarters for big musicals like *West Side Story, Funny Girl, Mame, Follies, Cats,* and *Mamma Mia!* This is one of Broadway's widest theatres, which means the seats on the far sides (especially in the Mezzanine) put you at an acute angle to the stage. Most directors compensate for this, but keep it in mind when buying seats. Some are sold, at a lower price, as "obscured view."

Marquee of the Winter Garden Theatre, tenanted by Mamma Mia!

CHAPTER SIX

SPECIAL GUIDE
TO OFF-BROADWAY

You recognize Broadway instantly: It's *42nd Street* and *The Producers* and *Death of a Salesman* and such. Big shows with big casts and big themes.

So what, then, is this Off-Broadway you've been hearing about? And how is it different from Off-Off-Broadway?

Off-Broadway evolved in the 1950s as a reaction against the rising costs and perceived lack of experimentation on Broadway. The Off-Broadway theatre movement began in the bohemian section of New York called Greenwich Village (between Houston St. and 14th St.) and spread throughout the city.

In the 1960s, an even cheaper, smaller and more experimental movement called Off-Off-Broadway emerged as complete rejection of commercial theatre.

Both continue to flourish. Off-Off-Broadway continues to explore challenging subject matter for tiny audiences. Off-Broadway has evolved into an increasingly commercial younger brother to Broadway, though most Off-Broadway shows today are still produced by not-for-profit companies. There are even some Off- and Off-Off-Broadway theatres functioning alongside the big for-profit theatres of Times Square. Off-Broadway hits sometimes find commercial producers and transfer to Broadway theatres. Several recent Tony winners including *Rent*, *Avenue Q*, *Contact*, *Proof*, and *Take Me Out* arrived via that route.

Location of the theatre is less important than size. As mentioned in Chapter Two, Broadway theatres have 499 seats or more, Off-Broadway theatres have 100 to 498 seats. Off-Off-Broadway theatres have 99 seats or fewer.

Off-Broadway theatres can be located anywhere in New York, but most are congregated in Greenwich Village, the upper West Side and, in recent years, the area east of Union Square, between Park Ave. South and Third Ave. in the teens. Tickets can cost as much as $78, not much different than those on Broadway, but most remain considerably cheaper than Broadway.

Off-Off-Broadway theatres also can be located anywhere in the city, though they seem to occur every other block in the East Village, the West Village and SoHo. Because of their tiny size, most charge little for tickets and pay actors and other employees very little as well. Because financial stakes are lower, OOB can take more chances. There's a lot of junk, but also a lot of brilliance. Lots of today's TV, film and Broadway talent got its start Off-Off-Broadway. Because so much of the work is specialized and has a limited audience, the small size of Off-Off-Broadway theatres is perfect.

OFF-BROADWAY THEATRE COMPANIES YOU SHOULD KNOW

Like Broadway, Off-Broadway puts on commercial productions that run until they stop making a profit ("open-ended run") and productions mounted by standing theatre companies that have a limited run because they are part of a pre-planned season of productions. The difference is, Off-Broadway and Off-Off-Broadway have far more of the latter than the former.

A description of the some the longer-running commercial productions can be found in Chapter Thirteen.

Here is a rundown of the larger Off-Broadway and Off-Off-Broadway theatre troupes, a brief description of their production philosophy, and a summary of their hits. Some of their missions are as simple as, "All new plays" or "Revivals of classics." These companies act as production engines for the American theatre, developing and showcasing new plays, writers, directors and actors. Many of those listed here have moved productions to Broadway and won major awards. Two have actually bought Broadway theatres and now operate in both worlds.

All thrive on subscriptions. Subscribers buy a whole season's worth of shows in advance and then take the good with the not-so-good, on the chance that somewhere in there will be something great. They also sell individual tickets, but because the theatres are small subscribers get the choice seats and spread the word on hits to their friends. Thus, hits usually sell out fast.

There are many more companies than those listed here, but I've included those that have produced that "something great" with some consistency.

Atlantic Theatre Company: 336 West 20th Street (Between Eighth and Ninth Avenues) New American plays, and imports of interesting new plays from Britain. *The Beauty Queen of Leenane*, Woody Allen's *Writer's Block*, *The Joy of Going Somewhere Definite*, *Blue/Orange*, *Dublin Carol*. 1-212-691-5919, x123. Web: www.atlantictheater.org.

The Flea Theatre: 41 White St. (between Broadway and Church St.) Hosts various Off-Off-Broadway troupes that develop new plays. *The Guys*, *No Mother to Guide Her*, *Billy the Kid*. 1-212-226-2407 Web: www.thefleatheatre.com.

HERE: 145 Avenue of the Americas (between Spring & Dominick Sts.) SoHo theatre space used by several Off-Off-Broadway companies and individual artists. *The Vagina Monologues*, *The Running Man*, *Symphonie Fantastique*, *The Women of Orleans*. 1-212-647-0202. Web: www.here.org.

Irish Repertory Theatre: 132 West 22nd St. (between Sixth and Seventh Aves.) "The very best in Irish drama." *The Irish . . . and How They Got That Way, The Shadow of a Gunman, The Colleen Bawn, The Shaugraun.* 1-212-727-2737. Web: www.irishrep.org.

La Mama ETC (La MaMa Experimental Theatre Club): 74A East 4th St. (between Second Ave and Bowery). Ellen Stewart's Off-Off-Broadway landmark still offers many productions "by artists of all nations and colors" on its three stages each year, usually for short runs. *I Can't Keep Running in Place, Why Hanna's Skirt Won't Stay Down, Balm in Gilead, Birdbath, The Unseen Hand, Viet Rock, The Rimers of Eldritch, Futz, The Dirtiest Show in Town, Reno: Rebel Without a Pause.* 1-212-475-7710. Web: www.lamama.org.

MCC Theatre (Manhattan Class Company): East 13th St. Theater, 136 East 13th St. (between Third and Fourth Aves.). Encourages "new American voices" through production of dramas and comedies by previously little-known playwrights. *Wit, The Mercy Seat, The Grey Zone, Trudy Blue, Nixon's Nixon.* Phone: 1-212-279-4200. Web: www.mcctheater.com

Manhattan Theatre Club: Biltmore Theatre, 261 West 47th St.; Stages I and II at City Center, 131 West 55th St. (between Seventh Ave. and Avenue of the Americas). Though MTC moved the heart of its operations to Broadway in 2003 after years as one of the most successful Off-Broadway troupes, it still maintains a strong Off-Broadway presence, programming two OB stages with new plays by MTC's stable of associated playwrights. *Proof, Ain't Misbehavin', The Tale of the Allergist's Wife, Love! Valour! Compassion! , Putting It Together, Frankie and Johnnie in the Claire de Lune, Crimes of the Heart, The Wild Party* (Andrew Lippa's), *Fuddy Mears, King Hedley II, Sylvia, Sight Unseen, The Piano Lesson.* 1-212-239-6200. Web: www.manhattantheaterclub.com.

Mint Theater Company: 311 West 43rd St. (between Eighth and Ninth Aves.) Rediscovering and reviving "worthy but neglected plays." *The Voysey Inheritance, Welcome To Our City, Mr. Pim Passes By, The House of Mirth, Miss Lulu Bett, Alison's House, Rutherford and Son.* 1-212-315-9434. Web: www.minttheater.org.

New Victory Theatre: 209 West 42nd St. Showcase for theatre companies from across the U.S. and around the world that offer theatre of all kinds for kids, teens and their families. Productions that have been showcased here include: *The Green Bird, It Ain't Nothin' But the Blues, A Year With Frog and Toad, Shockheaded Peter, Thwak, Peter and Wendy.* Phone: 1-212-239-6200. Web: www.newvictory.org.

The Public Theater/New York Shakespeare Festival: Public Theater, 425 Lafayette St. (near 8th St.) In summer: Delacorte Theatre, Central Park near West 81st St. New plays and musicals, often by eth-

nic authors, plus revivals of classics, especially Shakespeare. Shows
that originated here include: *A Chorus Line*; *Hair*; *The Mystery of
Edwin Drood*; *The Normal Heart*; *Caroline, or Change*; *Bring in 'da
Noise, Bring in 'da Funk*; *Two Gentlemen of Verona* (musical). Phone:
1-212-239-6200. Web: www.publictheater.org.

New York Theatre Workshop: 79 East 4th St. A collective of writers, actors, directors and other theatre talent who help develop one
another's work at all stages in their careers. Productions that have
emerged from that process include *Rent*, *Dirty Blonde*, *Quills*,
Lypsinka, *The Most Fabulous Story Ever Told*, *Blown Sideways
Through Life*, and *Bright Lights, Big City*. Phone: 1-212-239-6200 or 1-
800-432-7250. Web: www.nytw.org.

Pan Asian Repertory Theatre: West End Theatre in the Church of
St. Paul & St. Andrew, 263 West 86th Street, (between Broadway and
West End Ave.) "Forging a repertoire of new Asian-American works."
The Joy Luck Club, *Cambodia Agonistes*, *And the Soul Shall Dance*,
Yellow Fever, *The Legend of White Snake*. 1-212-868-4030.Web:
www.panasianrep.org.

The Pearl Theatre Company Theatre: 80 St. Mark's, 80 St.
Mark's Place. Revivals of classics. *The Chairs*, *The Rivals*, *The
Merchant of Venice*, *When We Dead Awaken*, *The Persians*. 1-212-505-
3401. Web: www.pearltheatre.org

Playwrights Horizons: Playwrights Horizons Theatre, 416 West
42nd St. (Theatre Row). New American plays and musicals. *Driving
Miss Daisy*, *Sunday in the Park With George*, *The Heidi Chronicles*,
March of the Falsettos, *Floyd Collins*, *Violet*. Phone: 1-212-279-4200
Web: www.playwrightshorizons.org.

Primary Stages: 59E59 Theatre, 59 East 59th St. (between Madison
and Park Aves.) Nurturing the development of playwrights. *All in the
Timing*, *You Should Be So Lucky*, *St. Nicholas*, *The Old Settler*, *Bovver
Boys*, *"2"* , *The Model Apartment*, *Mere Mortals*, *A Murder of Crows*.
1-212 279-4200. Web: www.primarystages.com.

P.S. 122: 150 First Ave. (at East 9th St.) Not-for-profit arts center
showcasing a variety of Off-Off-Broadway troupes and artists. *Matt &
Ben*. Artists whose work has been developed here: Eric Bogosian,

Spalding Gray, Holly Hughes, Karen Finley, John Leguizamo, Mac Wellman, Blue Man Group, Danny Hoch, Elevator Repair Service, Penny Arcade. 1-212-477-5288. Web: www.ps122.org.

Roundabout Theatre Company: American Airlines Theatre, 227 West 42nd St.; also runs Studio 54 and the Laura Pels Theatre on 46th Street. Revivals of classic plays and musicals, mainly from 20th century America, but also elsewhere. Formerly based Off-Broadway, the company refurbished Broadway's Selwyn Theatre as its new production headquarters, and renamed it for donor American Airlines. Still also produces Off-Broadway at the Pels Theatre. Revivals and transfers that originated here: *Cabaret, Nine, Side Man, The Man Who Came to Dinner, Follies, Assassins*. 1-212-719-1300. Web: www.roundabouttheatre.org.

Second Stage Theatre: 307 West 43rd St. Founded on the principle that new plays also need a second production, Second Stage showcases excellent productions from regional theatres around the U.S., and also does some debuts of new American plays and musicals. Productions showcased here have included: *Metamorphoses, Saturday Night, Jitney, Little Fish, Uncommon Women and Others, Tiny Alice, Ricky Jay and His 52 Assistants*. Second Stage Theatre at the corner with Eighth Ave. Phone: 1-212-246-4422. Web: www.secondstagetheatre.com.

Signature Theatre Company: Peter Norton Space, 555 West 42nd St. Theatre Row. The company devotes and entire yearlong season to new and revived plays of a single playwright. Among those so far: Sam Shepard, Lanford Wilson, Arthur Miller (debut of *Mr. Peters' Connections*), John Guare (debut of *Lake Hollywood*), Horton Foote, Adrienne Kennedy and Bill Irwin. 1-212-244-PLAY. Web: www.signaturetheatre.org.

Vineyard Theatre: Performs at Dimson Theatre, 108 East 15th Street, near Union Square. Showcases "bold and idiosyncratic theatre artists." *Avenue Q, How I Learned to Drive, Three Tall Women, Fully Committed, The Long Christmas Ride Home, Pterodactyls, Bed and Sofa, The Dying Gaul*. Phone: 1-212-353-0303. Web: www.vineyardtheatre.org.

The York Theatre Company: New "intimate" American musicals, and revivals of "underappreciated musicals of the past." Shows that were developed here include: *The IT Girl, Suburb, No Way to Treat A Lady, Fermat's Last Tango, The Show Goes On, The Fabulist, Exactly Like You*, and the annual "Musicals in Mufti" series. The Theatre at Saint Peter's in the Citigroup Center, 619 Lexington Ave. (at 54th St.). Phone: 1-212-935-5824 ext 11. Web: www.yorktheatre.org.

In addition to these companies, many great old ones are now out of business: Circle Rep, Café Cino, Circle in the Square, Equity Library Theatre, Light Opera of Manhattan, and the Ridiculous Theatrical Company.

WHERE TO BUY OFF-BROADWAY TICKETS

Ticket Central (www.ticketcentral.com) acts as a clearinghouse for tickets to Off-Broadway shows. Phone: 1-212-279-4200.

Most of the longer-running commercial Off-Broadway shows also have struck deals with one of the two big ticket agencies, TicketMaster or Telecharge, to handle phone and internet orders.

Theatres along Off-Broadway's Theatre Row on the far west end of 42nd St. have banded together to sell tickets through a common virtual box office at www.theatrerow.org. You can also call 1-212-714-2460.

Ticket policies at Off-Broadway shows are generally the same as for Broadway, though specific policies vary even more widely. Subscription theatres, which are more prevalent Off-Broadway, offer greater ticket flexibility to subscribers than to single-ticket buyers.

STATUS

One more issue: status. You'd think that the comparatively cozy world of legitimate theatre would pull together in a united and coordinated fashion. Ha!

In fact, there Broadway looks down on Off-Broadway the way a college senior looks down on a freshman: small scale and small time. Undaunted, Off-Broadway looks down on Broadway as overblown and overcommercialized.

Though production values have gotten to the point where they are roughly comparable, several determined efforts to get the Tony Awards to incorporate Off-Broadway have been firmly rebuffed. This is especially odd, since many Tony-winners of the last few decades began Off-Broadway.

Shows make the decision to invest in a transfer from Off-Broadway to Broadway when they prove (or believe) that they have enough commercial appeal to attract enough people to fill a larger theatre, and to pay more for tickets.

Broadway theatres generally have larger stages and therefore are able to present more extravagant shows. More seats also enable them to support higher salaries and, therefore, bigger-salaried stars. So the term "Broadway Musical" tends to suggest a specific kind of entertainment. Though, as *Rent* proved in 1996 and *Avenue Q* proved in 2004, a show that originates Off-Broadway can wind up the Best Musical on Broadway.

CHAPTER SEVEN

GETTING AROUND

You've got your tickets. Now it's time to plan the rest of your day or evening. Some people just pop out to the theatre on a whim. Others plan the trip like a military campaign. For the latter, here's a checklist:

- Plan transportation. If by car, plan your route and find a place to park. If by commuter train, make sure to plan how to get from the terminal to the restaurant or theatre. If by subway, remember to factor in possible delays. If by bus, remember to factor in traffic, especially if you're traveling crosstown (east to west or west to east), which tends to be slower.

- Plan child care. Babysitter or family?

- Plan a meal out. Make restaurant reservations. Check to estimate travel time from the restaurant to the theatre, figuring at least two minutes per short block, five minutes per long block; more if it's raining or snowing. Clock backward from 7:30 PM. Allot about an hour and a half for dining, including waiting for dinner to be prepared, and including the time it takes the waiter to bring the check, which can be considerable. You should call for that check by 7:15 at the latest, preferably by 7.

- Plan a post-theatre discussion session. Whether you go out for coffee, for cocktails, for cocktails at a piano bar, for a late-night club crawl, or simply for a chat on a post-theatre walk, in the train or car or bed, remember that talking about your experience with a companion is one of the most satisfying parts of the theatregoing experience. If you commute any distance, remember to keep an eye on the schedule for the last train or bus.

Some advice on how to get to and from the theatre:

The Times Square neighborhood, that is, the Theatre District, covers less than a square mile. The heart of this neighborhood runs from West 41st St. to West 54th Street, mostly between Avenue of the Americas (Sixth Avenue) and Eighth Avenue.

And yet it earns its nickname "Crossroads of the World" every day. My father used to say, "This place is like Times Square at Rush Hour!" And truly, it's no exaggeration. Even at 1 or 2 AM, it's still pretty bustling. There are several rush hours a day, each with different kinds of rushers.

That's because it's at the nexus of Manhattan streets, as well as subway and bus lines. Part of the reason the theatres are so successful is that so many people already crisscross its streets all the time. It's a high-traffic location in every sense of the word.

Times Square is bordered by several very different neighborhoods.

On the downtown or south side is the Garment District, which teems with designers, models and guys pushing wheeled racks of clothes during the day—and is comparatively quiet after dark (exactly the opposite of the Theatre District).

To the West lies the area once known as Hell's Kitchen for its lawlessness and violence, but now gentrified and re-nicknamed Clinton. Ninth Avenue and the cross streets leading to it have become restaurant meccas, though the neighborhood still gets grungier as you head west toward the Hudson River waterfront. Lots of actors and stage crew types have made homes here.

To the north (uptown), in the upper 50s, you are headed toward the tony precincts of Carnegie Hall, CBS and Columbus Circle, with Central Park and Lincoln Center beyond. Apartments are much more expensive and swanky than those just blocks away in Clinton, and there are world-class boutiques, especially along 57th Street.

To the east is Rockefeller Center, a cluster of huge boxlike office buildings that house the nation's media capital, with NBC, Fox, Time-Warner, *People* magazine, *Time* magazine, *The New York Post*, *TV Guide*, Sirius Satellite Radio, Simon & Schuster and dozens more broadcasters, publishers and periodicals within steps of one another.

A block farther east on Fifth Avenue, you find the great promenade of stores like Tiffany's, Sephora, Bendel, Cartier and Bergdorf Goodman, along with St. Patrick's Cathedral. If you come during the holiday shopping season, expect to take twenty minutes or more to swim through the crowds on just a few short blocks from 49th to 57th Streets.

At the heart of Rockefeller Center is a picturesque below-level skating rink, watched over by a gilded statue of Prometheus, and on Avenue of the Americas at 50th Street, Radio City Music Hall. Also nearby, on the block of 47th St. between Fifth and Sixth Avenues, is the Diamond District, flanked by tall, jewel-shaped towers at each end. Clusters of Orthodox Jews in traditional garb make a specialty of handling the gems, which glisten from nearly every window on the block.

SUBWAYS

The New York subway system is crowded, dirty, and confusing. It's also the best, quickest, and cheapest way to cover moderately long distances (more than ten blocks or so, about a half mile) in a jump.

The familiar subway tokens have been phased out. Instead, riders buy a yellow Metrocard at the former token booths, or at machines in each station. The machines take cash, credit cards and debit (ATM) cards. A single ride costs $2, but discounts are available if you program in $10 or more. You can also buy special cards that give you

Entrance to the Times Square subway station at 42nd Street.

The proper way to use the MetroCard for subways and buses. Magnetic strip down and to the right, colored side with the words "MetroCard" upright and to the left. Position it at the near end of the slot on the turnstile, then slide it through with one smooth movement.

unlimited rides for a day, a week or a month. These are well worth it if you are visiting the city and plan to do a lot of moving around. Unlike subway systems in most other cities, your two bucks allows you to travel anywhere you like in the system for the same price. Once you are inside the turnstiles, you can stay on the subway as long as you like. The song "Subway Directions" in the musical *Subways Are for Sleeping* takes delight in this fact. But like Toyland, once you pass its borders you cannot return—unless you pay another fare. (You can, however, get free transfers to the bus system.)

Some eighteen subway lines converge in the Theatre District from every corner of New York City, thirteen of them in the Times Square stop proper: 1, 2, 3, 7, 9, A, C, E, N, R, Q, S, and W.

The Metropolitan Transit Agency (MTA) is the New York City agency in charge of the buses, subways and commuter trains. Stops on its dozens of lines are marked with a white "M" in a blue circle, or the letters "MTA." Most subways run underground, as their name suggests. But in sections in Brooklyn and Queens, the subway also runs on huge trestles above the streets. These are called elevated subways or "el's."

Stations serving the Theatre District can be found at 47th and Seventh, 49th and Seventh, 50th and Broadway, 52nd and Eighth, 50th and Sixth, and 55th and Seventh and 53rd and Seventh. Each has its own strange personality. The 50th and Broadway station on the 1/9 Broadway express line, for example, is decorated with mosaics of "Alice in Wonderland." The station at 49th and Seventh is done all in orange-red tile.

And then there is the Times Square station itself. No map can do justice to this three-dimensional maze. A dozen platforms on four levels, connected by tunnels, elevators, stairs, escalators, and two dozen entrances spread over eight blocks, including one tunnel that seems to go on forever, a spiral ramp to Hades, and an arcade that suddenly turns into a mini mall. Twelve different subway lines from three different subway systems converge there. Even early in the morning and late at night, it's full of hurrying people, construction crews, ticket sellers, wranglers, commuters, hustlers and performers of all kinds.

Everybody wants to be a Broadway star, even if it's twenty feet *below* Broadway. In the course of a single week, the census of street performers in the Times Square station included breakdancers, a gospel singer, a living statue (all white), another living statue (of Liberty), Peruvian flute players, religious types handing out soul-saving literature (shades of Sgt. Sarah Brown), a classical violin player, a guy who danced to Latin music with a female mannequin strapped to his shoes, and a pair of teenagers who pounded out rhythms on plastic pails. All this, adding to the din of track announcements, squealing brakes, cranking turnstiles, shouted conversations, and thousands of crisscrossing footsteps.

In the wake of 9/11 there's also a lot of police. And, sometimes, soldiers. With carbines.

It's a tough place, and somebody at some point seems to have decided that newcomers should undergo a kind of bureaucratic hazing. You'd think, with all the visitors to the area, signs and directions would be clear and frequent. But no such luck. Train lines are identified by a system of letters and numbers that follows no rhyme or reason, and which are posted inside brightly colored, but otherwise mysterious circles and diamonds. One side of each platform is for local trains, the other for express trains—except when that's not the case. There are a few maps here and there, but almost nothing that clearly tells you which train or exit will get you to Shubert Alley, or the TKTS booth, or Madison Square Garden, or the World Trade Center site, or the Upper West Side. Attendants manning the ticket booths are sometimes able to help, but it's really not their job, and they can be spectacularly rude. Better yet, ask them for a copy of "The Map," a folded map put out by the MTA that lists all the bus, subway and train lines, and where they go. Deciphering it is up to you.

Here, in a nutshell, are the pros and cons of the New York subway system.

Cons: Confusing or non-existent signage. Mysterious schedules; local trains can turn into express trains without notice. Dirty stations. Loud and crowded trains.

Pros: Lots of trains running constantly, even late at night. If you miss a train by one second, just relax. Another one will be along in five or ten minutes. One standard fare ($2) gets you anywhere. No need to sift though long lists of destinations to figure out how much you must pay. Can get MetroCard for single trip, day or week or month, with discounts. Go anywhere you like, as often as you like.

BUSES

Eleven city bus lines converge on Times Square from various corners of the city: M5, M6, M7, M10, M16, M20, M27, M30, M31, M42, M50, M57 and M104. All stop within the Theatre District.

Like the subways, they cost $2 ($1 for seniors) to ride. Unlike the subways, they accept cash, but you must have exact change. You're better off buying a MetroCard at a subway station.

One of the most interesting and useful is the 104, which starts at the United Nations, runs along 42nd Street, then swings north on Broadway, right through the heart of Times Square, and up past all the theatres to Columbus Circle, then up the West Side past Lincoln Center, ending finally at West 129th St. and Amsterdam Avenue. It also runs back the same route.

A few suggestions on buses:

• Don't depend on them to get you anywhere in a rush. They are subject to all the same traffic tie-ups as the cars, and they make many, many stops.

• Signal to the driver when you want to stop by tugging on the cord that runs the length of the bus or (in some models), pressing a yellow plastic strip that runs along above the windows. Signal two blocks in advance of where you want to get off. In practice, this means the "Stop Requested" light is virtually always on, and the driver just makes his usual scheduled stops.

- Fares can be paid with exact change or by purchasing a MetroCard at any subway station. The same card can be used for buses and subways, and can be purchased for a single ride.

LONG-DISTANCE BUS LINES

At the southwest corner of the Theatre District, 42nd Street at Eighth Avenue, can be found the legendary Port Authority Bus Terminal, where Greyhound and other national bus companies arrive and depart from/to points across the U.S. This is also the terminal for the New Jersey public bus system. It's topped by a colossal and faceless shopping mall.

Complete bus schedules can be found at the Port Authority's website: http://www.panynj.gov/tbt/pabmain.HTM.

TOUR BUSES

For details on tour buses, see Chapter Eleven.

COMING TO BROADWAY BY CAR

New York City wasn't made for cars. It was laid out in the 19th century with horse-drawn carriages in mind. The oldest sections of the city, Greenwich Village and south, are a spaghetti of streets laid out according to no special plan, almost like a medieval European city. North of the Village, the streets are laid in a grid, with avenues running north and south, streets running east and west. Most are numbered: avenues numbered from First on the East River to Twelfth on the Hudson. Streets are numbered from 1st in Greenwich Village to 220th on the Spuyten Duyvil waterway. The theatre district stands on the southern half of the island, roughly between 41st and 54th Streets, and Sixth and Eighth Avenues, closer to the West Side of the island than the East Side.

In the can-do spirit of the early and mid-20th century, visionaries attempted to adapt Manhattan to the needs and requirements of the automobile. Most streets were made one-way, alternating eastbound and westbound. The shoreline was pushed out into the rivers, and highways built upon them. These are the best ways to approach Broadway by car.

Because the theatres are closer to the West Side, drivers should make their way to the Henry Hudson Parkway, which runs along the Hudson, natch. Exits are at 42nd Street and 56th Street.

From New Jersey, take the George Washington Bridge to the Henry Hudson Parkway, southbound. From Westchester, take the Cross County Parkway to the Henry Hudson Parkway south. From the

THE GYPSY ROBE

It all started in 1950 when chorus singer Bill Bradley from the original *Gentlemen Prefer Blondes* sent a dressing gown to a friend in the chorus of *Call Me Madam*. That person attached a rose from Ethel Merman's costume, as a souvenir, and sent the robe along to a friend in the chorus of another newly-opened show, and the tradition of the Gypsy Robe was born. Rules have been formalized: The dancer (or "gypsy") who has been in the most shows gets the robe on the opening night of her or his new show. That dancer must attach a piece of memorabilia, and pass the robe along to the most senior dancer on the next show. As robes have filled up with tchotchkes and been retired, they have been donated to Actors Equity Association, the Smithsonian Institution in Washington DC, or to The Museum of the City of New York, where they go on display. And the tradition goes on. You can see the latest gypsy robe and get a list of recent recipients at www.actorsequity.org/gypsyrobe/stories.html.

Bronx, take the Henry Hudson Parkway south. The Cross-Bronx Expressway also gets you there, but it is a dreaded traffic nightmare.

From Queens and Long Island, take the Long Island Expressway to the Midtown Tunnel, then follow 34th Street west to Eighth Avenue, and make a right. From Brooklyn and Staten Island, get to the FDR Drive, get off the 42nd Street exit, make a left and head west.

There is limited street parking. Your best bet is to get into one of the following list of parking garages.

Many commercial lots offer discounts if you bring your car in before 6 PM. Make sure you tell the attendant that you will be attending the theatre, and will be picking your car up before midnight. Cars going out early will be parked closer to the entrance, meaning less wait time when you come to pick them up. Expect to pay between ten and twenty dollars to park for the evening.

Here are some of the parking lots in the Times Square area:

Kinney, 220 West 41st St. 1-212-730-1777

Kinney, 236 West 41st St. 1-212-730-1777

Kinney, 250 West 41st St. 1-212-730-8333

Kinney, 264 West 42nd St. 1-212-997-5543

Meyers Times Square Garage, 141-143 West 43rd St. (also entrance on 44th St.) 1-212-997-7690

Advance Parking, 249-253 West 43rd St. 1-212-221-8902

Carter Hotel Parking Garage, 250 West 43rd St. 1-212-997-1550

Hippodrome Garage, 43rd Street at Avenue of the Americas (also entrance on 44th St.) 1-212-997-9096

Kinney, 100 West 44th St. 1-212-398-0464

Astor Parking Corp., 1515 Broadway at 44th St. 1-212-869-3543

Miro Parking Corp., 139 West 45th St. 1-212-944-5118

Resource Parking, 164 West 46th St. 1-212-840-7526

Quik Park, 303 West 46th St. 1-212-664-8224

333 West 46th St. Corp., 333 West 46th St. 1-212-245-9422

Trans-Parking, 223 West 46th St. 1-212-997-1636

Show-Biz Parking, 254-262 West 46th St. 1-212-757-7925

Quik Park, 145 West 47th St. 1-212-869-5479

Kinney, 253-255 West 47th St. 1-212-582-5711

West 47th Street, 257 West 47th St. 1-212-262-9778

Kinney, 754 Eighth Ave. between 46th & 47th Sts. 1-212-997-9421

GMC, 148 West 48th St. 1-212-575-9133

Kinney 155 West 48th St. 1-212-354-8904

Port Parking, 235 West 48th St. 1-212-245-9421

GMC, 225 West 49th St. 1-212-262-9779

Zenith, 790-806 Eighth Ave. at 49th St. 1-212-581-8590

GMC, 218 West 50th St. 1-212-262-9795

Circle Parking, 209-211 West 51st St. 1-212-397-9029

Zenith, 851-859 Eighth Ave. at 51st St. 1-212-581-8490

Parking 888, 888 Eighth Ave. at 52nd St. 1-212-245-0068

Park Service Inc., 166 West 53rd St. 1-212-397-9028

Central Parking, 810 Seventh Ave. at 53rd St. 1-212-974-9317

TAXICABS

Despite the expense, New Yorkers spend a lot of time and energy on taxicabs. Drivers themselves are a legendary part of the Manhattan landscape: sometimes garrulous and friendly, sometimes sullen, sometimes remarkably aromatic. Sometimes they sing.

Licensed cabs are yellow, with their rates stenciled on their doors, and a yellow bubble light on the roof. It's practically a law of physics that they can be seen everywhere and always—except where and when you want one. They somehow magically disappear just as the first drops of rain begin to fall. There was a move afoot in early 2004 to put nine hundred more taxis on New York's streets, which could ease the problem.

There are two ways to get a cab in New York: calling the dispatcher, and hailing. Calling the dispatcher is surer, but you have to wait longer. Hailing one is quicker, and you can make the decision whenever you want, but sometimes luck plays an outsize role in whether you wait twenty seconds or twenty minutes.

Here are just a tiny few of the cab companies in Manhattan.

Yellow Cab 277 Broadway 1-212-571-5412

Chelsea Taxi 250 Eighth Ave. 1-212-627-7575

All Star Taxi 545 West 37th St. 1-212-563-9696

The other way to get a taxi—also quicker and more colorful—is hailing them. Stand as close to the curb as seems safe, and simply raise your hand or umbrella, or other easily visible object. Hold it straight up and out and angled toward the oncoming traffic in the most visible way possible. Most streets in Manhattan are one-way, so keep your eyes and hand turned in the direction from which traffic is coming. On top of each taxicab is a gizmo that displays the cab's license number in light-up characters. If this roof light is off, the taxi is occupied or off-duty. Don't waste your time waving frantically at a cab with its light off. It won't stop.

However, if you see a cab with its roof light on, a little body English won't hurt your chances of attracting the driver's attention.

It's always easier getting a cab on one of the avenues (which go uptown or downtown) than one the cross streets (which go east or west). Better yet: stand on a corner, so you have two potential cab sources. Empty cabs prowl the avenues. Fortunately for you, cabs obey the law of supply and demand and tend to swarm into Times Square just about the time curtains are coming down. Unfortunately for you, the swarm of potential riders is always larger.

A tip if you are just coming out of a show and there are three dozen people who want a cab at the same time you do: Hailing a cab in Times Square itself is a challenge, and there's lots of competition. Also, traffic flows one way, downtown, on both Broadway and Seventh Avenue. If you're headed uptown, grabbing a downtown cab will only add to the expense because it will have to turn around on a crowded side street to get back to an uptown avenue.

You have a slightly better chance getting a cab on Sixth Avenue or Eighth Avenue, both of which flow uptown.

Another tip: if you are at the same corner with those three dozen other people, you might try walking a block or two over where the shows haven't let out yet.

Once inside, tell the driver, "Take me to . . ." He'll switch on his meter, which is set to run both by distance and time. There is an initial charge of two dollars and fifty cents when you enter the cab. While the cab is moving, it measures distance, which you pay at forty cents per one-fifth of a mile traveled. If the cab gets stuck in traffic, the meter starts running by time, which you pay at forty cents per two minutes. There is also a fifty-cent nighttime surcharge starting at 8 PM, and an afternoon charge of one dollar between 4 PM and 8 PM.

Tipping is not required, but customary. Twenty percent for a quick ride that delivers you someplace on time when you have a tight schedule. Fifteen percent for standard service. Zero for poor service.

Add all that up (you did remember to bring a CPA, didn't you?) and it may seem insanely expensive—as indeed it is—but also keep in mind that most travel distances in Manhattan are short. The whole island is only two miles wide and thirteen and a half miles long. Sitting in traffic, however, is another story.

There are official taxi stands—spots where taxis gather to pick up large numbers of passengers, who wait in a line. There is one at Penn Station and another at Grand Central station, but, oddly, none in Times Square. However, taxis often queue up on 46th Street between Broadway and Eighth Avenue, hoping to pick up fares at the Marriott Marquis Hotel. You can often get one there when you can't get one anywhere else.

Taxicabs should not be confused with limousines, liveries, or radio cars, which are substantially more expensive and generally cannot be hailed on the street.

PEDICABS

Since 1995 a new form of midtown Manhattan transportation has popped up: pedicabs. Passengers sit in a two-wheeled cushioned compartment in back, while the driver pedals a bicycle-like contraption in front. They're actually just glorified rickshaws. One of the companies, in fact, is called the Manhattan Rickshaw Company.

Drivers tend to be young, mainly students, who want to earn money while staying in shape. As Will Parker said in *Oklahoma*, "the whole thing don't sound very good to me." But it's your call. Pedicabs can be hailed from the street (and generally appear outside theatres in good weather just as the curtain comes down), or can be summoned by telephone. Fares are generally $1 per minute for two people. Most rides are $8 to $20, depending how far you want to go.

The three main companies are:

Pedicabs of New York (PONY) 1-212-766-9222

Manhattan Rickshaw Company 1-212-604-4729

Manhattan Pedicab Inc. 1-212-586-9486

HORSE-DRAWN CARRIAGES

One of the ironies of the high-tech 21st century Manhattan is that horse-drawn carriages, properly known as Hansom Cabs, still ply the traffic-packed streets of midtown. They line up along Central Park

South (what 59th Street is called between Fifth Avenue and Broadway), which, as the name suggests, runs long the south end of Central Park.

Hansom Cabs have been featured in films and TV shows, and many visitors consider a ride in one to be the ultimate in romance. The rides can be made considerably more romantic if you pick times when traffic is at a minimum, namely weekends and evenings, after rush hour.

Hay and stables aren't cheap, so expect to pay $40, including tip, for a twenty-minute ride.

Tip: Long lines form on Valentine's Day and on prom nights in June.

WALKING

New York is a city of walkers. The city blocks are designed with wide sidewalks, plus various widths of promenades, passageways, alleys, crosswalks, esplanades, overpasses, underpasses, breezeways, tunnels, escalators and ramps, all designed to accommodate, if not always to facilitate, foot traffic. Times Square itself is essentially a female space. It's not a tower you look at, like the Washington Monument. It's an open plaza. It's a place you go to *be in*, and be a part of, rather than just to look at. Unlike other tourist spots, self-contained parks like Disney World or Six Flags, etc., Broadway is also part of a living city. People live and work in the theatre district on things not necessarily tourist-related. Especially during the day.

The best way to see Times Square and Broadway is from street level, preferably after dark when the neon reveals its full glory.

New Yorkers think of sidewalks the way the rest of the country thinks of interstate highways. They like to keep things moving. Because sidewalks tend to get crowded, if you want to stop and look at something, step out of the main flow of foot traffic. Think of it as pulling over into a scenic rest stop. Also, if you're sightseeing, try not to walk three and four abreast slowly. Think of how you'd feel if three or four cars did this in front of you on the highway.

Tourists are easy to spot because they're always stopping to look up and marvel at the tall buildings. My attitude is: So what if they do? The sight is worth marveling at. Still, look around for a lamppost or a hot dog cart or a newspaper vending box or a trash bin. Park yourself in the lee of one of these existing obstructions and drink your fill of the sights without provoking the kind of tart commentary New Yorkers are justifiably famous for.

The morning starts with office workers who have arrived at Port Authority or coming up from Penn Station fanning out through Times Square as they head for their offices. Well-dressed, carrying leather and cloth cases, they are in a hurry to get where they're going. If you are in Times Square early in the morning, just let them go by, like express trains. They stop only to get coffee and Danish at carts that pop up like aluminum mushrooms, and vanish by lunch.

Morning is a time for tourists and for messengers, many on bicycles, many wearing the security chains, looking as if old Jacob Marley had joined the Tour de France. Delivery trucks are double-parked everywhere as they stock up the local markets. The morning light shines down the West Forties, and you can see the wrinkles on the faces of the old Broadway theatres, the first of which have begun to turn one hundred years old.

At lunchtime the restaurants are open, along with the surprisingly numerous delis and pizzerias in the area. Lunch carts with colorful umbrellas materialize out of nowhere to sell hot dogs, and more aromatic fare. The place starts to come into its own around this time of day, as the people who run the theatres begin coming to work for the day shift. You can see actors, painted like dolls and wearing their most flattering outfits, headed for auditions and, the lucky ones, to rehearsals.

This is when new shows do the "load-in" of their sets, all neatly painted or packed up in huge crates with the title of the show stenciled on.

This is also when closing shows do their "load-out." There are usually dumpsters.

A lot of the business of show business gets done around this time, and if you are there and know what to look for, you can see it happening.

On matinee days you can catch actors arriving at the theatre, about an hour or two before curtain. Then the buses roll up and the crowds start pouring from the subway entrances and getting off the buses, and lined up at the parking garages. The audience has arrived. And with them, come all the street vendors, eccentrics, buskers, barkers, haranguers, cops, and helpers who make their livings off the audiences.

On non-matinee days, there are always at the lines at the TKTS booth, which attract street musicians and people handing out flyers.

Things quiet down briefly in the late afternoon, but it's not long before 5:00 rolls around and the business people start streaming back through Times Square headed for the train or the bus.

Right around this time the crowds reach their peak as people pour in from every direction to find a place to eat, and to watch the lights go on, on Broadway. It's Times Square's nightly rush hour. One night in 1999 it took me forty minutes to squeeze my way up Broadway from 43rd St. to 49th St. Crowds haven't returned to exactly that density, yet, but make sure you leave yourself enough time. Streets are crowded, too, as dozens of taxis try to make drop-offs to the same theatre at the same time.

It's a really bad time to trying crossing any area street in the middle (unless traffic is completely gridlocked). Cross at corners, and only when you have the light with you. When you do step off the curb, keep an eye out for taxis. They're painted a bright yellow to give you a fighting chance.

Things reach a frenzy from 7:40 to 8 PM as some twenty-five thousand people try to squeeze through some twenty-five narrow doorways and settle into twenty-five thousand seats before the curtain goes up. At 7:45, the carillon atop 1501 Broadway begins playing "Give My Regards to Broadway" to remind people to step on it.

And then, at 8:01, silence. Or a reasonable approximation of silence. The Times Square lights and screens are still flashing, but the sidewalks return to being merely crowded, instead of actually impacted as they were a few minutes earlier.

Another rush will come raggedly from 9:45 PM to 11 PM as the various-length shows let out and people head back to their apartments, or their hotel rooms, or their commuter trains. The marquee lights go down on the Broadway theatres.

The late evening belongs to the night owls, party kids en route to one of the clubs in the area, shady characters, and then stragglers from 2 AM to 4 AM. This is not the best time to be out. Even the hookers around Port Authority give up and go home.

After this comes what gambler Sky Masterson in *Guys and Dolls* called "My time of day . . . a couple of deals before dawn . . . when the streetlamp light turns the gutter to gold." Street cleaners and garbage collectors do their work, bakers come in to start up the ovens, and, even before the sun is fully up, the commuters start scurrying through again.

SIDELIGHT: THE METRO EXPRESS

This isn't a bus, it's a shortcut.

Times Square, especially the west side and the cross streets that connect to Eighth Avenue, can be so mobbed in the half hour before curtain time that it's impossible to move quickly from one block to the next, especially if you're running late.

Shubert Alley is part of a network of midblock passages that enables people to move more quickly from street to street, especially as curtain time nears and the sidewalks on Broadway and Eighth Avenue become thronged to overflowing.

FEMININE INFLUENCE

Are most people who see Broadway shows gay men? According to the 2003 survey "Who Goes to Broadway? The Demographics of the Audience," 63.7 percent of theatregoers are women.

If you need to make a quick transit uptown or downtown, there are midblock connections from 44th to 45th Streets via Shubert Alley (public), or through the Minskoff Theatre passage (semi-public); from 45th to 46th via the two Marriott Marquis passages (semi-public); from 46th to 47th through the Edison Hotel lobby (private); from 47th to 48th through the Dean Witter passage (semi-public); and from 48th to 49th through the Crown Plaza carport (semi-public). There's also a connection from 50th to 51st via the Gershwin Theatre passage.

I call it the *Metro* Express because in the early 1990s I was working on a book about a musical from Poland called *Metro*. Always running late, the show's young dancers would hustle from their hotel on 48th to the Minskoff Theatre near Shubert Alley. This is the route they ran.

HOW TO STAY SAFE IN TIMES SQUARE

Comedians and talk-show hosts like to paint New York as a place populated almost exclusively by thieves and killers. You might expect that the minute you step off the plane or train, you'll take a bullet in the chest. The fact that millions of people live out their entire lives in the city relatively unmolested refutes that image. Since the renaissance of the 1990s, New York, and especially Times Square, is a substantially safer place for visitors than it was in the 1960s to 1980s. One survey found it the safest big city in the nation.

Nevertheless, it's not your backyard. A few safety tips will help ensure you to have a secure visit to the Theatre District.

To avoid pickpockets, keep your wallet in a safe place, like an inner jacket pocket, and not in the back pocket of your pants. If you carry a purse, don't leave it open. The same applies to shopping bags. Anything that you put down and leave unattended is likely to attract the attention of a pilferer—or a police officer. Since 9/11, any package or bag left unattended is treated as a potential threat.

- Pickpockets often work in teams. One person distracts the intended victim, or "mark," and the other lifts the goods. Sometime one will bump into you, hoping you will immediately feel for your wallet to make sure it's still there. That lets the partner know exactly where your wallet is, so he can lift it more subtly once your guard is down.

- Be especially vigilant around street musicians, soapbox lecturers, news crews and the MTV fan crowds. All of these are situations where a visitor's attention is focused on something beside their wallet. It's like a shopping mall for crooks.

- If you come with children, hold their hands and keep them within sight at all times. If you get separated, it doesn't automatically mean they've been kidnapped. But even getting lost can be a scary and disorienting experience for a child, not to mention a parent. Have your child carry a note at all times with your name and phone number, especially if you own a cell phone and are carrying it with you. Make sure the child has two quarters for a pay phone, as well.

- Avoid arguments. If someone gives you a hard time, seek out a police officer, of which there are now many in Times Square. Don't try to duke it out yourself. You may find your assailant is carrying a concealed weapon.

- Watch out for street scams, especially from people selling things. It's OK to buy hot dogs, pretzels and chestnuts on the street. But anything worth any major money is not going to be sold on the street. There is no such thing as a ten-dollar Rolex or a two-dollar pashmina. Also watch out for 3-card-Monte scams. A scruffy-looking guy sets up a little table with three playing cards on it. He shows you all three. One is the ace of hearts. He switches them all around and bets you twenty dollars that you can't guess which is the ace of hearts. You usually win the first time, but you never win again. If someone comes up to you and tells you he's found a wad of cash, and is willing to share it with you if you'll give him your bank account and PIN number. Say "no thanks," even if he shows you the cash. There are psychics, palm readers and all manner of sage-looking soothsayers operating out of storefronts. Avoid them, even as a goof. Or, if you must use their services, get the fee written in advance. They often quote one price, then claim to have stated another, far higher.

- Street prostitutes have been pushed out of the Theatre District and off 42nd Street entirely. As stated elsewhere, to find them (or to be found by them) you have to stay out later and prowl further west and south. Prostitution is illegal in New York and both hookers and johns are subject to arrest, fine and possible jail time. And let's be honest. *Pretty Woman* notwithstanding, street hookers tend to be mean and addicted to drugs—not to mention being petri dishes of disease. They're just not worth the trouble, even with a condom.

ATMS IN TIMES SQUARE

If you need quick cash, here are some of the most convenient places where you can find bank ATMs around Times Square.

- Fleet Bank in the Marriott Hotel underpass on 46th Street near Seventh Avenue (southwest corner).

- Chase Bank at the corner of 42nd Street and Seventh Avenue (northwest corner).

- Washington Mutual Bank at the corner of 47th Street and Broadway (northwest corner). This is not only the most convenient

ATM to the TKTS booth, which is right across the street, it also charges no transaction fee.

- Wachovia Bank at the SE corner of 47th and Seventh, similarly adjacent to TKTS.
- Times Square Visitors Center on the east side of Seventh Avenue between 46th and 47th Sts.

There are also private ATMs in delicatessens and convenience stores throughout the Times Square area. These charge higher fees than the banks—$2 or $2.50 per transaction versus $1 or $1.50 for the banks. A few recently started advertising 99-cent transactions. But after a 2003 news story about how one of these owners (elsewhere in the city) found a way to harvest people's PIN numbers and drain their accounts, I no longer use the private ATMs, and recommend you don't use them either.

RESTAURANT ROW

Though there are restaurants tucked into every stray corner of the Times Square area, there is a special concentration on West 46th Street, between Eighth Avenue and Ninth Avenue. The ground level of nearly every lovely old brownstone on this block has been converted to use as a restaurant (sometimes a restaurant/nightclub, sometimes a restaurant/theatre, but all involving the provision of victuals. This block is aptly nicknamed Restaurant Row—which brings up the subject of where to eat.

CHAPTER EIGHT

HOW TO PICK A RESTAURANT

There are tens of thousands of restaurants in New York City. It sometimes seems there are at least that many in the Theatre District alone. Every price range, every ambience, and nearly every ethnic cuisine can be found there.

New Yorkers love to eat out, and the city is constantly thronged with eateries catering to the latest food craze. The turnover can be brutal. A Mexican place turns into a Thai place turns into a Nouvelle place, turns into a Vegan place turns into an Asian-fusion place turns into an Atkins Diet place. It never stops.

Sadly for foodies who are also theatre fans, relatively few of these fad-surfing places open in the Theatre District. Restaurants here tend to be conservative and middle-of-the road. Gastronomic experiments tend to happen further east in midtown, or in SoHo fifty blocks south, or on the Upper East Side.

But all is not lost, as the gourmets among you will tell you of course.

There was a time in the late 1970s and early 1980s where the Theatre District had become notorious for having some of the worst restaurants in New York. Since the boom of the late 1990s, this situation has made something of a turnaround. The recession of the early 2000s knocked out the sillier and more horrible of the crop, and what's left is a marked improvement over years past.

The people who live and work in the Theatre District know where to find good food for a reasonable price because if they didn't they'd get sick or broke or both. They know where to get a sandwich or a burger just as well as where to take a valued client or family member out for a night to remember. I asked a dozen of them for their recommendations, added them to my own, and came up with a dining geography of Times Square.

DINING GEOGRAPHY OF TIMES SQUARE
You'd expect Times Square itself to have some of the greatest restaurants on the planet—and you'd be wrong.

There's the nice Blue Fin restaurant in the W Hotel at the corner of 47th Street, but right across the street at the uptown end of Times Square is the ersatz Italian eatery Olive Garden. Not exactly a point of pride. There are two McDonalds within five blocks of each other—one on 42nd St. next door to Disney's New Amsterdam Theatre, and one on Seventh Ave. near the Palace. Along the west side of the Square there's the overpriced Roxy delicatessen and a Howard Johnson's that hasn't significantly changed its menu since the Eisenhower administration (and which has announced its closing). Bubba Gump Shrimp Co. recently joined the throng, offering seafood in a former bank space at the corner of 44th Street. But that's about it.

Suffice to say, most of the significant restaurant action is on the side streets.

The best concentration of reasonably-priced quality restaurants is to the west of the Theatre District, just beyond Eighth Avenue. West 46th St. between Eighth and Ninth Avenues is known as Restaurant Row because nearly every building on the street houses a restaurant, from the chi-chi Orso to the pub-like O'Flaherty's to the theatre-insider Joe Allen's. There are some two-dozen along this block, and it's worth your time to just walk up one side and down the other, reading the menus posted in the windows, to find something that exactly suits your taste and pocketbook.

Go to the Ninth Ave. end of that block and turn either left or right. You're in ethnic restaurant heaven. Every block features something new: a Louisiana Cajun place, a Vegan restaurant, Ethiopian, Brazilian, Thai, etc. And in general they are significantly cheaper than the restaurants just a block or two to the east. If you're willing to walk just one extra city block west, you can find a significantly cheaper and more diverse eating experience.

The west side of Eighth Ave. is also known for pubs where food is secondary, but still OK. But not what you'd think of as cosmopolitan.

A cluster of moderately priced ethnic restaurants can be found on 49th St. east of Seventh Avenue. Forty-fourth St. opposite Shubert Alley has some large, busy ethnic places, too, though the prices are generally a bit steeper.

McHale's bar and grill, clubhouse for Broadway's techies.

More upscale places are located on the side streets in the 50s, though 50th St. itself between Broadway and Sixth Avenue seems to be serving as a magnet for chain family restaurants like Applebees and TGI Friday.

There has been a fair amount of turnover of restaurants along the revived West 42nd St.—mainly fast-food places catering to tourists— but the gustatory character of the block hasn't yet asserted itself.

THEATRE-RELATED RESTAURANT TIPS

Many New Yorkers go out to eat as a form of entertainment. At some of the finer restaurants, people linger two or even three hours over multi-course gourmet meals.

If you, on the other hand, just want something to eat before you see a show, you need to plan accordingly. Most of the restaurants in the Theatre District know that when the clock strikes 8, most customers have to be nestled snug in their theatre seats, or there will be trouble.

It's optimum to leave at least an hour for dinner and at least a half-hour to get to the theatre and get settled in. That means you should arrive at the restaurant no later than 6:30. Six or 5:30 makes for a more leisurely repast.

If time is tight, however, tell your waiter that you have an eight o'clock curtain. He and the kitchen are likely set up for exactly these kinds of situations, and he'll be able to suggest tasty dishes that can be prepared quickly. Often, the daily specials are ready to go. In other words, if you get to your table at seven, don't ask for the Peking Duck.

TIPPING

Standard tip in New York is 15 percent for standard service. Tip eighteen, twenty percent or more for extraordinary service. But don't reward poor service. A long wait for food may not be the waiter's fault; more likely the kitchen's, for which the waiter should not be penalized. But inattentiveness is the waiter's fault, and rudeness certainly is. I knock off five percent for each slight. Three strikes, and they're out. If they don't like ten percent—or zero—perhaps they'll do better next time.

PICKING A RESTAURANT

There are a million Manhattan dining guides out there, including *Zagat's*, which allows patrons to rate restaurants. Mostly, though, the choice of a restaurant is a personal one. Examine the menu in the front window, look around inside, sniff the air. If you don't get a good feeling about a place—if it doesn't look clean, if it smells odd, or if it's too formal or not formal enough—just move on. There are dozens and dozens more within easy walking distance.

I've been recommending Theatre District restaurants to people all across the country for years, and they tend to fall into a few typical groups. In my own listing below I've tried to adhere to these. People generally want to

- Save money
- Take the kids somewhere they'll like
- Impress a date or client or other VIP
- Eat a specific cuisine
- Go someplace famous, or where they have a chance to see someone famous
- Be near the theatre. Oh, and
- Have a good meal.

The list below has good examples of each of these kinds of restaurants. All have been tested either by the author personally, or a picked group of people who eat in Times Square regularly. The author has sent in-laws and people he has to face every day to these restaurants, and they've come back with thumbs up. For more detail, you may also wish to consult one of the *Zagat* guides or Zagat.com, which lists the reactions of respondents who are, or purport to be, actual customers.

Moderately Priced places for a nice dinner

Barrymore's (American bistro) Named after the acting dynasty, this relaxed theatre-oriented place offers burgers, pasta, and associated pub food, served by (mostly) friendly waiters. 267 West 45th Street, 1-212-391-8400. Closest theatres: Imperial, Golden, Royale, Plymouth.

Ben's Delicatessen (Jewish deli) Just past the southern end of the theatre district is this kosher Everest. Oak paneled dining rooms on two levels serve up big, fat deli sandwiches of pastrami, lox, etc. Their slogan: "We cure our corned beef ourselves. Our chicken soup cures everything else." Who could argue? 209 West 38th St. (between

---

MONSTER FLOP

Dracula has long been a stage favorite, with two successful revivals of the hit 1927 play plus a new musical. However, *Frankenstein* has had a much harder time of it. A 1981 stage adaptation of *Frankenstein* was hailed for its imposing set and dramatic special effects costing hundreds of thousands of dollars—but it flopped spectacularly, closing on opening night.

Seventh and Eighth Aves.). 1-212-398-2367. Closest theatres: New Amsterdam, New Victory, Ford Center.

Bombay Masala (Indian) The second-floor white-tablecloth eatery claims to be the oldest Indian restaurant in New York. Biryanis, tandoori dishes and curries are standouts. 148 West 49th St. 1-212-302-8150. Closest theatres: Winter Garden, Ambassador, Cort, Palace.

Bubba Gump Shrimp Company Restaurant and Market (seafood) Recently-opened second-floor spot near the downtown end of Times Square, this chain eatery specializes in all sort of shrimp dishes, along with grilled chicken, ribs, etc. 1501 Broadway at 44th Street, 1-212-391-7100, www.bubbagump.com. Closest theatres: Minskoff, Shubert, Hayes, Broadhurst.

Café Edison (Russian/Polish/Jewish) Nicknamed "The Polish Tea Room," this extremely informal restaurant offers, brisket, derma, borscht, matzoh-ball soup and other shtetl delicacies, usually accompanied by a plate of mixed pickles. As gathering place for Broadway's old guard. No credit cards accepted. Located next to the entrance of the Hotel Edison, 228 West 47th Street, 1-212-354-0368. Palace, Barrymore, Atkinson, Biltmore.

Café Europa (Continental) Big windows on two sides look out on Avenue of the Americas and 46th St. as diners nosh on Italian and French dishes, with a special emphasis on fresh vegetables in season. Part of a chain that's been popping up around the city. 1177 Ave. of the Americas, 1-212-575-7272. Closest theatres: Cort, Belasco, Palace, Lunt-Fontanne.

Carmine's (Italian) The successor to dear departed Mamma Leone's, this Southern Italian dining room diagonally opposite Shubert Alley is always noisy and packed, often with a line out the door. A giant painting of opera singer Enrico Caruso gazes down as waiters deliver colossal portions in what seem to be bathtub-size platters. Good for bigger parties. 200 West 44th Street, 1-212-221-3800, www.carmines-nyc.com. Closest theatres: Minskoff, Shubert, Hayes, Broadhurst.

Don Giovanni Ristorante (Italian). The speciality of the house is some two dozen kinds of brick-oven style pizza. But try instead the ample pasta dishes, bruschetta, and big salads. The décor is vintage opera pictures, posters and memorabilia. 358 West 44th St. (between Eighth & Ninth Aves.) 1-212-581-4939, www.dongiovanni-ny.com. Closest theatres: St. James, Majestic, Second Stage.

Encore (American bistro) Pleasant family-style restaurant in the eighth floor lobby of the Marriott Marquis Hotel, looking up at the indoor atrium, and down at the hum of 45th St, and Times Square. If you buy a meal, your kids eat free. 1-212-704-8900. Closest theatres: Marquis, Lunt-Fontanne, Minskoff, Booth, Music Box.

Hakata (Japanese) Cozy spot for classy sushi and other East Asian dishes. 230 West 48th Street, 1-212-245-1020. Closest theatres: Walter Kerr, Biltmore, O'Neill.

Hunan Chef (Chinese) The name notwithstanding, the kitchen can handle all the various cuisines of China at the Restaurant Row favorite. 360 West 46th Street, 1-212-315-2770. Closest theatres: Lunt-Fontanne, Al Hirschfeld, Atkinson, Biltmore, Golden.

Iroha (Japanese) Noodle dishes and soups are specialties of this restaurant, part of a cluster of ethnic restaurants on the south side of 49th St. near the corner of Seventh. Good if you're in a rush. 152 West 49th Street, 1-212-398-9049. Closest theatres: Winter Garden, Ambassador, Cort, Palace.

Joe Allen (American bistro) Legendary hangout of actors and other theatre folk on Restaurant Row. Not as hot as a decade ago, but rare is the night when you don't spot a famous or at least recognizable face. Décor note: one wall is plastered with window cards from some of Broadway's infamous flops. 326 West 46th St. 1-212-581-6464, www.joeallenrestaurant.com. Closest theatres: Lunt-Fontanne, Al Hirschfeld, Atkinson, Biltmore, Golden.

Joe Allen's restaurant, a gathering place for Broadway's old guard.

JR Restaurant (American bistro) Similar atmosphere to Joe Allen's but lower-key, and lower-priced. Good salads, burgers and chicken dishes. Offers discounts for Broadway ticket holders. A Restaurant Row-style restaurant, but on the nearer side of Eighth Avenue. 264 West 46th St. 1-212-719-5694. Closest theatres: Imperial, Richard Rodgers, Lunt-Fontanne, Golden, Royale.

Judson Grill (American) Tastefully-designed restaurant at the upper end of the moderate price range, but new and attractive—a good place to make a good impression without going broke. 152 West 52nd Street, 1-212-582-5252. Closest theatres: Broadway, Virginia, Neil Simon.

Kodama (Japanese) A personal favorite. This friendly place has a first-rate sushi bar, in addition to quietly excellent tempura and other standard dishes. One of the specials, the Broadway Box, offers a sampling of their best. Actors often can be seen picking up a light dinner before showtime. 301 West 45th St. 1-212-582-8065. Closest theatres: Al Hirschfeld, Golden, Royale, Imperial.

Lindy's (New York Deli/Diner) Not the location immortalized in Damon Runyon's "Guys and Dolls" (as "Mindy's"), but they do their best to evoke the same old-time Broadway atmosphere. PS: I checked: In the 21st century, they're still selling more cheesecake than strudel. 1525 Broadway at 45th St. 1-212-626-7306, and 825 Seventh Ave. at 53rd Street, 1-212-767-8343, www.rieserestaurants.com. Closest theatres: Broadway, Studio 54, City Center.

Manhattan Chili Co. (Tex-Mex) Chili in all its many varieties is the specialty at this busy restaurant just steps from Times Square. 1500 Broadway (entrance on 43rd St.) 1-212-730-8666, www.manhattanchili.com. Closest theatres: Henry Miller's, Town Hall, Minskoff, Belasco.

O'Flaherty's Ale House (Irish) Irish stew, corned beef and other Gaelic favorites are on the table at this Restaurant Row hotspot. From the street it looks like a rowdy pub—which it is—but it also has a quieter dining room set up like a library with shelves of books. 334 West 46th Street, 1-212-246-8928. Closest theatres: Lunt-Fontanne, Al Hirschfeld, Atkinson, Biltmore, Golden.

Ollie's (Chinese) Informal Chinese restaurant with an emphasis on handmade noodle dishes and steamed buns packed with meat and vegetables. Almost as good as the original on the Upper West Side, and one of the best lower-priced Chinese spots in Times Square. 200B West 44th St. 1-212-921-5988. Closest theatres: Minskoff, Shubert, Hayes, Broadhurst.

Orso (Italian) The next step up from Joe Allen, with snootier waiters, this attractively designed trattoria has good Northern Italian food that attracts its share of famous Broadway faces. 322 West 46th St. 1-212-489-7212, www.orsorestaurant.com. Closest theatres: Lunt-Fontanne, Al Hirschfeld, Atkinson, Biltmore, Golden.

Pergola Des Artistes (French) Family-run Continental restaurant, snuggled next to the stage door of the Imperial Theatre. 252 West 46th Street, 1-212-302-7500. Closest theatres: Imperial, Lunt-Fontanne, Golden, Royale, Plymouth.

Pongsri Thai Restaurant (Thai) Wonderful Thai restaurant, once so crowded that they expanded into the neighboring storefront. Good seafood. Specialty of the house is the sweet and hot Bangkok Chicken. All the basics are done well. 244 West 48th Street, 1-212-582-3392. pongsri1.citysearch.com. Closest theatres: Longacre, Walter Kerr, Biltmore, O'Neill.

Siam Inn (Thai) Understated Thai restaurant with delicious red and yellow curries. 854 Eighth Ave. near 51st St. 1-212-757-3520. Closest theatres: Neil Simon, Virginia, Gershwin.

Southside Café (Italian) Tucked away a step below street level on 47th St. between Broadway and Eighth Ave. A dozen tables in a cozy space. Pasta and seafood. Southern Italian but refined, and restrained décor. Big plates, good food. 252 West 47th St. 1-212-354-0566, www.southside-cafe.com. Closest theatres: Atkinson, Barrymore, Biltmore.

Virgil's Real Barbecue (Southern/Texan) Times Square's temple to any sort of meat (or vegetable) you can smear with barbecue sauce and sear. 152 West 44th St. 1-212-921-9494, www.virgilsbbq.com. Closest theatres: Minskoff, Shubert, Hayes.

Kid/family places/Fast Food Joints

Only you know whether your children are mature enough to eat out at a tablecloth restaurant. If you aren't sure, here are some places that welcome family trade. Be prepared for Manhattan prices at chain restaurants to be considerably higher than you're used to back home. Key to your choice should be picking someplace close to your theatre, so you don't have to pay the bill and run ten blocks with a child in tow. I've spread these out so they are close to various parts of the Theatre District. If your kid is likes more sophisticated food, skip back up to the section where I talk about moderately priced places.

Applebee's: Franchises in a national chain of family-style restaurants that go in for a décor of old movie and sports posters and memorabilia hanging on the walls. Then menu is a similar hodgepodge, but does include meat and seafood and salads that parents will like, alongside burgers, chicken fingers and other stuff for kids. Special menus change every few weeks, but always manage to include something Tex-Mex. Is it gourmet? Uh, no. But it will feed a family of four respectably well, without a lot of attitude, on dishes, with a waiter, for under $100 in the heart of midtown Manhattan. Which, you will find, is no mean feat.

50th St. between Seventh Ave. and Broadway. Closest theatres: Winter Garden, Gershwin, Circle in the Square.

234 42nd Street, south side between Seventh and Eighth Aves. 1-212-391-7414. Ford Center, New Amsterdam, New Victory.

Art Café: (American diner) Despite the left-bank name, it's just a diner near the north end of the theatre district. But a good spot for families going to one of the big theatres in the area, or Radio City. There are some abstract prints on the walls, but basically it's a no-frills place to get a cheeseburger deluxe, a basket of fried clams, an open-face turkey sandwich, etc. 1657 Broadway, SW corner of Broadway at 52nd Street. 1-212-246-9797. Closest theatres: Neil Simon, Virginia, Gershwin, Broadway, Winter Garden.

Fast Food Court: Can't decide what to have? A mall-style fast food court offering no-frills Mexican, Chinese, burgers, ribs, chicken, and just about everything else has opened in a storefront on the west side of Eighth Ave. between 44th and 45th St. Amenities are spartan. Closest theatres: Golden, Majestic, St. James, Al Hirschfeld.

Hamburger Harry's: More than a dozen different kind of hamburgers are on the menu at this family-friendly restaurant that serves its mounds of curly fries with gusto. 145 West 45th St. 1-212-840-2756. Closest theatres: Lyceum, Minskoff, Marquis.

Kentucky Fried Chicken: 50th St. at Seventh Ave. Closest theatres: Winter Garden, Gershwin, Circle in the Square.

Mars 2112: This is the cool place to take kids, if you have money and time. The concept is that you are going out to dinner . . . on Mars. You travel to the dining area in an elevator like a space ship, and the menu consists of earth food, with some little twist that makes it "alien." It's fun. Employees get dressed up like aliens. Birthday parties are a specialty. Located in the sunken plaza at 1633 Broadway, SW corner of 51st St. and Broadway. 1-212-582-2112, www.mars2112.com. Closest theatres: Gershwin, Circle in the Square, Winter Garden.

McDonalds: 42nd Street, South Side between Broadway and Eighth Ave. Closest theatres: New Amsterdam, New Victory, Ford Center.

1585 Broadway (near 46th St.) Closest theatres: Palace, Marquis, Minskoff.

1633 Broadway (near 50th St.) Closest theatres: Winter Garden, Gershwin, Circle in the Square.

1700 Broadway (near 53rd St.) Closest theatres: Neil Simon, Virginia, Studio 54, City Center.

Popeye's: Seventh Ave. at 48th St. Closest theatres: Walter Kerr, Longacre, Palace.

Subway: 351 West 42nd St. Closest theatres: New Victory, Ford Center, New Amsterdam.

    West side of Eighth Ave. near 47th St. Closest theatres: Atkinson, Biltmore

TGI Friday: A competing chain of restaurants roughly similar to Applebees, though pitched a little bit more toward a single crowd. Still, families are treated just as well as at Applebee's, and for a similar price. Seventh Ave. at 50th St. Closest theatres: Winter Garden, Gershwin, Circle in the Square.

    Broadway between 53rd and 54th St. Closest theatres: Neil Simon, Virginia, Studio 54, City Center.

Wendy's: 1211 Ave. of the Americas (at 47th St.) Closest theatres: Cort, Palace.

White Castle: 525 Eighth Ave (near 36th St.) Closest theatre: Nederlander.

Places With Something Extra

Some of these are super-insider hangouts, some are big fat commercial theme parks. But they all offer something beyond what's on the plate.

Angus McIndoe (Eclectic) Trendy theatrical restaurant du jour. Started by some of the folks involved in *The Producers* at the St. James next door, and run by the former maitre d' of Joe Allen, it is now place to be seen. Post columnist Michael Riedel prowls here, and famously got into a dustup with a director whose show he'd been slagging. There's also food: Traditional dishes with a twist, like roasted half duck with soft polenta and peach-pineapple chutney or roasted monkfish with red curry, coconut milk and saffron jasmine rice, and so on. 258 West 44th St. 1-212-221-9222, www.angusmcindoe.com. Closest theatres: St. James, Majestic, Broadhurst, Hayes, Shubert.

B.B. King Blues Club & Grill (American) A supper club in the late Forties tradition, with jazz and blues floor shows. There's even a Sunday Gospel Brunch. 237 West 42nd St. 997-4144, bbkingblues.com. An entertainment destination in itself, but closest theatres include American Airlines Theatre, Ford Center, New Amsterdam, Second Stage, Nederlander.

Ellen's Stardust Diner (Diner) Great name for a retro Fifties diner that tries to do what it does with a little magic. Since they booted *Forbidden Broadway* from its longtime "Under Broadway" performance space in the basement (now the Iridium Jazz Club), the main attraction has been wacky singing waiters. 1650 Broadway at 51st St. 1-212-956-5151, www.ellensstardustdiner.com. Closest theatres: Winter Garden, Gershwin, Circle in the Square.

ESPN Zone (American) The ultimate sports restaurant. How about *two hundred* TV monitors tuned to every imaginable sport? He-man menu features Buffalo wings, steaks, chops, etc. NE corner of Broadway at 42nd St. 1-212-921-3776, www.espnzone.com. Closest theatres: New Amsterdam, Nederlander, New Victory, Ford Center.

Planet Hollywood (American) 1540 Broadway at 45th St. Why the flagship of a chain called Planet Hollywood is in New York baffles me. And its museum-like collection of memorabilia (there's a vintage motorcycle in the foyer) manages to pay as little tribute to the surrounding world of Broadway as it possibly can. And the prices are crazy for the quality level. Nevertheless, there is an undeniable carnival appeal to the place. For people who must have glitz. 1-212-333-7827, www.planethollywood.com/restaurants/new_NYtimes.shtm. Closest theatres: Shubert, Minskoff, Lyceum, Marquis

Ruby Foo's (East Asian) This stylish Chinese/Japanese/Thai invention has been designed within an inch of its glamorous life, and looks right out on Broadway. 1626 Broadway at 49th Street, 1-212-489-5600, Closest theatres: Ambassador, O'Neill, Winter Garden.

Sardi's (Italian/French) This is that place. You know: the place in every movie and cartoon about the New York showbiz scene. The place with all the caricatures of the famous people on the walls. Like a bristlecone pine, this place has survived in the same spot forever (or at any rate since the 1920s) and still, after an interregnum, in the hands of the Sardi family. Its dining rooms have been the scene of countless opening night parties. The anguish and joy of those nights has soaked into the very walls. The famous dish in cannelloni. The first floor is cooler, but the second floor is more intimate. 234 West 44th Street, 1-212-221-8440, www.sardis.com. Closest theatres: Shubert, Hayes, Broadhurst, St. James, Majestic, Minskoff, Booth.

The Supper Club (American) A recreation of a Forties supper club, a la B.B. King, but with a Big Band as the floor show, plus dancing. 240 West 47th Street, 1-212-921-1940. Closest theatres: Atkinson, Barrymore, Biltmore.

The View (Italian/French) Perched atop the Marriott Marquis like a top hat is this romantic but expensive revolving restaurant with a three-hundred-sixty-degree panorama the Big Apple from high above the center of Times Square. If you liked the vistas in Woody Allen's *Manhattan*, you've found your dinner spot. Inside the Mariott Marquis Hotel, 1535 Broadway, between 45th and 46th Streets, 1-212-704-8900. Closes theatres: Marquis, Minskoff, Lunt-Fontanne, Music Box, Booth.

Upscale places

If you don't mind spending a small fortune for really good food, New York is the place for you.

Above (American Gourmet) Regional, seasonal domestic ingredients prepared in original ways are the hallmark of Chef Larry Forgione, creator of An American Place, located high above 42nd Street. 234 West 42nd Street, 1-212-642-2626. Closest theatres: New Amsterdam, New Victory, Nederlander, Ford Center.

Barbetta (Italian) The oldest surviving dining room on Restaurant Row (already planning its centenary in 2006), specializing in the white truffle dishes of Italy's Piedmont region, with a chandeliered interior and a garden patio out back in summer. 321 West 46th St. Restaurant Row, 1-212-246-9171, www.barbettarestaurant.com. Closest theatres: Lunt-Fontanne, Al Hirschfeld, Atkinson, Biltmore, Golden.

Becco (Italian) Make sure to try the osso bucco and the chocolate cake at this Restaurant Row spot run by TV chef Lydia Bastianich. If you're not sure what you want, there's always the pasta sampler. 355 West 46th St. Restaurant Row, 1-212-397-7597, www.lidiasitaly.com/restaurants.html. Closest theatres: Lunt-Fontanne, Al Hirschfeld, Atkinson, Biltmore, Golden.

Blue Fin (Seafood) Spiffy new place in the W Hotel at the NW corner of Times Square. Marvelous fresh seafood is beautifully presented (don't miss the clam chowder) And it's right in the center of the action. 1567 Broadway at 47th Street, 1-212-918-1400 Closest theatres: Palace, Barrymore, Marquee, Biltmore, Atkinson.

Café Un Deux Trois (French bistro) French-influenced food served in a huge open dining area a half block in from the east side of Times Square. Named for its address: 123 West 44th St. 1-212-354-4148. Closest theatres: Minskoff, Shubert, Hayes.

Citarella (Seafood) This popular restaurant (founded by the people who run the gourmet food shops) in the McGraw-Hill building offers seafood with an Italian touch, with a magnificent view of the passing show on Avenue of the Americas. 1240 Avenue of the Americas at 49th Street, 1-212-332-1515, www.citarella.com. Closest theatres: Cort, Radio City Music Hall, Ambassador.

Esca (Italian) Neapolitan food is on the menu at this restaurant, named for its signature dish (literally "bait"), consisting of a boldly spiced mixture of raw seafood. 402 West 43rd Street, 1-212-564-7272. Closest theatres: St. James, Majestic, Second Stage, and the theatres of Restaurant Row.

FireBird Cafe (Russian) Caviar is the specialty at this elegant spot on Restaurant Row. 363 West 46th St. Restaurant Row. 1-212-586-0244, www.firebirdrestaurant.com. Closest theatres: Lunt-Fontanne, Atkinson, Biltmore, Golden, Royale, Al Hirschfeld.

Frankie & Johnnie's (Steakhouse) Up a flight of steps from St. level, this is Theatre District landmark grill. 269 West 45th Street, 1-212-997-9494. Closes theatres: Imperial, Royale, Golden, Plymouth, Booth, Music Box.

Gallagher's (Steakhouse) A theatre district landmark. Its steaks are aged in all their well-marbled glory in a cold-storage locker that has a window on the street. Inside, it's all red wine, sharp knives and sizzling beef in this meat-and-potatoes paradise. 228 West 52nd Street, 1-212-245-5336, www.gallaghersnysteakhouse.com. Closest theatres: Neil Simon, Virginia. Broadway, Winter Garden.

Le Bernardin (French) Seafood is the order of the day at one of New York's classiest, most sophisticated and priciest French restaurants. 155 West 51st Street, 1-212-489-1515, www.le-bernardin.com. Closest theatres: Gershwin, Circle in the Square, Winter Garden, Neil Simon.

Limoncello (Northern Italian): Beef, veal and seafood cooked with an international flair characterize this spot, which is popular with publishing moguls from nearby magazine headquarters. 777 Seventh Ave. at 51st Street, 1-212-582-7932, www.limoncellorestaurant.citysearch.com. Closest theatres: Gershwin, Circle in the Square, Winter Garden, Neil Simon.

Osteria Al Doge (Italian) A trattoria atmosphere pervades this classy, two-level dining room. 142 West 44th Street, 1-212-944-3643. Lunch Monday through Saturday; dinner nightly. Closest theatres: Minskoff, Shubert, Hayes, Broadhurst.

Trattoria Dopo Teatro (Italian) Despite the name, this comfortable trattoria is a shrine to the movies, especially Italian movies, and the cuisine reflects its Roman origins. 125 West 44th Street, 1-212-869-2849, www.dopoteatro.com. Closest theatres: Minskoff, Shubert, Hayes, Broadhurst.

Quick cup of coffee places

One of the best developments in recent theatre is the tendency for audiences to grab a cup of coffee before a show, rather than an alcoholic drink. You'll notice it has cut way down on the snoring, and cranked up the standing ovations.

Broadway has not escaped the Starbucks invasion; new ones seem to open hourly. But there are a few other places, too, to grab a cup of designer java as you're headed for the theatre.

Bagel Express Company: Northeast corner of Eighth Ave. at 51st Street.

Cosi: Southwest corner of Broadway at 51st St.

Europa Café: NE corner of Broadway at 53rd St.

Europa Café: SW corner of Seventh Ave. at 43rd St.

Starbucks: Across from the north entrance to Shubert Alley at 45th St.

Starbucks: 251 West 42nd Street, near Eighth Ave.

Starbucks: Northwest corner of Broadway at 47th St.

Starbucks: Northeast corner of Broadway at 51st St.

Starbucks: Northeast corner of Eighth Ave. and 43rd St.

Starbucks: West side of Seventh Ave. at 49th St.

CHAPTER NINE

WHERE TO STAY

> "Broadway . . . is statistically trivial, and normally
> its product is trivial, too. But every so often, it isn't,
> and it's those 'every so oftens' that we remember . . .
> Broadway's strength is that the people are alive."
>
> —WILLIAM GOLDMAN

If you saw the 1988 movie *Big*, you may remember the scene where young Josh (played by Tom Hanks) comes to New York and spends his first night in a hellhole Times Square hotel, a filthy rat's nest full of drug addicts and hookers fighting with their pimps.

This needn't be your experience.

There are hundreds of hotels, inns, motels, hostels, bed-and-breakfasts, fleabags, roach motels, and pleasure domes in New York, facilities to suit every taste and price level. Several prominent specimens of each of these groups are located in the Theatre District, and it will relieve you to know that thanks to the renaissance of the late 1990s, overall they are generally of far better quality than the ones of the *Big* era. Still, it pays to look before you sleep. The roach motels still exist, like a hangover from the bad old days.

Here are some of the best ones in the immediate vicinity of Times Square.

Hotels are listed here by cross street so you can book them for convenient access to whichever shows you plan to see.

Because this is midtown Manhattan, expect to pay top dollar, even for surprisingly tiny rooms. In New York, visitors don't spend many waking hours in their hotel rooms anyway. The cheapest acceptable accommodations run about $90, though fleabags (not included here) can be found cheaper. On the top end, well, the sky's the limit. Most rooms will run you between $125 and $300 a night.

If a Times Square hotel is not listed here, there is generally a good reason. It's either dirty, offers poor service, or is hilariously overpriced for the quality level.

WEST 42ND STREET

Hilton Times Square—234 West 42nd St., 1-212-930-7400. www.hilton.com. In the heart of the craziness of the new 42nd Street, with a back door out onto 41st St. diagonally opposite the Nederlander Theatre (where *Rent* is playing). Other nearby theatres: Ford Center, New Amsterdam, New Victory.

WEST 43RD STREET

Westin New York at Times Square—270 West 43rd St., 1-212-201-2700, www.westinny.com. Exuberantly designed brand-new hotel that forms part of the gateway to the new 42nd Street. The main entrance is at the corner of 43rd and Eighth Ave. Closest theatres: American Airlines, Ford Center, St. James, Majestic.

Casablanca Hotel—147 West 43rd St. just off the east side of Times Square. 1-212-869-1212, 1-888-922-7225, www.casablancahotel.com. A romantic little boutique hotel, a favorite with the guests who have discovered it. Closest theatres: Henry Miller's Theatre, Town Hall Theatre.

WEST 44TH STREET

Algonquin—59 West 44th St., 1-212-840-6800, www.algonquin-hotel.com. Legendary meeting place of the 1920s Algonquin Round Table. "Old New York" elegance, on the east side of Times Square, beyond Avenue of the Americas. Look for the hotel's guardian spirit, Matilda the cat. Closest theatres: Belasco, Lambs'.

Iroquois—49 West 44th St., 1-212-840-3080 or 1-800-332-7220, www.iroquoisny.com. Next door to the Algonquin. Closest theatres: Belasco, Lambs'.

Milford Plaza—270 West 45th St., 1-888-288-5700, www.milford-plaza.com. An older, no-frills hotel, popular with tourists, partly owing to its unbeatable location, opening on one side onto 45th St. and on the other onto Eighth Avenue. The Celebrity Diner at street level gives an immediate taste of New York. Closest theatres: Majestic, Golden, Royale, St. James, Imperial.

Millennium Broadway—145 West 44th St., 1-212-768-4400, 1-800-622-5569, www.millenniumhotels.com. Shiny new hotel that incorporated a former Broadway theatre, the Hudson, into its construction, and uses it for corporate meetings. Closest theatres: Belasco, Lambs', Shubert, Helen Hayes.

WEST 45TH STREET

Best Western Ambassador—132 West 45th St., 1-800-784-1180, bestwestern.worldexecutive.com. No-frills hotel on the east side of Times Square, near Avenue of the Americas. Closest theatres: Lyceum, Belasco, Lambs', Minskoff.

WEST 46TH STREET

Marriott Marquis—1535 Broadway, between 45th and 46th Sts. 1-212-398-1900, 1-800-228-9290, www.marriott.com. They tore down three classic Broadway theatres to build this two thousand-room hotel, but compensated by incorporating a new and excellent house into its construction, the eponymous Marquis. The inside is the signature Marriott hollow shell with elevators rising up a central column overlooking a twenty-plus-story atrium. The rooms and public spaces look out on the center of Times Square, and there are several restaurants including one on the roof, with great views of the city. The hotel uses theatrical themes in the naming of corporate meeting rooms, and hosts many theatrical events. Closest theatres: Marquis, Lunt-Fontanne, Rodgers, Minskoff, Music Box, Booth.

Paramount—235 West 46th St., 1-212-764-5500, 1-800-225-7474, www.ianschragerhotels.com. Quietly elegant hotel that is a favorite with visiting celebrities. Closes theatres: Rodgers, Lunt-Fontanne, Marquis, Atkinson.

Broadway Bed and Breakfast Inn—264 West 46th St., 1-800-826-6300, www.broadwayinn.com. Cute budget hotel with a real "inn" feeling, right around the corner from the busiest block on Broadway. Extremely helpful staff, quite knowledgeable about finding Broadway discounts. One of the best bargains in the Theatre District. Closest theatres: Rodgers, Lunt-Fontanne, Marquis, Golden, Imperial.

The Muse—130 West 46th St., 1-212-485-2400, www.themusehotel.com. Quiet, dignified, clean hotel on the east side of Times Square (toward Rockefeller Center). Some rooms include a balcony. Closest theatres: Palace, Marquis, Lunt-Fontanne.

WEST 47TH STREET

Edison—228 West 47th St., 1-800-305-0991, www.edisonnewyork.com. A bustling, well-kept older hotel, whose art deco passageway between 46th and 47th St. brings a lot of the color and life of Broadway spilling into its lobby. Also home of the legendary Broadway meeting spot, the Café Edison, known to theatre folks as the "Polish Tea Room." Close to the geographical center of the Theatre District. Closest theatres: Atkinson, Barrymore, Biltmore, Rodgers.

West Times Square—1567 Broadway at 47th St. 1-212-930-7400, www.whotels.com. Brand-new (2002) and trendy hotel that anchors the northwest corner of Times Square. Some sensational views. Closest theatres: Palace, Barrymore, Atkinson, Biltmore.

Doubletree Guest Suites—1568 Broadway at 47th St. above The Palace Theatre. 1-212-719-1600, www.doubletree.com. Located in the northeast corner of Times Square, directly across from the TKTS booth, with stunning views of Times Square. Gets consistently high ratings on hotel websites for cost, service, and location. Closest theatres: Palace, Marquis, Barrymore, Cort.

WEST 48TH STREET

Days Inn—790 Eighth Ave. between 48th and 49th Sts. 1-212-581-7000, www.daysinn.com. Bare-bones budget hotel. Avoid rooms on side of building facing firehouse (the 48th St. side). Closest theatres: O'Neill, Longacre, Walter Kerr, Ambassador.

Crowne Plaza Manhattan—1605 Broadway between 48th and 49th St. 1-212-977-4000, www.crowneplaza.com. Mid-level hotel with rooms and public spaces that feature views up and down Broadway. Closest theatres: Ambassador, Walter Kerr, O'Neill, Longacre.

Best Western President—234 West 48th St. 1-866-608-9330, www.bestwestern.com. Budget hotel with minimal amenities. Closest theatres: Longacre, Walter Kerr, O'Neill, Barrymore.

Renaissance New York Times Square—714 Seventh Ave. (at 47th St.) 1-212-765-7676. marriott.com/renaissancehotels This luxury hotel occupies the entire small block at the north end of Times Square and, while pricey, delivers good service in a unique location. Closest theatres: Palace, Cort, Longacre, Walter Kerr.

WEST 49TH STREET

Mayfair New York—242 West 49th St., 1-212-586-0300. Budget "European style" hotel near Times Square. Display of Broadway photos in the guest lounge. Closest theatres: O'Neill, Ambassador, Walter Kerr, Winter Garden.

The Time—224 West 49th St., 1-212-246-5252. Functional hotel near Times Square. Closest theatres: O'Neill, Ambassador, Walter Kerr, Winter Garden.

WEST 51ST STREET

Sheraton Manhattan—790 Seventh Ave. 1-212-581-3300, 1-800-625-5144, www.starwood.com/sheraton. This big chain hotel takes up the entire block bounded by Broadway, and Seventh Ave between 51st and 52nd Sts. Closest theatres: Winter Garden, Broadway, Virginia, Neil Simon.

Michelangelo—152 West 51st St. at 51st Street. 1-212-765-1900, 1-800-237-0990, www.michelangelohotel.com. A boutique hotel favored by those who are turned off by the bustle of the big chain hotels. Closest theatres: Winter Garden, Gershwin, Circle in the Square, Ambassador.

WEST 52ND STREET

Novotel New York—226 West 52nd Street at Broadway. 1-212-315-0100. Fax: 1-212-765-5365, www.novotel.com. Modern-looking chain hotel fronting on Broadway. Closest theatres: Virginia, Neil Simon, Broadway, Ed Sullivan (where David Letterman tapes his show).

Sheraton New York Hotel and Towers—811 Seventh Avenue (at 53rd St.) 1-212-581-1000, www.starwood.com/sheraton. Large meeting rooms and dramatic frontage on Seventh Ave. makes the Sheraton a magnet for conventioneers. Luxury tower rooms are also available. Closest theatres: Broadway, Virginia, Neil Simon, Studio 54.

DISCOUNTS

Hotel bookings have become like airline seats: no two people on the same floor pay the same rate.

A smart travel agent will be able to steer you to all sorts of discounts, at even the trendiest hotels (except on New Year's Eve!)

But you can also arrange these yourself. AAA membership gets you an automatic ten percent off at participating hotels, which is nearly all of them.

The wonderful world of the web offers several large websites that book rooms at wholesale rates. Among the best of these:

Cheaprooms.com

Expedia.com

Hotels.com

Orbitz.com

Citybase.com

Some sites offer hotel and theatre packages, notably www.nyc.com and www.broadway.com.

Aware of this, some of the hotels themselves have begun offering discounts and packages that are exclusive to those who book through the hotels' own websites. I've included these with the listings.

TONY AWARDS

The person who won the most Tony Awards is director/producer Harold Prince, whose mantelpiece is crowded with twenty of the mounted medallions. His projects have included the original *Fiddler on the Roof*, *Cabaret*, and many of Stephen Sondheim's greatest musicals including *Follies*, *A Little Night Music*, and *Sweeney Todd*.

The only time there was a tie in the Tony Awards category of Best Musical was in 1960 when *Fiorello!* and *The Sound of Music* shared the award.

TIPS

- Avoid rooms on the first few floors that face the street. New York streets in this neighborhood remain noisy until the wee hours, and even the not-so-wee-anymore hours.

- If you come by car, make sure to check whether the hotel has its own parking facility, or offers a discount at a nearby commercial garage. This could turn out to be a considerable cost, so make sure to check!

- Websites like www.tripadvisor.com let you read recent reviews by actual customers who paid their hard-earned money. Read these reviews before you book.

- Among Times Square hotels, older tends to mean crummier and newer tends to mean nicer. There are exceptions. A few of the older hotels have made major renovations to stay competitive, but regular visitors have found that most of the spiffiest renovations have been done to the priciest rooms and suites. Smaller and cheaper rooms at these hotels tend to have remained shabby.

- Make sure you get what you reserved and stand your ground if you don't. One of the most common complaints I've heard is that people booked one level of room, and found, upon arrival, that they'd been bumped down under the pretense that the hotel was overbooked. Make sure you get everything in writing, including size of bed (queen, twin, etc.) smoking or non-smoking room, etc. If you order on web or through a travel agent, make sure to bring the print-out of your reservation.

- Don't let the staff give you attitude. Most places have great, courteous service, but a few places have employees whose rudeness borders on the French. Don't take it. Demand what you paid for.

CHAPTER TEN

WALKING TOUR OF THE BROADWAY THEATRE DISTRICT

"Theatre represents, at its best, a victory of
civilization over barbarism."
—EMORY LEWIS

If you are coming to New York for the first time, try to arrange your schedule so you get your first glimpse of Broadway at night. It was designed to be beheld in the evening.

You can approach from almost any direction, but the most dramatic approach is from the north, or uptown. And as you crisscross Broadway on this tour, headed south, or in New York parlance, downtown, you'll get flashes of Times Square getting closer and closer, until you finally wind up in its very heart.

As you walk, notice how residential mixes with business, the architectural details, the marquees. There's a special magic in marquees. They strive to project the personality of what's within, like flowers growing on the building to attract, not bees, but you.

PART ONE—57TH STREET TO 47TH STREET

If you've a classical bent, you can start your walking tour at 57th and Seventh Avenue, **Carnegie Hall**, temple of orchestras, soloists, occasional pop moments, even theatre moments, like the 1992 Sondheim celebration concert. Built by 19th century robber baron/philanthropist Andrew Carnegie.

Otherwise, an appropriate place to start is Broadway and 56th, where you'll find bank ATMs on three corners—this is New York and stocking up on cash right now might not be such a bad idea.

Continue a block downtown to 55th Street and turn to the left, continue across Seventh Avenue and another half block to the exotic-looking Moorish palace, built in 1923 as a home for the Ancient and Accepted Order of the Mystic Shrine (i.e., the Shriners). It was saved from the wrecker's ball in the Forties by Mayor Fiorello H. LaGuardia, of *Fiorello!* fame, as a temple of the arts for the common man, called **The New York City Center of Music and Drama**. The production policy has evolved continually since then. For a stint in the 1960s it was home to a series of revivals of earlier musicals that brought older stars like Ethel Merman back in *Annie Get Your Gun,* and showcased younger stars in classics, including Barbara Cook as Mrs. Anna in *The King and I.*

The City Center, as it's generally called, now hosts a great deal of dance, but each spring, the "Encores! Great American Musicals in Concert" series regularly sells out. The series finds lesser-known shows that might never get a full-scale Broadway revival, and presents them with big stars for performances over five days. Ironically two of these, *Chicago* and *Wonderful Town*, moved to Broadway. And *Chicago* subsequently became an Oscar-winning film. Its renaissance began here at the City Center, which also contains two downstairs Off-Broadway theatres used by Manhattan Theatre Club.

Make an about-face and head back west on 55th Street, crossing both Seventh Avenue and Broadway, and continuing west. On the downtown side of 55th you'll seen the green-lit sign of **McGee's Irish Pub**. Proceed nearly to the end of the block. On your right, you'll see a small storefront soup store at 259-A, officially named **Al's Soup Kitchen International**. It's better known to fans of the old "Seinfeld" TV series as home to the prototype of the infamous "Soup Nazi." He still works there, and really detests this name, so please don't bring it up if you go. You know how he can be.

At the end of the block turn left, cross 55th Street, and continue downtown one block to 54th Street. Cross to the downtown side of this street, turn left and head east. You'll find yourself under the marquee for the infamous **Studio 54**. It opened in the 1920s as the Gallo Opera House, but fared poorly in this first incarnation. It was used for many years as a television studio on 54th Street, hence the name. In the 1970s it finally achieved its place in history as the headquarters of the Manhattan disco scene. It was also the headquarters of sex, drugs and the music of The Village People. Long before "American Idol," young hopefuls queued up at the original velvet rope hoping to be judged cool enough to enter it's disco-ball-swept interior. Many waited in vain.

But the discotheque went into steep decline with the death of disco music, and was reconfigured as the environmental home for Roundabout Theatre Company's hit revival of *Cabaret*, which spent most of its long run here. Roundabout bought the theatre in 2003 and now operates it as a regular Broadway theatre.

Continuing east on 54th Street, you'll notice a modest doorway saying **Sound One Recording Studio**. Don't be fooled: This is one of the major recording studios in the city. Many of your favorite cast albums were made here. If you peek in, you'll see posters from the many pop and rock acts that laid down tracks here.

Further down this block you'll see **Gold's Gym**, where many Broadway dancers keep themselves buff. On the left is the local branch of the **Kinko's** copying chain where many of the aspiring playwrights who live and work in the area dupe their latest scripts to

The Ed Sullivan Theatre at 53rd Street, where "The Late Show With David Letterman" tapes Monday through Thursday.

send out. Also on the left is **Paradise DVD**, the first porno shop on this walk, but not the last.

At the the of this block, you're back on Broadway. Make a right and look up. It's the marquee of **The Ed Sullivan Theatre**, where "The Late Show With David Letterman" is taped Monday through Thursday. The Sullivan was originally a Broadway house, Hammerstein's Theatre, built in 1927 by Arthur Hammerstein, of the theatrical Hammerstein family. It went through several names before being purchased by CBS in the 1930s, and has been a TV studio ever since. Ed Sullivan's Sunday night variety show originated from here, as hosanna'd in *Bye Bye Birdie*. This was the stage where Sullivan introduced The Beatles to the American public in 1964.

As you approach the corner with 53rd Street, things may look familiar. This is the corner where Letterman does many of his wacky stunts. Turn right and continue on the north side of 53rd a few steps. You'll see Rupert Jee's **Hello Deli**, a modest storefront not much different from a million others in the city, except that Letterman enlists Jee in many of his on-air sketches. The tranquil-seeming block outside is frequently transformed into a stage for Letterman-related events like motorcycle jumps, the smashing of piles of fruit, rock concerts, make-believe taxi accidents, and who knows what all. The show tapes around 5 PM if you want try catching one. They are almost never announced in advance.

Turn back eastward on 53rd Street and return to Broadway. Cross 53rd and look up again. This is the **Broadway Theatre**, which has been given a sleek new art deco marquee. Originally designed as a house for both cinema and vaudeville, this large (nearly 1,800 seats) theatre became a headquarters for Broadway musicals in 1930, and has stayed thus ever since. This is where Ethel Merman first sang "Everything's Coming Up Roses" in *Gypsy*, where Patti LuPone first sang "Don't Cry for Me, Argentina" in *Evita*, where Colm Wilkinson gave the U.S. its first taste of his Jean Valjean in *Les Misérables*, and where that big helicopter took off in *Miss Saigon*.

Continue to the end of this block and make a right onto 52nd Street. About halfway down on the right, you'll pass the entrance to **Roseland**, the Swing-era dance hall where partner-dancing is still king. The club hosts certain annual Broadway events including *Broadway Bares*.

Further down this block are two famous Broadway theatres facing each other, the Virginia and the Neil Simon.

The **Virginia Theatre** opened in 1925 as home to The Theatre Guild, a play-producing company that specialized in introducing New York to the works of international playwrights like Shaw, Molnar, Turgenev and Pirandello, along with works by American Eugene O'Neill, whose five-hour *Mourning Becomes Electra* was a triumph in 1931. The Guild's trump card was the husband-wife acting team of Alfred Lunt and Lynn Fontanne who appeared in at least one play a season here. More recent successes have included *City of Angels*, *Jelly's Last Jam*, and *Smokey Joe's Café*.

Facing the Virginia is the **Neil Simon Theatre**, which today houses Hairspray. Originally named the Alvin Theatre for its original owners, Alex Aarons and Vinton Freedley, it's one of Broadway's most successful theatres, having hosted dozens of long-running hits since its opening in 1927, including original productions of *Anything Goes*, *The Boys From Syracuse*, *Red, Hot and Blue!*, *A Funny Thing Happened on the Way to the Forum*, *Shenandoah*, and *Annie*.

Proceed past the Neil Simon to the far end of the block, turn left onto Eighth Avenue, go south one block, cross 51st Street and turn left again onto this block. Directly in front of you, to the right, is a traffic pass-through cutting through the middle of the block. Though designed as a pedestrian walkway and car drop-off for the Gershwin and Circle in the Square theatres, now the only cars allowed in are those headed for the building's parking lot. Pedestrians are still welcome, especially those headed for the two theatres.

The upstairs one, the **Gershwin Theatre**, is the biggest on Broadway, with nearly 2,000 seats. Having opened in 1972, it's also one of Broadway's newer theatres. It has hosted its share of hits, including the original *Sweeney Todd* and *Wicked*, the U.S. premiere of *Starlight Express*, a long engagement of *Riverdance*, and major

The crowd of pedestrians on Avenue of the Americas seems to go on forever.

revivals of *Show Boat*, *Mame*, *1776*, and *Fiddler on the Roof*. The right side lobby of the theatre's orchestra level (up the escalator) contains the **Theatre Hall of Fame**.

At the far end of the breezeway is the **Circle in the Square Theatre**, opened in 1972 as the uptown showcase for the venerable Greenwich Village Off-Broadway troupe, offering an annual slate of interesting revivals and original plays. Like the downtown space on Bleecker Street, the Circle in the Square has Broadway's only full thrust stage, meaning the audience sits on three (and sometimes four) sides, surrounding the playing space. The troupe has since gone bankrupt, but the theatre lives on as a place to find ambitious stagings of shows, including recent productions of *The Rocky Horror Show* and *Metamorphoses*, the latter played around a huge pool of water occupying nearly the entire stage.

Return to 51st Street and continue east. On your left you'll see the marquee to the **Times Square Church**. If it looks like a Broadway theatre, there's a good reason. This is the old Mark Hellinger Theatre, home to the original *My Fair Lady*, and many other great musicals. Regrettably, it was sold to the church in 1994, just before the boom in musicals put a premium on theatres just its size. Too bad.

The building across the street from the church is the Paramount Building, home of the Showtime cable service, along with many other broadcast entities and magazines. At the corner is a sunken plaza that contains the **Mars 2112** theme restaurant, which offers a simulated trip to the Red Planet. Cross Broadway to a legendary block. On the corner is **Ellen's Stardust Diner**, featuring singing waiters in a Fifties atmosphere. Next door is the **Iridium Jazz Club** in a downstairs space that once housed the *Forbidden Broadway* revue. Dominating the street is the block-straddling **Cadillac Winter Garden Theatre**, where Al Jolson serenaded his "Mammy" from a specially built runway. The theatre hosted *Hellzapoppin*, Stephen Sondheim's Broadway debut with *West Side Story*, and his triumph with *Follies*. This is where Barbra Streisand first sang "People" in *Funny Girl*, and where Angela Lansbury strutted in *Mame*. This is also where *Cats* rolled up its record run of eighteen years, 1982 to 2000. It's now home to *Mamma Mia!*

Just past it is the site of the original **Lindy's** restaurant, hangout of Damon Runyon, who chronicled the street life of Broadway from a corner booth, in stories that became *Guys and Dolls*. The site is now occupied by a bakery/café and one of Times Square's ubiquitous electronics stores.

Return to 51st Street and continue east to Seventh Avenue. Cross it to a seemingly undistinguished block. As you continue east, you enter a forest of tall, concrete-and-glass-clad office buildings. This is **Rockefeller Center**, capital of American broadcast and print media. When you reach the Avenue of the Americas (Sixth Avenue) turn right and walk past a pedestrian plaza. Across the way on the NE corner with 50th Street, you can see the art deco marquee of one of New York's most recognizable landmarks, the 5,000-seat **Radio City Music Hall**, where the Rockettes still garner automatic applause with their synchronized kick line. Today the theatre houses mainly concerts and awards events, including the annual Tony Awards, which arrive the first weekend in June.

Kitty-corner from Radio City is a faceless Rockefeller Center office tower with a very nice reflecting pool in a plaza. To build it, they demolished The Roxy, sister theatre to Radio City, which advertised itself for a time as the biggest theatre in the world. A 1960 photo of actress Gloria Swanson amid its ruins is said to have inspired the musical *Follies*. So maybe it was worth it after all.

The Art Deco marquee for Radio City Music Hall.

Skip 50th Street, and continue down to 49th Street. Then turn right and head back toward Broadway. Toward the end of this block, on the left, you'll encounter a cluster of mid-level ethnic restaurants, including the **Bombay Masala**, which claims to be the oldest Indian restaurant in New York. Cross Seventh Avenue, pass the subway entrance and proceed across this short block to Broadway.

On the NE corner of this intersection you'll see the stylish **Ruby Foo** Asian restaurant. Beyond it at midblock is **Caroline's Comedy Club**, the city's premier standup venue, which books top comedians from talk shows and cable specials.

Now cross Broadway and note the **Colony Record Store** on the NW corner, with its vintage neon logo of a bobby-soxer leaping into the air while clutching a 45. This store offers a first-rate inventory of sheet music and cast albums, though the prices won't have anyone leaping for joy.

It's appropriate that this corner has a music store on it: this once was the gateway to Tin Pan Alley, a three-block stretch of Broadway once the epicenter of the American music industry. One remnant of this glorious past remains. Inside the Colony, at 1619 Broadway, is the famed **Brill Building**, recognized by its brass art deco doorway. Many music companies still have their offices here.

Continuing west on 49th Street, you'll come to the marquee of the **Ambassador Theatre**, where Spencer Tracy's career got a boost in *The Last Mile*, where Savion Glover tapped the history of America in *Bring in 'da Noise, Bring in 'da Funk*, and where Kristin Chenoweth brought down the house and became a star in the 1999 revival of *You're a Good Man, Charlie Brown*. This house is beloved by theatre historians because the architect configured the stage and performing space diagonally on the too-narrow plot. There is a hint on the theatre's exterior: the entrance doors also are canted at a 45-degree angle.

The entry to the Brill Building (right), headquarters of Tin Pan Alley.

THE SIDEWALKS OF NEW YORK

The sidewalk in front of the Palace Theatre was once known as "The Beach." Vaudeville performers would camp out there, and do their act for anyone who came or went, hoping against hope for a fluke booking at what was then the pinnacle of their profession.

The west side of Eighth Avenue running from 40th Street up to about 50th was once known as the "Minnesota Strip" because of the many Midwestern girls who wound up plying the Oldest Profession there.

If you look across to the downtown side of 49th Street you'll see the Crowne Plaza Hotel. A passageway allows guest to drop off their cars, and for pedestrians to pass through to 48th Street. This is the north end of the *Metro* Express, a series of midblock walkways that allows pedestrians to move quickly from here down as far as 44th Street.

Continuing west on 49th Street, on the same side at the Crowne Plaza you'll see the **Eugene O'Neill Theatre**, built in 1925 as the Forrest Theatre. This was where the 1934 hit, *Tobacco Road*, played all of its remarkable 3,182 performances. Other distinguished O'Neill tenants have includes *A Thousand Clowns*, *Big River*, *The Bad Seed*, *A View From the Bridge*, *All My Sons*, the legendary flop *Moose Murders*, and several plays by Neil Simon, who owned it for a time.

Just past it is a small **Cyber Café** where you can check your email or research one of the shows you'd like to see.

The last landmark on 49th Street is again on the uptown side of 49th Street is **St. Malachy's Church**, also known as The Actors' Chapel. This Roman Catholic church has served since 1920 as a refuge for theatre folk to pray to St. Genesius, the patron saint of actors, for all the things theatre folk pray for.

It's likely that not a few streetwalkers have prayed there, too. For at the next intersection, Eighth Avenue, you can look across to the SW corner. The west-side sidewalk from there down to 42nd Street, lined with frowzy storefronts, was nicknamed the **Minnesota Strip** for the great number of Midwestern girls who came to the city with stars in their eyes, and found themselves trapped into a life as hookers cruising there. Though they moved elsewhere during the 1990s crackdowns by Mayor Rudolph Giuliani, pros once again can be found plying their trade there, though generally in smaller numbers and not until the theatre crowd has cleared out.

Before you turn this corner, look across Eighth Avenue again to the NW corner. This imposing building, **Worldwide Plaza**, home to EMI,

Polygram, Universal and other music companies, stands on the former site of Madison Square Garden—one of several sites it inhabited since leaving Madison Square proper in the early part of the 20th century. The latest incarnation of MSG is at 34th Street and Seventh Avenue.

Turn downtown once again and walk one block past the Days Hotel to 48th Street and cross to the SE corner. This brick building is **Engine Company 54/Ladder Company 4/Batallion 9**, known as "Broadway's Firehouse" because it protects the theatres of Times Square and has to inspect any open flames used in the shows. Their slogan is, "Never missed a performance."

Tragically, they were among the first companies to respond to the call from the World Trade Center on September 11, 2001. More than a dozen of its firefighters never came back. The folk of Broadway responded by building a shrine of candles, flowers and testimonials on the sidewalk in of its doors. The firefighters' sacrifice is remembered now with a bas-relief plaque by A. Kotler.

Turn east on 48th Street, past **Pongsri** Thai and **Hakata** Japanese restaurants. To the left is the towering **Ritz Plaza**, which stands on the site of longtime Theatre District landmark Mamma Leone's restaurant. The stacks of chianti bottles and wandering violinists are now gone, replaced by luxury apartments. About halfway down the block you'll come to two Broadway theatres facing each other across the way, the Longacre and Kerr Theatre. The one on the right, the **Longacre Theatre**, was roused in 1935 by Clifford Odets' *Waiting for Lefty* with Elia Kazan and Lee J. Cobb. Since then it has offered Dorothy Parker's *The Ladies of the Corridor*, Zero Mostel in *Rhinoceros*, *Children of a Lesser God*, and the long-running, Tony-

Looking uptown through Times Square from 44th Street.

winning musical *Ain't Misbehavin'*.

Across the street, the **Walter Kerr Theatre**, long known as the Ritz, had an unremarkable career for its first seven decades. But in the 1990s it came alive with a series of Pulitzer-winning dramas, including *The Piano Lesson, Proof*, and *Angels in America*, both part one, *Millennium Approaches*, and part two, *Perestroika*.

On the NW corner with Broadway is a large retail store devoted to candy, candy, candy, notably the products of the **Hershey** company, which are packaged in various witty ways as souvenirs. Cross both Broadway and you'll come to facing businesses that may comfort some who miss home: the Texas Restaurant and Saloon, purveyor of ribs and other barbecue, and Popcorn, Indiana, which sells flavored popcorn that you can't take into the theatres with you.

Continue east on this short block and cross Seventh Avenue. The stretch of 48th Street between Seventh and Avenue of the Americas is known for its congregation of more than a dozen music stores, most of them specializing in one type of instrument, e.g. guitars or brass or strings or percussion, plus sheet music and accessories. If you play an instrument, you may wish to browse here.

Continue east until you come to the **Cort Theatre**, home of *Boy Meets Girl, Advise and Consent, The Diary of Anne Frank, The Magic Show, Ma Rainey's Black Bottom*, and *Sarafina!*

Now look both ways and cross over to the other side of the street, in the shadow of the **McGraw-Hill Building**. You are standing on the site of the Playhouse Theatre, which was demolished in 1968, but not before it made one last bid for glory. It is where Mel Brooks' movie classic *The Producers* was filmed. If you stand in the lobby near the

Looking downtown through Times Square from 45th Street.

newsstand, you're standing on approximately the spot where the chorus sang "Springtime for Hitler." One trace remains. If you go back outside, look across the street and you'll see the marquee of the Cort Theatre, just as it appears in the film.

Resume your walk eastward to Avenue of the Americas, and turn right, headed downtown once again. A spacious granite-floored plaza leads you to **1211 Avenue of the Americas**, an office building that serves as headquarters to **The New York Post**, **FOX News**, and **TV Guide**. That's right, "Picks & Pans" get picked and panned right upstairs.

At the next corner, turn right. This block of 47th Street between Sixth and Seventh Avenues is fairly sleepy today with small restaurants and hotels, and no theatres at all. But in the 1920s, as Damon Runyon memorably reported, this block was known as **Dream Street**, a place of theatrical hotels, rooming houses and speakeasies inhabited by vaudevillians and would-be vaudevillians who were "great hands for sitting around and dreaming out loud about how they will practically assassinate the public in the Palace if they ever get a chance."

And The Palace is near at hand. On the SE corner of 47th Street at Seventh Avenue is the entrance to the **Doubletree Hotel and Suites**, which was built above and around the legendary **Palace Theatre**, where "playing the Palace" was once considered the pinnacle of American vaudeville. Built in 1913, this stage has seen performances by the top luminaries of the first half of the 20th Century: Judy Garland, The Marx Brothers, Houdini, Fanny Brice, Ethel Barrymore, Jack Benny, Sarah Bernhardt—the long and distinguished list goes on. It was refurbished in the 1960s as a Broadway musical house. Tenants over the year included original runs of *Sweet Charity, George M!, Woman of the Year, La Cage aux Folles,* and *The Will Rogers Follies*. It's been occupied for a decade by two Disney musicals, *Beauty and the Beast* and *Aida*.

The patch of pavement in front of it was known as **The Beach**, where denizens of Dream Street would perform their acts, hoping someone going in or out would recognize their genius and move their act inside. It rarely happened, but show business is the business of hope.

Now, turn around. You have arrived at last in **Times Square**, the crossroads of the world. So many lights, so many signs, so many cars, so many people. It's dizzying to try taking it all in at once. Better to focus on a detail here, a detail there. There's a powerful energy rising up out of the earth here. Enter its vortex.

Directly in front of you is a large, triangular traffic island officially known as Father Duffy Square. A large **statue of Father Francis P. Duffy**, wartime chaplain of the 165th Infantry, and pastor of the Holy

Cross Church on 42nd Street, stands at the center of the island, but it is overwhelmed by an abutting theatrical landmark, the **TKTS** discount ticket booth, with its characteristic red-and-white canvas panels. Erected as a temporary structure in 1973, the booth now sells about one in ten Broadway tickets. People queue up daily in two long lines that run down to another statue, that of entertainer **George M. Cohan** at the 46th Street end, then fold back on themselves. Walk down to the Cohan statue and you can look out on Times Square as he does.

Strange note: Cohan's statue attracts the attentions of flocks of pigeons who do what pigeons have always done to statues. But not Father Duffy's spotless statue just a new dozen feet away. Miracle on 47th Street? You decide!

Time to rest... but there's nowhere to sit. Even Father Duffy must stand. But you needn't. Just south of The Palace on Seventh Avenue is the **Times Square Visitors Center**, whose marquee calls it the **Times Square Information Center**, built inside what used to be the Embassy cinema. There are kiosks and booths and concessions, selling every type of theatre-related ticket, tour and memorabilia. But, best of all, there are seats. Free seats, where you can rest as long as you like. There's even a video game for the kids to use while you can "sit, sit you down, sit," and recharge for a few minutes.

The statue of George M. Cohan, the man who wrote and performed "Give My Regards to Broadway," stands guard at the center of Times Square.

GEORGE
• M •
COHAN
1878-1942

★ Give my Regards to Broadway ★

The marquee of the Palace Theatre (left) and the entrance of the Times Square Information Center, topped with billboards for current shows.

PART TWO—47TH STREET TO 41ST STREET

Cross back over Seventh Avenue to the TKTS booth and continue west across Broadway, then past the **Blue Fin** restaurant onto the rest of West 47th Street. To your right is the **Morgan Stanley** headquarters topped by its immense illuminated multi-story digital stock ticker. On the ground floor is the cramped and busy **Starbucks** where so many theatregoers stop to fortify themselves with mochaccinos at 7:30 each night before heading off to catch their curtains.

On the left, just past the entrance to the brand-new **W Times Square Hotel** (built on the site of the old Central Theatre where Rodgers and Hart debuted their first musical, *Poor Little Ritz Girl*), notice a small doorway with a faux half-timbered logo. This is the old **Theatre Guild** building, onetime headquarters of the producing powerhouse that hosted Eugene O'Neill's plays, the acting team of Lunt and Fontanne and, in 1942, *Oklahoma!* Lawrence Langner kept an office here, and here is where Rodgers and Hammerstein first cemented their legendary collaboration. If you peek in the glass door and look to the left, you can see a beautiful marble panel with the masks of comedy and tragedy.

Just past it on the same side of the street is the **Café Edison**, part of the **Hotel Edison**. Nicknamed "The Polish Tea Room," this unassuming eatery is a favorite among the older generation of showbiz types, who come for the borscht, blintzes, flanken and stuffed derma. It's the setting for Neil Simon's comedy, *45 Seconds From Broadway*.

Beyond the entrance to the Edison Hotel entrance you'll find **The Supper Club**, a popular nightclub. This space was for many years a small Broadway theatre, the **Edison Theatre**, home to the long-running hit, *Oh! Calcutta!*

Just past it is the **New Dance Group Arts Center**, which serves as a rehearsal hall for Broadway shows, and offers classes for dancers.

Across from The Supper Club you'll see the looping wrought-iron trim on the marquee of the **Ethel Barrymore Theatre**, built for one member of the regal Barrymore and Drew acting clans, today represented by—who else?—Drew Barrymore. Ethel starred in the inaugural production *The Kingdom of God*. Memorable productions over the years included *Design for Living* with Noel Coward and the Lunts, Clare Boothe Luce's *The Women, Pal Joey* with Gene Kelly, Wendy Wasserstein's *The Sisters Rosensweig*, and the Stephen Sondheim revue *Putting It Together* with Carol Burnett. But the theatre's greatest moment came when Marlon Brando bellowed "Stella!" in Tennessee Williams immortal *A Streetcar Named Desire* in 1947.

At the end of the block, you'll come to two facing Broadway houses, the **Biltmore Theatre** on the right, and the **Brooks Atkinson Theatre** on the left. The 1925-vintage Biltmore, known for housing Neil Simon's *Barefoot in the Park* and the long-running "tribal love-rock musical" *Hair*, was virtually abandoned in the 1980s. It nearly was torn down in the 1990s before the ubiquitous Manhattan Theatre Club took over the site, arranged a development deal that included the huge **Biltmore** residence tower at the corner, refurbished it at a cost of more than $27 million, and reopened it as the company's flagship.

The Atkinson, named for a longtime theatre critic at *The New York Times*, housed Neil Simon's Broadway debut, *Come Blow Your Horn*, Dustin Hoffman's Broadway debut in *Jimmy Shine*, and a series of acclaimed plays and comedies including *Lenny, Talley's Folly, The Dresser, Buried Child*—and even the musical, *Jane Eyre*.

Past the Atkinson you'll see the **China Club**, a popular night spot that landed in the headlines in the early 2000s when rapper P. Diddy and then-girlfriend Jennifer Lopez became involved in a shooting after an evening roistering here.

At the end of this block, look across Eighth Avenue to the right. About midblock between 49th and 50th is a marquee for the **New York Sightseeing Visitors Center**:, a privately-owned center for booking tours on the Gray Line buses. See Chapter Eleven for details.

Cross Eighth Avenue, turn left and go down one block past a series of bars and adult video stores. At the next corner, turn right onto 46th Street. This block contains one of the thickest clusters of eateries in the city. Known as **Restaurant Row**, the block between Eighth and Ninth Avenues serves up French, Indian. Chinese, Irish. Italian and American restaurants, some for the wealthiest gourmets, some for the most budget-conscious tourists. There are a few legends here as well. **Joe Allen** has been a gathering place for the stars and decision-makers of Broadway for at least two generations. **Don't Tell Mama** is a cornerstone of the city's thriving cabaret scene. A hefty percentage of each day's pre- and post-theatre dining is done on this street, partly because it's so conveniently located near so many theatres. It's worth your while to make a turn around this block and pick up some of the sample menus and postcards that many of them post at their doors.

On the downtown side of the block near Eighth Avenue is the meeting hall of **IATSE**, the stagehands and electricians' union. From its door, there is a clear sightline eastward back across Eighth to a rundown-looking building at the NE corner. Cross over to it to get a good look. Barely legible over the door is the sign reading **McHale's**. Inside is a bar and grill where a considerable part of Broadway's technical people get hired. They meet here, in a virtual annex to their union hall, to drink and schmooze about the latest incoming shows, and who's going to be working on them.

Landmarks will begin to come faster now, as you approach the heart of the Theatre District.

Across 46th Street you can see the wood-paneled face of **JR** restaurant and the friendly **Broadway Inn**. Continuing eastward on the uptown side of the street, you'll pass the **Paramount Hotel** and the **Church of Scientology**. Across the way you'll see a parking lot where you can pass through to 45th Street. Next to it is the rear marquee for the Imperial Theatre. The main auditorium is here on 46th, but the front entrance is on 45th.

Beyond it is the **Richard Rodgers Theatre** (nee the 46th Street Theatre), which saw the openings of Frank Loesser's biggest hits, *Guys and Dolls*, and *How To Succeed in Business Without Really Trying*, plus *Good News*, *Anything Goes*, Ethel Merman and Bert Lahr in *DuBarry Was a Lady*, *Finian's Rainbow*, Gwen Verdon in both *Damn Yankees* and *Redhead*, Mary Martin and Robert Preston in *I Do! I Do!*, *1776*, *No No Nanette*, *Nine*, *Lost in Yonkers*, *Side Show*, *Footloose*, *Seussical*, and Billy Joel's *Movin' Out*—not to mention both the original and revival of *Chicago*.

Just past it, on the uptown side of the street, is the back entrance to the Edison Hotel. Next to that is the **Lunt-Fontanne Theatre**, named for the husband-wife acting team, where originated several 1920s editions of the *Ziegfeld Follies*, the Lunts themselves in *The Visit*, Richard Burton's *Hamlet*, Burton again with his ex-wife Elizabeth Taylor in *Private Lives* and the original *The Sound Of Music*, not to mention *Titanic*. More recently the theatre has housed Disney's long-running *Beauty and the Beast*, which moved here from the Palace.

Up a steep and narrow stairway next to the Lunt-Fontanne and you'll come to the second-floor **Harlequin** rehearsal studio. Right next to that is another stairway that leads to the **Gaiety Male Burlesque**, which is just upstairs, incongruously, from a **Howard Johnson** that's stood there since Year One, but recently announced it will be closing.

Facing this panoply of olde Times Square is a monolith of new Times Square, the **Marriott Marquis Hotel**, which takes up the entire end of the block between 46th and 45th fronting on Times Square. To build it, they had to tear down three working Broadway theatres, the Morosco, the Bijou and the old Hayes, plus the shells of two more. In return for this loss, the hotel incorporated one new Broadway space, the beautiful **Marquis Theatre**, which has housed *Victor/Victoria*, Paul Simon's *The Capeman*, Bernadette Peters' *Annie Get Your Gun*, and the Tony-winning *Thoroughly Modern Millie*.

The hotel also hosts a variety of Broadway events throughout the year (see more in Chapter Eleven). For pedestrians it offers two mid-block walkways to 45th Street. A wide one for taxis and auto dropoffs, and another strictly for walkers, which features a mural of scenes from musicals, including *A Chorus Line*, *West Side Story*, *Hello, Dolly!*, and other classics.

When you're done admiring it (and seeing how many of the shows you can name), head east again on 46th Street. Cross Broadway to the traffic island, wave at the statue of George M. Cohan as you pass, then proceed across Seventh Avenue. Look up and to your left at the building that now houses a TGI Friday restaurant. It once housed the Miller Shoe Shop, which served the theatre trade. Its slogan is still carved into the building's façade: "THE SHOW FOLKS SHOE SHOP DEDI-CATED TO BEAVTY [sic] IN FOOTWEAR." Below it are four statues set in faded-gilt niches, representing the greatest actresses of their age, as selected by the readers of Playbill in the 1920s: Ethel Barrymore as Ophelia, Marilyn Miller as Sunny, Mary Pickford as Little Lord Fauntleroy, and opera singer Rosa Ponselle as Norma. These ladies have been watching over 46th Street for eight decades (despite the fact that Ethel's first name is now covered by the TGI Friday sign).

This next block features the offices of **Actors' Equity**, the actors' union, on the left at number 165. Down the block on the same side is an Off-Broadway space, the **Laura Pels Theatre**, which is now operated by Roundabout Theatre Company. The glassed-in entrance leads to esca-lators that take you down to the playhouse, which is below street level.

This block also once also contained the legendary **High School for the Performing Arts**, setting of the film *Fame* and the song "Nothing" in *A Chorus Line*. *Fame*'s big dance number, with its mem-orable choreography on the top of car roofs, was filmed on this block. The school has since moved uptown near Lincoln Center.

At the end of this block on the right is the cozy **Café Europa**. You can continue beyond Avenue of the Americas to a block of 46th Street known as **Little Brazil** for its many Brazilian restaurants and asso-ciated businesses.

Or, you can make a right, go one block downtown, and turn right again onto 45th Street. Two-thirds of the way down on the right, you come to the oldest continuously-operating theatre on Broadway, the 1903-vintage **Lyceum Theatre** with its distinctive, columned façade and wavy-fronted marquee.

Beyond it you return to Times Square. Seventh and Broadway crisscross here, meaning you're now at the very center. The next block will also be the heart of the Broadway Theatre District.

You may wish to detour to the right at this corner, passing both the **Planet Hollywood** theme restaurant and the huge **Virgin Megastore**, which sells CDs and DVDs.

Return to the corner of 45th and Broadway. Look up at the building looming on the west side of the block between 45th and 44th. If you're there on a weekday morning, there's a pretty good chance you'll see a mob of teens holding signs and screaming at something on the third floor. **MTV** tapes concerts there, in a studio with huge windows gazing onto Times Square. The star du jour often comes to the window and waves at the fans below, prompting screaming that may remind you of bobby-soxers screaming for Frank Sinatra at the old **Paramount**—which, coincidentally was located two blocks south at 43rd Street.

But we're getting ahead of ourselves. MTV is in the **Viacom Building**, which uses the vanity address One Astor Plaza. Where is Astor Plaza? No such place. But it takes it name from the old Astor Hotel that once stood on the site with a lobby that was a popular rendezvous for theatre-bound friends. Meeting "under the clock at the Astor" was a familiar World War II expression. Also in this building, above the MTV studio, is the **Minskoff Theatre**, home to Debbie Reynolds' *Irene*, the crazy Polish musical *Metro*, one of several versions of *The Scarlet Pimpernel*, and Glenn Close in Andrew Lloyd Webber's *Sunset Boulevard*.

The Minskoff is accessed through a breezeway that cuts under the Viacom building to 44th Street, but don't go through, yet. Though surrounded by the modern towers of multimedia capitalism, the nerve center of Manhattan is dominated by a concentration of two- and three-story buildings, most of them erected in the 1920s, that earn income just two or three hours a day, and are devoted to the arts. This stretch of 45th Street is chockablock with prime Broadway theatres, a killer's row of top legitimate houses.

As you continue west on 45th Street you have arrived at Broadway's innermost sanctum, **Shubert Alley**. Like Times Square itself, it's not so much a thing to look at as a place to be, a place to gather. Ultimately it's just a passage, lined with posters, two tan-brick theatres, the Booth on the 45th Street side and the Shubert on the 44th

Street side, with a souvenir shop in between. Why should such a place have magic? Perhaps because all the theatre lovers who have passed through leave a little of their excitement and enthusiasm there. Over the decades, the energy has built up. You will feel it, and add your own. Interestingly, nobody stays in Shubert Alley very long. It's a place that speeds you to the theatre, and that's enough.

I know of only one Broadway show scene that's actually set in Shubert Alley: the opening number of *The Producers*, "The King of Old Broadway." It's the perfect place for such a king to hold court.

The Booth Theatre at the north end is one of Broadway's most intimate, with fewer than 800 seats. Over the years it's stage has held, Kaufman and Hart's *You Can't Take It With You*, William Saroyan's *The Time of Your Life*, Noel Coward's *Blithe Spirit*, and Stephen Sondheim's *Sunday in the Park With George*, along with *The Elephant Man*, *Butterflies Are Free*, and *For Colored Girls Who Have Considered Suicide*.

Snuggled right next door to the west is the **Plymouth Theatre**, home to *The Odd Couple*, *The Skin of Our Teeth*, *Equus*, *The Life and Adventures of Nicholas Nickleby*, *Plaza Suite*, *Passion*, and *Jekyll & Hyde*.

At its side is the **Royale Theatre**, where Tennessee Williams' Gentleman Caller first knocked in *The Glass Menagerie*, where Julie Andrews made her American debut in *The Boy Friend*, where Laurence Olivier embodied postwar Britain in *The Entertainer*.

Downtown side of West 45th Street, showing the facades for the Golden, Royale, Plymouth, Booth, and Minskoff Theatres.

Across the street is the columned façade of the **Music Box Theatre**, built by Irving Berlin to house his intimate 1920s revues. Since then, it has seen the opening nights of Berlin's *As Thousands Cheer*, the Gershwins' *Of Thee I Sing* (the first musical to win the Pulitzer Prize), George S. Kaufman's *The Man Who Came To Dinner*, Bobby Clark and Gypsy Rose Lee in *Star and Garter*, Marlon Brando making his debut in *I Remember Mama*, and TV's "West Wing" creator Aaron Sorkin having his big break with *A Few Good Men*.

Next to the Music Box is the **Imperial Theatre**, which has housed relatively few shows overall through the years—but only because so many have been long-running hits: *Rose-Marie, The New Moon, Annie Get Your Gun, The Most Happy Fella, Oliver!, Fiddler on the Roof, Pippin, Dreamgirls, The Boy from Oz*, and the transfer of *Les Misérables*.

Past it is the entrance to a parking garage, followed by a knot of small restaurants, including Sam's piano bar and restaurant, **Barrymore's**, **Puleo's**, and **Frankie and Johnny's**.

Back on the south side of the street again is the tiny **Golden Theatre**, which has showcased *Avenue Q, Waiting for Godot, Beyond the Fringe, Falsettos, Master Class, The Blood Knot, Side Man*, and Pulitzer-winners *The Gin Game* and *Glengarry Glen Ross*.

The Milford Plaza Hotel provides a bookend to the block, and its **Celebrity Delicatessen and Restaurant** at the SE corner of 45th and Eighth is not a bad place to have lunch, though it's rare to see actual celebrities.

So you think the corner means you're at the end of killer's row? Wait, there's more. You now cross Eighth Avenue again, and there, blinking in neon, is the newest and oddest marquee on Broadway, that of the **Al Hirschfeld Theatre**, which had been known as the Martin Beck from its construction in 1924 until June 2003. Beck was a manager who booked acts at the Palace and decided to build his own theatre, he pioneered the far side of Eighth Avenue, but no one followed his lead. Hirschfeld was a famous artist who drew caricatures of the various shows, which appeared each Sunday in *The New York Times*. He once drew a self-portrait of himself, using his own head as an inkwell for a quill pen that has a drop of ink hanging from it. This image has been rendered in neon on the marquee of his new namesake theatre.

Across the street is the Japanese restaurant **Kodama**, where theatre folk often order a light dinner before shows. Right past it is a landmark apartment building, the appropriately named **Camelot**, which is home to many of the actors, writers and technicians who run Broadway. Further down on that same side is the **Triton Gallery**, the city's most comprehensive dealer in theatre posters, new and old.

Return to Eighth Avenue and walk one block south, then turn east again at 44th Street and cross Eighth Avenue. This is Broadway's second-most theatred block, also nicknamed **Rodgers and Hammerstein Row**, because so many of their blockbusters bowed here.

On the right is the **St. James Theatre**, scene of their first hit together, *Oklahoma!* They returned there with *The King and I* and *Flower Drum Song*, but the theatre has seen plenty of other hits as well, including Lillian Gish and John Gielgud in *Hamlet*, plus *Where's Charley?* , *The Pajama Game*, *My One and Only*, *The Secret Garden*, *On the Twentieth Century*, and *The Who's Tommy*. This is where Carol Channing made her entrance in a red dress as the chorus sang the title song of *Hello, Dolly!* It's also where audiences were treated to the sight of Adolph Hitler doing a fair impression of Judy Garland in Mel Brooks' *The Producers*.

Meanwhile, across the street at the **Majestic Theatre**, Rodgers and Hammerstein enjoyed successes with *Carousel* and *South Pacific*, before giving way to a string of classics including *The Music Man*, *Camelot*, *The Wiz*, and current long-run champ, *The Phantom of the Opera*.

Continuing down the hallowed ground of this block, you will pass, on the right, offices of most of Broadway's biggest producers, including the Dodgers, Jujamcyn, and Tony Awards Productions. Also on this side is Broadway's smallest house, the **Helen Hayes Theatre**, which has offered Tony-winners *Torch Song Trilogy* and *The Last Night of Ballyhoo*, along with the original productions of Eugene O'Neill's *Beyond the Horizon*, Albert Innuarato's *Gemini* and Claudia Shear's *Dirty Blonde*.

Right after the Hayes, you'll see Broadway landmark **Sardi's** theatrical restaurant, followed by the loading docks of *The New York Times*, for which Times Square is named. The *Times* building stands on the site of World War II hangout the **Stage Door Canteen**, at which servicemen on shore leave got to mingle with top Broadway stars before being shipped back out to war.

Across the street you'll see the marquees for neighbors, the **Broadhurst Theatre** and the **Shubert Theatre**.

The Broadhurst was one of choreographer Bob Fosse's favorite theatres. He staged *Dancin'* there, and after his death Anne Reinking choreographed the revue *Fosse* there. Other tenants: *Cabaret*, *Amadeus*, *Kiss of the Spider Woman*, *Grease*, Woody Allen in *Play It Again, Sam*, the real Humphrey Bogart in *Petrified Forest*, and Helen Hayes in *Victoria Regina*.

At the downtown end of Shubert Alley is the **Sam S. Shubert Theatre**, flagship of the Shubert producing and theatre-managing empire, whose elegant offices can be found upstairs. Notable productions here have included *A Chorus Line*, *Big*, *Crazy for You*, *Babes in Arms*, *A Little Night Music*, *Can-Can*, *Bells Are Ringing*, Katharine Hepburn in *The Philadelphia Story*, and *Promises, Promises*.

Once you pass the Loewe's Cinema on the uptown side, and the popular restaurants **Ollie's** and **Carmine's**, and the new **Bubba Gump** on the downtown side, you're back in Times Square.

Look up, to your right and you'll see the most photographed building in the area, **One Times Square**, better known as the building where the ball comes down on New Year's Eve.

One Times Square was once *The New York Times* headquarters, which didn't look a lot different from The Flatiron Building. After the *Times* moved its operations a half block west on 43rd Street, the building wound up with a white masonry sheath as The Allied Chemical Building. It's gone through several owners, and the sheath turned out to be perfect for turning the whole building into a giant jukebox-like neon monument. It's a towering American light sculpture, tiaraed in front with a giant steaming cup of Japanese ramen—the Cup Noodles sign.

Cross Seventh Avenue and Broadway to the southeast corner of 44th Street and you'll wind up in front of **ABC-TV**, with its wavy, multi-leveled news crawl and video screen. Passersby can watch shows being taped in the windowed street-level studio there, which stands on the site of Rector's restaurant, another Broadway landmark from the early 20th century. Across the street on the NE corner is the giant **Toys 'R Us** store with Times Square's newest landmark, a three-story indoor ferris wheel.

Forty-fourth Street quiets down considerably on the east side of Times Square, being occupied mainly with quiet hotels and restaurants, including the Osteria al Doge and Virgil's. But there are two theatres. On the downtown side there is the **Lambs' Theatre**, an Off-Broadway space that occupies what used to be a private club for actors, The Lambs. On the uptown side of the street is the venerable **Belasco Theatre**, which was built, owned, operated and now, some say, haunted by impresario David Belasco. Shows there include the original *Dead End*, *Awake and Sing*, the original (pre-film) *Rocky Horror Show*, and, for a time, the long-running nudie revue, *Oh! Calcutta!*

Another onetime Broadway theatre is hidden on this street. The **Millennium Broadway Hotel** bought the old **Hudson Theatre** and incorporated it into the new building, though it is no longer used for Broadway productions, but for corporate meetings. Still, it's there if you look for it.

The end of the block returns us to Avenue of the Americas. If you look across to the block between 44th and 43rd, you can see the site of the old **Hippodrome Theatre**, which housed epics and extravaganzas, including the legendary "drowning pool" into which an army of chorus girls would march a disappear, much to the horror and delight of audiences. The Hippodrome was ripped down to build a car-park, which at lease retains the name: the **Hippodrome Parking Garage**.

If you're interested, you can cross Avenue of the Americas to explore the block of 44th Street beyond, which still has the **Algonquin Hotel**, gathering place of the 1920s Algonquin Round Table. Across the street, and marked with a plaque, is the office building that once housed *The New Yorker*, which employed many of the Round Tablers, like Dorothy Parker.

Otherwise, swing downtown and around, past the **International Center of Photography**, and onto 43rd Street.

On the right is the **Town Hall**, not the seat of government, but a theatre that hosts concerts, dance troupes, lectures, and the occasional traveling show. On the left is a construction site. The Durst family bought up most of the block, including **Henry Miller's Theatre**, which housed a hit run of *Urinetown*, and is tearing down everything to put up another skyscraper. Henry Miller's is closed during construction, but the Dursts have said it will be incorporated into the new building, a la the Palace and Hudson, and will reopen about 2008. We'll see.

Back now in Times Square. On the NE corner is an office building with curious plaque. It marks the birthplace of playwright Eugene O'Neill, who entered the world, auspiciously, in a hotel that once stood on the site. On the SE corner is the headquarters of the corporate parent of the **NASDAQ** stock exchange, which continually broadcasts stock news. On the traffic islands between Broadway and Seventh Avenue you can see the **U.S. Marines** recruiting kiosk, with its neon American flag, and the **New York Police Department** post, decorated with two beautiful mosaics of the five boroughs.

On the west side of Times Square at 43rd Street is the pyramid-topped office building at **1501 Broadway**. This is another beehive of the theatre industry, home to press agents, talent agents, producers, et al. It's even got its own website, www.1501Broadway.com, for industry

The NYPD station in Times Square.

folk. It is surmounted by a giant clock that contains a carillon. At 7:45 each evening, it plays George M. Cohan's "Give My Regards to Broadway" as a little reminder to tardy theatregoers that it's time to find your theatre and your seats.

A noteworthy landmark on this stretch of 43rd Street west of Times Square, is the main entrance to the Square's namesake, *The New York Times*. Reporters for the Grey Lady can be seen hustling in and out all day long, just like something out of *The Front Page*. The rest of the block functions as something of a back door for 42nd Street, so we'll skip it, and instead, turn downtown one short block. As you pass the Café Europa's sandwich and coffee shop and the entrance to the Reuters building, pause for a moment to remember **Gray's Drug Store** that stood here in the 1920s. In the basement, Joe Leblang ran a cut-rate ticket service that allowed two generations of young people to afford Broadway shows, and served as an inspiration to the folks who founded today's TKTS booth.

As you pass the **Chase Bank** at the corner, brace yourself. Turn to the right and there, spread out before you, is **The New 42nd Street**. It's built on the sites and within the shells of old 42nd Street, for good or ill. It assumes that because the 42nd Street of myth and legend was a neon legend that it was aggressively commercial, and that's what they've gone for, with a gaudiness that goes beyond crass and excessive to a kind of transcendent neon orgasm.

Somewhere in there, someone remembered that the original neon was about Broadway, so you'll see that several vintage theatres on the block have been rehabilitated, notably the **New Amsterdam** on the downtown side of the street. This theatre for many years housed the *Ziegfeld Follies*. Fixed up and owned by Disney, it now houses *The Lion King*, and seems likely to continue to do so for years to come.

Our walking tour of this block should start on the uptown side near the subway entrance. As you go west, you'll pass what turns out to be the oldest existing theatre in Times Square (though technically Off-Broadway) the **New Victory Theatre**, which today specializes in theatre for kids. Beyond that is Broadway's newest theatre, the **Ford Center for the Performing Arts**, built by the now-defunct Livent Inc. from components of two older theatres the Lyric and the Apollo (different from the Apollo Theatre in Harlem, which is still in operation). Built in 1998, the Ford Center has already housed two big hits, *Ragtime* and a revival of the appropriately named *42nd Street*.

Down past the Ford Center you come to the **American Airlines Theatre**, home to the Roundabout Theatre Company. Originally the Selwyn, the AA was named by Roundabout for a generous corporate sponsor. The building also houses the **New 42nd Street Studios** where most of the biggest Broadway shows now hold their rehearsals.

If you look up to the second story between the Ford Center and the American Airlines you may spot the façade of something that looks like another theatre. It is. Or was. The **Times Square Theatre** was judged too small to be profitable, so it was being converted to a hip-hop showcase as this edition went to print.

The north side of 42nd Street features the **Broadway City** arcade, **B.B. King's** soul and R&B concert hall, and an ever-changing variety of restaurants and retail stores. Near the end of the block, the **Loewe's** cinema chain operates a thirteen-screen multiplex. If you don't find anything you like there, just cross to the south side of the street where **AMC** operates a *twenty-five*-screen multiplex inside the shell of the old Eltinge Theatre. That's nearly forty movie theatres in the space of about an acre. It's like cable, but live. Sort of.

From the AMC cinemaplex, turn back east now and pass the **Times Square Hilton Hotel** and **Madame Tussaud's Wax Museum**, a branch of the famous London tourist attraction. Look for the **easyEverything** cyber café, and the sprawling **McDonald's** restaurant before returning to the **New Amsterdam Theatre**, which just happens to be accompanied by a massive **Disney** merchandise store.

We have one more stop to make. Return to the corner of 42nd Street and Seventh Avenue. Turn downtown and go one block to 41st Street, past the **Red Lobster** restaurant with its very tasteful giant oscillating plastic lobster over the door. Instead, look to the right and you'll see the last outpost of Broadway, **The Nederlander Theatre**, flagship of the Nederlander chain.

It looks terrible—but that's on purpose. Since 1996 it has played host to *Rent*, the musical about young bohemians trying to survive in the scruffy East Village. To help recreate that world, the producers chose this theatre beyond the fringe of Broadway, and distressed it inside and out to create something of an environmental theatre experience.

The Nederlander is last remnant of the great lost Theatre District of **The Rialto**—the stretch of Broadway between Times Square and

Herald Square. At its peak in the late 1920s, the Nederlander (then known as National Theatre) was accompanied in this neighborhood by the **Empire**, the old **Broadway, Maxine Elliott's, Knickerbocker, Princess, Casino,** and other theatres. All of them have been swallowed up by the garment trade, which is headquartered here.

The only trace, other than the Nederlander, is the **Chase Bank** branch at 39th street, which stands on the site of the old Metropolitan Opera House. Its downstairs teller area boasts opera-themed decorations, the last evidence that this was the place the great Caruso made his American reputation. The whole area consists of office buildings and fabric stores, though there has been some recolonization of this area by businesses serving Broadway, including producers, press agents, rehearsal halls and Playbill.

You've now come to the end of your walking tour of Times Square. Take a moment to stop and look back uptown, and contemplate the neon canyon of Times Square. Whatever the time of day, those lights will be flashing.

CHAPTER ELEVEN

OTHER THINGS TO SEE AND DO

THEATRE TOURS

Going backstage at a real Broadway house is a thrill for any theatre lover. To see the dressing rooms, the racks of costumes, the carefully stored props and sets, and, best of all, seeing the theatre from center stage, the way the actors see it, can make you feel like you're part of the magic.

To share this feeling, there are several organized guided backstage tours to some of Broadway's great old playhouses:

Broadway Open House Tour—The League of American Theatres and Producers hosts two-hour tours that stop at fifteen classic Broadway theatres, and goes inside at least two. Guides tell the theatres' histories, and allow you glimpses of theatre folk at work. Tours start at 10 AM Wednesday and Saturday mornings (additional days during the warmer months). Tickets: $25. Call 1-212-239-6200 or 1-800-223-7565. Web: www.LiveBroadway.com. Tickets can also be purchased in person on the spot at the Times Square Information Center, 1560 Broadway (near 46th Street), where the tours set out.

Lincoln Center—A chance to go backstage at one of America's biggest arts complexes, including the Metropolitan Opera House, Avery Fisher Hall, New York State Theatre (home of New York City Opera and New York City Ballet), and the center's Broadway theatre, the Vivian Beaumont. Call 1-212-875-5350.

Disney's New Amsterdam Theatre—Disney hosts its own tour of its crown jewel, the restored 1903-vintage New Amsterdam Theatre, onetime home of the *Ziegfeld Follies*, including a peek at how its tenant, *The Lion King*, gets put together each night. Tours are given at 10:30 AM Mondays and Thursdays. Tickets: $12 for adults, $5 for children under 12. Call 1-212-282-2900 or fax a request to 1-212-282-2918.

NYC Showbiz Insiders Tour—A commercial tour company offers the New Amsterdam tour in a package that also includes backstage visits to Radio City Music Hall, the NBC Television Studio, and lunch at Planet Hollywood Restaurant. This is a full-day (eight hours plus) expedition that costs $89 per person. Call 1-800-669-0051 or 1-212-445-0848.

The Radio City Stage Door Tour—A one-hour walking tour of the art deco landmark includes a meeting with one of the famed Rockettes dancers. Call 1-212-465-6100.

TOUR BUSES

Several tour bus companies service midtown Manhattan, but the most ubiquitous is the Gray Line, which operates a fleet of open-topped double-decker buses. These depart from the Gray Line headquarters at 777 Eighth Avenue (west side) between 47th and 48th Streets, and offer several different loops around the city. For a fee of $71 per person ($50 per child), for instance, you get a two-day unlimited pass that enables you to get on or get off the bus wherever and whenever you like for forty-eight hours.

For example, the "Classic New York" bus takes you down Seventh Avenue and Broadway through the heart of Times Square, but then ranges out to classic New York sights like the Empire State building, Madison Square Garden, Greenwich Village, Chinatown, Little Italy, the United Nations, Rockefeller Center, and Central Park.

Website: www.NewYorkSightseeing.com. Phone: 1-800-669-0051.

SHUBERT ALLEY

If the Theatre District has a heart, it is this short pedestrian passageway connecting West 44th Street and West 45th Street. Both a haven and a shortcut, it's a little oasis between the Shubert and Booth theatres on one side, and the Viacom building on the other. Fans waiting for stars to emerge from the stage doors of the two theatres can peruse the full-size three-sheet posters from the latest shows, or pick up memorabilia in the tiny One Shubert Alley store. The annual Stars in the Alley event is held here each May or June (www.starsinthealley.com), allowing fans to meet many of the stars from those shows. And the Broadway Flea Market and Grand Auction (www.bcefa.org/events/auction.html), held each September, also spills out of this space onto adjacent streets. A plaque placed above the door to the Shubert Theatre in 1963 dedicates "this short thoroughfare" to "all those who glorify the theatre." It's a don't-miss pilgrimage destination for every theatregoer.

RUNYONLAND

One night I was taking my younger son to see a Broadway show when we passed a fashion photo shoot in the middle of Times Square. It was chilly and the model would hide inside an ankle-length fur coat waiting for her cue. When it was time to shoot, the umbrella lights went on, she flung off the coat and started posing, as passersby applauded.

"It's always an adventure in Times Square," my son said.

He's right. One of the best shows on Broadway takes place on the streets outside the theatres, as performed by its characters and street entertainers. Damon Runyon's portrait of the 1930s-era rogues' gallery was immortalized in the "Runyonland" sequence that opens *Guys and Dolls*. The pin-striped gamblers may be gone, but a whole new cast of mugs has taken their place.

In addition to the tourists of all nations jockeying for good camera angles, there's a man who parades around carrying a giant snake on his shoulders; street musicians at the TKTS booth playing every manner of musical instrument for the quarters of passersby; Asian sketch artists who will draw you or render your name in calligraphy; incense sellers; comic book sellers; people who will sell you everything from pocketbooks to pictures of the late lamented twin towers painted on black velvet. And, of course, there are hot dog carts, pretzel carts, Latin kebab carts, carts that sell candied nuts and, in winter, carts that sell hot roasted chestnuts, all belching aromatic smoke into the air. On every other corner are newsstands that also sell everything from aspirin to umbrellas.

On all but the coldest days you may find Robert Burck, a street performer known as "The Naked Cowboy," who struts around Times Square playing his guitar and singing, while wearing nothing but a white cowboy hat and silver briefs.

Visitors often provide their own kind of show. Hundreds of teenagers gather outside the MTV studios on the west side of Broadway and 45th Street holding signs and hoping to catch a glimpse of the latest pop star waving from the big windowed studio on the third floor. When one acknowledges them, you can hear the screaming for blocks. A slightly more sedate crowd gathers at windowed TV studios on the east side of Broadway and 44th Street (ABC-TV) and in Rockefeller Center on the downtown side of the skating rink (NBC-TV).

David Letterman tapes his show at the Ed Sullivan Theatre, Broadway at 53rd Street, Monday through Thursday starting at 5 PM, and often stages wacky stunts on 53rd Street between Broadway and Eighth Avenue that the public can watch.

And people are always ready to talk to you. People seeking money for the homeless, people offering free samples of new products, (I've gotten everything from candy and jerky to energy drinks and mulled cider with creme fraiche), people handing out free tickets to the many TV shows that tape in the area, young comedians from local comedy clubs who get paid based on how many people they personally can drag in, people trying to convince you to vote for this candidate or boycott that product. Evangelists warn you to look after your soul, for Jesus is coming again. Reporters from all the newspapers and networks roam the square daily looking for man-on-the-street interviews. And then there are the Black Israelites, no great fans of Caucasians, who loudly preach on passages from the Bible that they feel support their views. The love to involve unwary tourists in debates.

Also among the people all too willing to talk to you are scam artists, dealt with in a separate section in this chapter.

Though most of these things happen during the day, Times Square doesn't really become itself until nighttime, when the iconic neon lights come on, and provide their own unique *son et lumiere* show. Huge billboards and news zippers proclaim everything from soup to stock prices.

And right in the middle of it all—Broadway shows. Every night and twice a day on Wednesday, Saturday and Sunday, people pour into and out of the theatres, talking about shows. That's where *you'll* come in, and become part of Runyonland.

The bottom line: Times Square isn't just a place to pass through heading for the theatre. Make time to go through at a leisurely pace, and let your Broadway adventure happen to you.

When things happen to America, great or terrible, people instinctively gather in Times Square. There's the famous photo of a sailor kissing a girl there on victory day at the end of World War II. On the morning of 9/11, I was part of a crowd watching the terrible events unfold on the giant TV screen over the ABC studios. If you turned to the right, you could see the actual smoke from disaster rising over downtown.

THE NEW 42ND STREET

In less than ten years, the block between Broadway and Eighth Avenue has been transformed from one of the sleaziest strips in the Western world, to a family-friendly theme park. Developers and city agencies have downplayed the naughty and the bawdy in favor of the sporty and gaudy. (For those who get the reference to the lyric in *42nd Street*, all these words rhyme in a New York accent.)

Gone (or at least moved elsewhere) are the hookers and drug dealers who nicknamed the block "the deuce." And good riddance. But you know something? They were never what bothered theatre lovers the

BELASCO'S GHOST

In life, prolific Broadway playwright and producer David Belasco created the stories that became operas *Madame Butterfly* and *The Girl of the Golden West* before his death in 1931. Of Broadway's many fabled ghosts, his remains, characteristically, the busiest. He was seen many times as a robed figure sitting in the mezzanine of the Broadway theatre that bears his name. He reportedly was not seen for many years after the nudie revue *Oh! Calcutta!* played there in the early 1970s, but reports began popping up again after the theatre housed a 2001 revival of *Follies*—a musical about ghosts of many kinds that haunt an old theatre.

most. What bothered us the most was the fact that all those great old theatres, some dating back to the turn of the 20th century, were not being used for shows. Their dressing rooms were used for storage, their murals painted over, their prosceniums covered with stained movie screens. Forty-second Street had once been the heart of Broadway, and it was always painful to see it being used for something else, especially something that was such a tawdry mockery of real theatre.

But, after decades of neglect, politicians' broken promises, and plans that went nowhere, the renaissance got underway in the mid 1990s. The New Amsterdam was gorgeously restored by Disney. The Hammerstein family's New Victory Theatre was restored as a children's theatre. The old Selwyn, home of Maugham, Coward and Nazimova, returned as the American Airlines Theatre, home of the Roundabout Theatre Company. The old Lyric and Apollo were torn down and replaced by the handsome new Ford Center. Even the venerable and long-forgotten Eltinge was saved (or at least its façade and proscenium were) though it now houses a multi-screen cinema.

Ultimately, all the porno theatres have either been converted back to their original use as legitimate theatres, turned into multiplex family cinemas, converted to retail use, or razed.

The filth may be gone, but there is still a potent honky-tonk atmosphere, conjured by colossal neon signs and hucksterism raised to a high art. Madame Tussaud's opened a New York branch of its famed London waxworks. B.B. King Jazz Club's offers live music. Chevy's offers Mexican food. BroadwayCity is a giant videogame arcade. The McDonalds claims to be one of the nation's biggest. Broadway was always about excess.

No matter what you may think of its commercial excesses, if you walk down this block, pause for a moment and marvel that you're in the presence of a legitimate miracle. The neon lights are brighter than ever on this classic corner of Broadway.

THEATRE-RELATED MUSEUMS

The Billy Rose Theatre Collection/New York Public Library— Exhaustive collection of sheet music, theatre books, and newspaper clippings going back to the 19th century—plus the legendary Theatre on Film and Tape Archive (TOFT) videotapes of all Broadway shows since 1970 (available to theatre professionals and researchers only). Address: 40 Lincoln Center Plaza (next to the Vivian Beaumont Theatre) Phone: 1-212-870-1639. Web: www.nypl.org

Museum of Television & Radio maintains viewing and listening rooms so visitors can access its amazing collection of archived television and radio programs. Old TV musicals, Broadway stars appearing on shows, and special programs like the recent "A Celebration of George Balanchine." Address: 25 West 52 Street, between Fifth Ave. and Avenue of the Americas. Phone: 1-212-621-6800. Web: www.mtr.org.

Museum of the City of New York—Lots of archived photos, props, costumes and other memorabilia from more than a century of New York theatre. Once ran a special exhibit just on *Guys and Dolls*. Located outside the Theatre District, but on the so-called "Museum Mile" of Fifth Avenue, that includes many world-class art museums. Address: 1220 Fifth Ave. at 103rd St. Phone: 1-212-534-1672. Web: www.mcny.org.

Shubert Archive—The closest thing Broadway has to a theatre history museum, but focused only on those scripts, photos, sheet music, business records and memorabilia of theatres owned by, and shows produced by, the Shubert Organization. Open mainly to writers, researchers and historians, and only by appointment. An admission application can be found at www.Shubertarchive.org. Address: Inside the Lyceum Theatre, 149 West 45th Street, NY, NY 10036. Email: information@shubertarchive.com.

International Center of Photography—Operating in a ground-floor space with huge windows looking out on West 43 St. at Avenue of the Americas (Sixth Ave.), the ICP presents and ambitious schedule of shows and collections with social, political and or historical content, including many of Broadway and Times Square through the years. www.icp.org.

Theatre Hall of Fame—The Theatre Hall of Fame is located on the second floor of the Gershwin Theatre, 51st Street between Broadway and Eighth Avenue, an elevator ride up from the lobby, on the left. A shrinelike spot for devoted theatregoers since it opened in 1971. There is no razzmatazz, just the names of the greats engraved on tablets on the wall. Administrator Terry Hodge-Taylor has also been collecting memorabilia from the inductees to display in cases on the Hall level. It's a place to contemplate the magnitude of the talent that has chosen to reveal itself on the few small blocks surrounding this spot. New inductees are announced each November, and a private induction ceremony takes place late each January. Right now the only people who can see it are those who have tickets to whatever show is playing at the Gershwin, but organizer Terry Hodge-Taylor says he's hoping to open it to the general public sometime in 2005.

PLACES MENTIONED IN SHOWS

Many Broadway shows mention buildings, neighborhoods and other locales in New York City. Because the city is always changing, many are gone. But many, too, are still standing. You can visit them, or their sites. Here is a sampling:

Castle Garden and **Tony Pastor's**—*Hello, Dolly!* has many New York references. "I might join the chorus of the Castle Garden show" from "Dancing" and "We'll join the Astors at Tony Pastor's . . ." from "Put on Your Sunday Clothes." The Castle Garden Theatre once stood in what is now Battery Park at the southern tip of Manhattan. Tony Pastor's New Fourteenth Street Theatre, once on the uptown side of 14th Street near Third Avenue, is credited as the birthplace of vaudeville in the 19th century.

The Bronx and **The Battery**—"New York, New York" in *On the Town* points out that "The Bronx is up and The Battery down." The Battery is the southernmost tip of Manhattan Island, now a park where a ferry departs for The Statue of Liberty. The Bronx is one of the five boroughs, or major geographical divisions of the city of New York, and the only one on the mainland. The Bronx is also mentioned in *A Chorus Line*, as being "uptown, and to the right."

The Tenderloin—The title and setting of the musical *Tenderloin* refers to the 1890s-era red-light district that was located on the West Side of Manhattan roughly in the area of today's Theatre District and westward into what is now Clinton. Late at night, the area pays homage to its legacy.

The Deuce—Mentioned in *The Life*, nickname of 42nd Street between Broadway and Eighth Avenue. This is the same block (in better days) referenced in the *Follies* song "Broadway Baby": "pounding 42nd Street to be in a show." And, of course, it's the block mentioned in the show *42nd Street* as being "naughty, bawdy, sporty, gaudy," once the headquarters of theatre in New York.

Morgan Library—Site of Coalhouse Walker's standoff in *Ragtime*, now a museum, 29 East 36th St. (near Fifth Ave.), but closed to the public until 2006 for renovations.

Union Square—Heard in the *Ragtime* song "The Night That Goldman Spoke in Union Square." A park and still a public gathering place where Broadway crosses 14th Street, though public speakers are less common than in the past. Recently, Union Square was the site of 9/11 vigils and memorials, and anti-war protests.

Christopher Street—The place where "such interesting people live" in *Wonderful Town*. Not only is it still there, a major thoroughfare in the West Village section of Greenwich Village, but, if anything, people living there today are even more "interesting" than those in the Sherwood sisters' era. In fact, the further west you go, the more interesting it gets, especially after dark. Site of Off-Broadway's Lucille Lortel Theatre.

The Park and **Washington Square**—In the *Sweet Charity* song "Where Am I Going," she says no matter where she runs, "to the park, or Washington Square" she only meets herself there. "The Park" probably means Central Park, which covers a swatch of Manhattan from 59th to 125th Street, and from Fifth Avenue to Eighth Avenue (which becomes Central Park West at 59th Street). Washington Square is also a park in the heart of Greenwich Village, at the foot of Fifth Avenue.

East Village, Alphabet City—The setting of the musical *Rent*, the eastern section of Greenwich Village beyond First Avenue, surrounding Tompkins Square Park, where the avenues are lettered instead of numbered. Still a bohemian area, but considerably gentrified since the mid-1990s setting of *Rent*.

Hippodrome, Aquarium, Flatiron Building, *Tobacco Road*—All onetime Manhattan landmarks mentioned in the On the Town song "My Place" from an out-of-date guidebook. Most were already gone by 1944 when *On the Town* opened, which was the joke of the song. *Tobacco Road* was a long-running hit about rural life. It played at the Theatre Masque, since renamed the Golden Theatre, and still standing at 252 West 45th Street, though *Tobacco Road*, and even its successor *Angel Street*, are both long gone. The site of the titanic Hippodrome Theatre is now a parking garage—The Hippodrome Garage—on Avenue of the Americas, between 44th and 45th Sts. The one still standing is the Flatiron Building at 23rd Street, Broadway, a triangular building on a triangular plot, once the tallest building in the world, replaced by "The Empire State [Building]," as the song says. The latter is at 34th St. and Fifth Ave. The Aquarium was located in Battery Park, but relocated to Brooklyn's Coney Island in the 1920s.

Radio City Music Hall—Where Daddy Warbucks takes Annie their first evening together in *Annie*. At 5,000 seats, still the biggest theatre in Manhattan, and still standing at Avenue of the Americas and 50th St.

Fifth Avenue—In the film *Easter Parade*, the title song takes place on Fifth Avenue, one block east of the Theatre District. Sure enough, every Easter morning, people still dress up and promenade down the avenue.

Shubert Alley—Not mentioned by name, but the setting of the song "The King of Old Broadway," the opening number of *The Producers*. Still there, connecting 44th and 45th Sts. between Seventh and Eighth Aves.

The Palace—*Minnie's Boys*, *Once Upon a Mattress* (jokingly), and many other shows mention this legendary theatre, for decades the top of the heap in vaudeville. It's still there, at Seventh Avenue and 47th St. on the northeast side of Times Square; now a Broadway theatre.

Minsky's—Referenced in *Gypsy* and the film *The Night They Raided Minsky's*, a onetime notable burlesque theatre. Burlesque king Billy

Minsky presented strippers and comics at several different theatres around New York from 1914 until they were banned in 1937.

Tin Pan Alley—Once the site of a unique gathering of businesses that effectively controlled the writing, publishing, and broadcasting of American popular music, the name was coined by songwriter Monroe Rosenfeld for the sound of dozens of musicians playing simultaneously, which poured out of the open windows of the various buildings. The area originally referred to was 28th Street between Fifth Avenue and Broadway in the early 20th century; the district moved to around Broadway and 32nd Street in the 1920s, and ultimately landed on Broadway between 42nd and 50th Streets. Once evoking ballads, dance music, and vaudeville songs, the name ultimately became synonymous with U.S. popular music. Its demise resulted from the rise of film, audio recording, radio, and TV, which created a demand for more and different kinds of music, and the growth of commercial songwriting centers in cities such as Hollywood and Nashville.

The Brill Building—Still standing at 1619 Broadway, the last—but greatest—remnant of Tin Pan Alley. The center of American music publishing in the 1950s and early 1960s, writers including Gerry Goffin & Carole King and Neil Sedaka wrote many of their biggest hits in its notoriously factory-like environments. The distinctive brass art deco entryway still proclaims, in capital letters, "The Brill Building."

Lindy's—A restaurant, originally on Broadway, next to the Winter Garden Theatre, made famous by the many mentions in Damon Runyon's *Guys and Dolls* stories, where it was called "Mindy's." A restaurant by the name of Lindy's operates near Times Square today, and tries to recapture the ambience of the original Lindy's. See Chapter Eight for details.

PLACES TO SHOP

Footlight Records—There are several respectable record stores in the Times Square area, including the mass-market Virgin Megastore in the center of Times Square at 46th Street (cast albums are downstairs to the right, with classical), and Colony Records at the corner of Broadway and 49th (which also has a first-class selection of sheet music). But the really serious show music collector takes the R or N train downtown to Greenwich Village to visit Footlight Records. Not only do they get all the new cast albums, solo CDs, and studio recordings, they have many vintage recordings in various formats, plus international theatre recordings from around the world. They deal in used, out-of-print and collectible recordings. And what they don't have in stock, they will seek for you. The crowning glory of the shop is its collection of vinyl records, old LPs, and even 78s. The salespeople are not the friendliest you ever encountered, but they tend to be extremely knowledgeable—when they deign to speak at all. Address: 113 East 12th Street. Phone: 1-212-533-1572. Website: www.footlight.com.

The Drama Book Shop—The best place to buy theatre books in New York, since it opened in 1917. Recently moved to a new location just south of the Theatre District. For those who remember the lumbering elevator at its two previous locations, some good news: the new shop is at street level. A great place to browse for every sort of new and old book on theatre and film, plus a stock of theatre-related videos and other related merchandise. There's even a small theatre downstairs where they have meet-the-author events, and play readings. Address: 250 West 40th Street. Phone: 1-800-322-0595. Website: www.dramabookshop.com.

Triton Gallery—From the front of the Al Hirschfeld Theatre, cross 45th Street and continue a short distance west, and you'll have entered the mecca for poster lovers. The store claims to have the "world's largest collection of theatrical window cards and posters," and looks it. The long, street-level store showcases all the posters from current shows and classics, plus shows from other countries and long ago, plus collections of the works of James McMullan and other notable poster artists. They sell reproductions of those posters, as well as the original posters themselves, some of them rarities and collector's items.

Example: Not only do they have the 1981 original production of *Little Shop of Horrors*; they also have the poster from the first attempt at the 2003 revival, which closed in Florida, featuring the name of the previous leading lady. The latter sorts of posters are only for dedicated fans, and for them, Triton is heaven. Address: 323 West 45th Street, between Eighth and Ninth Avenues. Phone: 1-800-626-6674. Website: www.tritongallery.com.

NEW YEAR'S EVE

Times Square is also the traditional gathering place for revelers on New Year's Eve. In a party televised throughout the world, people gather to watch a brightly lit Waterford crystal sphere descend a pole atop the triangular building at the downtown end of the square, then shout, dance and get buried in confetti. A few tips if you go:

- Get there early. Depending on the temperature, anywhere from a quarter million to three-quarters of a million people pack into a fourteen-square-block area. To prevent people from getting hurt, police herd people into a network of fenced-in enclosures. Once you are in one, you may not wander around. You may leave, but cannot return.

- Bring comfortable shoes. People start arriving in the afternoon, and eight hours is a long time to stand anywhere.

- Back to the point about temperature. New York is a seaport, and in January it can get down into single digits on the Fahrenheit scale. Bundle up.
- No booze allowed. It's true.
- There are no convenient toilets. If you stand out in the freezing cold for hours drinking, expect nature to take its course with your bladder. Go beforehand, and drink sparingly.
- The best way to take care of all the above problems is to sign up for a New Year package at one of the area restaurants. You'll have warmth, amenities and access to the heart of the action at the big moment.
- In the post-9/11 world, security is tight. Expect to have bags searched. And don't even think of bringing a firearm—probably a good precept about visiting New York in general.
- At midnight, prepare to be smooched by strangers.

OTHER INTERESTING SPOTS

Sardi's Theatrical Restaurant—Caricatures of theatre stars of the present and past adorn the walls above the crimson banquettes in this classic Theatre District landmark, which has been pushing the cannelloni (and hosting Broadway opening night parties) since 1927. It's worth popping in for a drink or a meal just to say you've been. The main floor is the classiest, though the second floor has a great view of 44th Street and Shubert Alley, which is diagonally opposite. Details in Chapter Eight. Address: 234 West 44th Street, between Broadway and Eighth Avenue.

Don't Tell Mama—Of the many cabarets and nightclubs in New York, this one on Restaurant Row may be the one closest related to the theatre world. It has three stages and presents live shows seven days a week. Named after the song in the musical *Cabaret*, Don't Tell Mama Piano Bar and Cabaret offers a nightly rotating schedule of comedians, singers, songwriter showcases, and variety. Broadway performers often appear in late shows here after the curtain comes down on their main gig. Among regulars are "Seth's Broadway Chatterbox," a Thursday night series of interviews between raconteur Seth Rudetsky and theatre stars, and "Judy Garland Live!" a late-night Saturday show with impersonator Tommy Femia. There's also a piano bar for after-theatre get-togethers. Address: 343 West 46th St. Phone and reservations: 1-212-757-0788. Web: www.donttellmama.com.

Don't Tell Mama has two sister clubs in Manhattan with similar show-reference names: Mama Rose's at 219 Second Avenue (at 13th Street) between the East Village and the Union Square neighborhoods. Rose's Turn at 55 Grove Street (near Bleecker Street) in Greenwich Village.

Don't Tell Mama nightclub on Restaurant Row is one of the busiest in the city. It's named for a song in Cabaret.

Other prominent cabarets that often feature theatre talent:

Danny's Skylight Room, 346 West 46th Street, 1-212-265-8133

The Oak Room at the Algonquin Hotel, 59 West 44th Street, 1-212-419-9331

Café Carlyle at the Carlyle Hotel, 35 East 76th Street, 1-212-744-1600

The Supper Club, 240 West 47th Street, 1-212-921-1904

Ars Nova Theater, 511 West 54th Street, 1-212-868-4444

Westbank Cafe's Laurie Beechman Theater, 407 West 42nd Street, 1-212-695-6909

The Triad, West, 158 West 72nd Street; 1-212-787-7921

Marie's Crisis, 59 Grove Street (Greenwich Village), 1-212-243-9323

ONE TIMES SQUARE

Everybody who comes to Times Square wants to know the same thing: "Where's the building where the ball comes down?" That's the lighted globe that descends a post each New Year's Eve at the precise moment of midnight, local time, setting off the riotous celebrations in the thronged streets below. It's been doing so since 1904.

The spot is at the south or downtown end of Times Square, on the triangle bordered by Broadway, Seventh Avenue, and 42nd Street. If you look closely, you can see the post all year long. The globe itself is packed away each New Year's Day, and brought out in the final days of December the following year.

The building, once the headquarters of *The New York Times* (which gave the square its name), was renamed Allied Chemical Building after the *Times* moved a half block west on 43rd Street decades ago. It has since been renamed the more neutral One Times Square, and is now swaddled in billboards and illuminated signs. A news "zipper," which runs the latest headlines around the building several floors up, is maintained by the Dow Jones company, publishers of *The Wall Street Journal.*

ROCKEFELLER CENTER

This complex of office buildings on the northeast side of the Theatre District houses many of the major American media outlets: NBC-TV, The Associated Press, *Time, People, The New York Post, TV Guide,* and McGraw-Hill Books, to name just a handful among the hundreds.

Two landmarks are traditional favorites with theatre folk: the skating rink and Radio City Music Hall.

Radio City Music Hall—This 5,000-seat art deco masterpiece is home to concerts and touring shows throughout the year, many of which are of interest to theatre people. Most notable is the annual Tony Awards, held the first Sunday in June. Tickets go on sale the first or second week in May, the day the nominations are announced. There's also the annual *Radio City Christmas Spectacular*, featuring the iconic kick-line, The Rockettes, and Santa Claus. In season (November through January), the ninety-minute show can be seen up to six times a day, just like the bad old days of vaudeville. But most of the performances sell out, especially on the weekends. Tickets go on sale in late summer. Address: East side of Avenue of the Americas at 50th Street. Website: www.radiocity.com. Phone: 1-212-247-4777 or the "Christmas Hotline" at 1-212-307-4100.

Rockefeller Center Skating Rink—Zooming around the ice, surrounded by the towers, shops and fluttering banners of Rockefeller Center is one of those quintessential New York experiences. The rink (which turns into an outdoor restaurant March to October), is recessed below street level, but watched over by the shining statue of Prometheus and, during the holidays, an immense sparkling Christmas tree. Admission is $7.50 adults, $6 kids, during the week, $9 adults and 6.75 kids. The prices jump another couple of dollars during the peak of the holiday season. Even so, there's often a line on weekends. Address: Inside the block bounded by 50th and 51st Streets, and between Fifth Avenue and Avenue of the Americas. Phone: 1-212-332-7654.

LINCOLN CENTER

Wonders roll out nightly from the cultural cornucopia of Lincoln Center. This temple of the arts stretches over three city blocks on Manhattan's West Side, not far from Columbus Circle, about ten blocks north of the Theatre District.

The entire complex of half a dozen white travertine marble buildings is clustered around a plaza and fountain. This is where Leo Bloom shouted "I want everything I ever saw in the movies!" in the film of *The Producers*.

The most prominent component is the Metropolitan Opera House with its Chagall murals. If you're facing it, to the right is Avery Fisher Hall, longtime home of the New York Philharmonic. To the left is New York State Theatre, home of New York City Ballet and New York City Opera. Through a passage between the Met and Avery Fisher is a reflecting pool and the special New York Public Library branch that houses its performing arts collection, notably the Billy Rose Collection of theatre books, sheet music, video and archival clippings, and the Jerome Robbins Dance Archive. Countless shows and books, including this one, were researched there.

The building standing next to the library is the one of primary interest to theatre lovers: the **Vivian Beaumont Theatre**, which is the Broadway theatre on the site. Along with the Off-Broadway **Mitzi Newhouse Theatre** downstairs, these two spaces are programmed by **Lincoln Center Theater**, a company (not an actual theatre building) that specializes in revivals of classics, and in sponsorship of new American plays and musicals. Among recent offerings was the 2000 Tony-winner as Best Musical, *Contact*. Web: www.lct.org. Phone: 1-212-239-6200 or, outside metro NY area, 1-800-432-7250.

Here are phone numbers for Lincoln Center's major constituents:

New York City Opera—In addition to the regular opera repertory, this company has done lush productions of sophisticated musicals like *Sweeney Todd* and *A Little Night Music* with big voices and a big orchestras, and is promising to do more in the future. 1-212-870-5570 Web: www.nycopera.com

New York City Ballet—Annual highlight is the holiday-time production of *The Nutcracker*, choreographed for them originally in 1954 by George Balanchine. This is the one that began them all. 1-212-870-5570 Web: www.nycballet.com

Big Apple Circus—Sets up an actual big-top tent in Lincoln Center's Damrosch Park for a lively one-ring circus each holiday season. Web: www.bigapplecircus.org.

Alice Tully Hall, 1-212-362-1911

Avery Fisher Hall, 1-212-874-2424

Chamber Music Society, 1-212-362-1900

Great Performances, 1-212-362-1913

Metropolitan Opera, 1-212-362-6000

Overall website: http://www.lincolncenter.org.

ADULT ENTERTAINMENT

The enduring image of Times Square is a fleshpot. That image has been compromised considerably in recent years with a massive cleanup of the area, backed by legislation that limits the number of XXX bookstores, by police patrols that have chased away most of the street hookers and drug peddlers, and by the video and DVD revolution that made porno cinemas obsolete.

Nevertheless, the law of supply and demand is still in effect. The grungy Times Square still sort of exists, though it is no longer at center stage. You have to stay out a little later, and go a few blocks further west and downtown to find it. Or for it to find you.

Prostitutes—Prostitution is illegal in New York, and so is patronizing a prostitute. Police sometimes set up stings and arrest the customers, known as johns or tricks. Nevertheless, street prostitutes still roam the west side of Eighth Avenue (a.k.a. the Minnesota Strip) late at night after show curtains have come down, and can be found in the streets further west and around the Port Authority Bus Terminal. Male prostitutes work further south, near the piers west of Greenwich Village.

However, these tend to be the bottom of the barrel. A (small) step up can be found in several publications including *The Village Voice*, *The New York Press* (both available free in honor boxes) and Al Goldstein's venerable (if that's the right word) *Screw* magazine (available in adult bookstores). These have extensive ads, many with color photographs, in the back pages. The prostitutes—male, female, and "she-male"—list themselves as offering "body work," a throwback to the old massage parlor days. These are available for "in-call" (at an apartment or brothel) or "outcall" (your place) and many take credit cards.

Adult Video, DVD, and Book Stores—The number of these in the Times Square area is less than a tenth of what it was in their 1970s heyday. When you enter, they may look at first like a regular video store. Under city law, no more than forty percent of such businesses can be devoted to porno. So you must navigate past racks of traditional video and DVD releases to reach a cordoned-off section of the shop where the real business is done.

Show World Center—West side of Eighth Avenue, between 42nd and 43rd Streets.

The Playpen—West side of Eighth Avenue between 43rd and 44th Streets.

Gotham City Video—West side of Eighth Avenue between 43rd and 44th Streets.

Peepland—West side of Eighth Avenue between 43rd and 44th Streets.

Nilupul—West side of Eighth Avenue between 46th and 47th Streets.

DVDs Palace—West side of Eighth Avenue at the NW corner of 46th Street. Adult entrance on 46th Street, downstairs.

Extreme—West side of Eighth Avenue between 46th and 47th Streets.

Bare Elegance—South side of 50th Street near Broadway.

Peep Shows—Some stores also have "peep shows" where you enter a private booth to watch short segments of adult films by dropping coins in a slot. The ease and privacy of home video viewing has all but rendered the once-ubiquitous peep shows extinct. Some of the above video stores also maintain a bank of peep booths in the back.

"BURLESQUE"/TOPLESS BARS/STRIP CLUBS

Only a few traditional strip joints remain in the Times Square area:

All American Male Revue—240 West 52nd Street, 1-866-872-6366

Bare Elegance Gentlemen's Club—216 50th Street near Broadway, above the video store, 1-212-245-3494

Executive Club—603 West 45th Street, 1-212-245-0002

Fresh Players Gentlemen's Club—West 53rd Street near Broadway

Gaiety Burlesque (Male strippers)—West 46th Street near Seventh Avenue (second floor)

Lace—725 7th Avenue, East side of Seventh Avenue near 48th Street, 1-212-840-9139

Peepland—West side of Eighth Avenue between 43rd and 44th Streets

Private Eyes—320 West 45th Street, 1-212-978-0000

Silk—552 West 38th Street, 1-212-594-5100

Stiletto @ Club 44—689 Eighth Avenue, 1-212-765-5047

CENTRAL PARK

Don't miss a trip to this magnificent oasis, just five blocks from the north end of the Theatre District. Landscaped with sublime elegance by Frederick Law Olmstead, its winding paths thread a new activity or vista around every turn. There's the Hecksher Playground, Bethesda Fountain, the Central Park, the Carousel, Belvedere Castle, Wollman Skating Rink, Tavern-on-the-Green, The Ramble, Strawberry Fields, the horse-drawn carriages, the jogging paths, Central Park Lake, the Metropolitan Museum, and, best of all, the Delacorte Theatre, where the Public Theater mounts one or two Shakespeare plays each summer. Admission: free. Find details at www.shakespeareincentralpark.org.

Central Park has been the setting of a hundred movies, perhaps most memorably in the "Let's dine al fresco" sequence in *The Producers*; and even a musical: *Up in Central Park*.

PLACES TO KEEP COOL IN SUMMER AND WARM IN WINTER

New York can be frigid in the winter and tropical in the summer. Visitors from other climes should check the calendar and the Weather Channel and dress accordingly.

But if you spend many hours on the street sightseeing, you may start to long for a refuge. Shopping or "shopping" are time-honored ways of warming up or cooling down, but New York shopkeepers know all the tricks, and no matter how well-dressed you are, they will start tapping their feet if you don't buy something. It helps to be dressed nicely. If you carry a big open bag and don't buy anything, they should not be blamed for being suspicious.

So, where can you go for free to adjust your temperature?

The best hassle-free spot is the Times Square Visitors Center at 1560 Broadway (near 46th St.) which has rows of theatre-style seats where you can kick back and catch your breath as long as you like.

A network of passageways stretches for blocks beneath Rockefeller Center. These can be accessed from most of the subway entrances in the area. Some sections are air-conditioned or heated in season, some are not.

The Marquis Hotel on the west side of Times Square between 45th and 46th Sts. has an immense atrium starting on the 8th floor full of comfortable seats. They do prefer that you buy refreshments from the stand there, but traditionally have been accommodating to hotel guests—or those who could conceivably pass as hotel guests.

BROADWAY SPECIAL EVENTS

Broadway stars are remarkably accessible to the public. Aside from appearing in-person every night on the stage (and at the stage door afterward) they also take part in special events throughout the year where they perform for, and meet, their audience—often as a fundraiser for a good cause, but sometimes for free. If you are in the Theatre District for these events, make an effort to attend. They're well worth it. Dates listed here are subject to change, so make sure to check the contact number or website before you go.

JANUARY

Kids Night on Broadway: Last Tuesday in January or the first Tuesday in February. Half-price tickets for kids, when accompanied by an adult who buys a full-price ticket. Tickets go on sale in November. 1-888-BROADWAY. Web: www.kidsnightonbroadway.com.

FEBRUARY

Nothing Like a Dame: Monday in late February or early March. Female Broadway stars are showcased in this annual fundraising concert for the Women's Health Initiative. Tickets go on sale in December. 1-212-840-0770. Web: www.bcefa.org.

Broadway Bears: The Sunday of Presidents Day Weekend. Each show designs a teddy bear to look like a character in that show, then auctions it at this fundraiser for Broadway Cares/Equity Fights AIDS. Bears can be previewed at www.bcefa.org. 1-212-840-0770.

City Center Encores!: This celebrated series of vintage musicals-in-concert hosted revivals of *Chicago* and *Wonderful Town* that wound up on Broadway. The annual series of three productions begins each February on the week before Presidents Day weekend. 1-212-581-1212. Web: www.citycenter.org/encores.

MARCH OR APRIL

Easter Bonnet Competition: A Monday and Tuesday in March or April, roughly corresponding to Easter. Shows compete to raise the most money to benefit Broadway Cares/Equity Fights AIDS, and to present the most creative Easter bonnet in this revue, usually accompanied by a skit or song. Tickets go on sale about a month ahead. 1-212-840-0770. Web: www.broadwaycares.org/events/easter.html.

MAY

Ninth Avenue International Food Festival: Third weekend in May. The diverse ethnic restaurants of Ninth Avenue, one block west of the Theatre District, sell samples of their bounty. Admission is free.

LATE MAY OR EARLY JUNE

Stars in the Alley: The Wednesday before the Tony Awards. Stars from Broadway shows gather in Shubert Alley for a lunchtime concert and block party to celebrate the end of one Broadway season and the beginning of the next. Free. 1-212-764-1122. Web: www.starsintheal-ley.com

JUNE

The Antoinette Perry (Tony) Awards: First or second Sunday in June. Annual awards ceremony saluting the best of Broadway. If held at Radio City Music Hall, as in previous years, tickets go on sale to the public on the day the nominations are announced, usually the first or second Monday in May, at a phone number announced that day. You'll be able to find it at www.tonyawards.com.

Broadway Under the Stars: Weekend following the Tony Awards. Broadway songs performed in late evening at Bryant Park, 42nd St. and Avenue of the Americas. Free. 1-212-484-1222. Web: www.nycvisit.com.

Broadway Bares: Third or fourth Sunday in June. Not to be confused with Broadway Bears, this event presents the buffest male and female Broadway dancers performing striptease numbers and dances with an absolute minimum of costuming, as a fundraiser for Broadway Cares/Equity Fights AIDS. 1-212-840-0770 Web: www.broadwaycares.org/events/bares.html

JULY

Free Shakespeare in Central Park: Presented by the Public Theater at the Delacorte Theatre, near the West 81st St. entrance to the park. People come early in the day and get on line for the free tickets, which are distributed at 1 PM for that evening's performance. 1-212-539-8750. Web: www.publictheater.org.

Lincoln Center Festival: Month-long festival of theater, ballet, opera, and music performances in and around the performing spaces of Lincoln Center, Broadway at 65th St. 1-212-721-6500. Web: www.lincolncenter.org.

AUGUST

New York Fringe Festival: Two weeks in mid-August. Dozens of shows, many avant-garde or experimental, are showcased in the mid-summer festival, presented at Off-Off-Broadway spaces around the city. In NYC 1-212-420-8877.Outside NY: 1-888-FRINGENYC. Web: www.fringenyc.com

SEPTEMBER

Broadway on Broadway: First or second Sunday in September. Times Square becomes a pedestrian mall for two hours as actors from the incoming fall musicals—and some long-running shows—perform excerpts from their scores on a huge stage set up near 43rd St. Free. Web: www.broadwayonbroadway.com.

Broadway Flea Market and Grand Auction: Third Sunday in September. Vendors sell posters, rare cast albums and other theatre memorabilia in Shubert Alley, followed late in the day by an auction of rarer and autographed props from Broadway shows. You can meet and talk to Broadway stars all day at the Celebrity Table, where they will sign autographs as a fundraiser for Broadway Cares/Equity Fights AIDS. 1-212-840-0770 Web: www.broadwaycares.org/events/auction.html.

Next Wave Festival: September through December at Brooklyn Academy of Music, 30 Lafayette Avenue, Brooklyn. Innovative and experimental theatre from the U.S. and around the world. Single tickets go on sale in early September. 1-718-636-4100. Web: www.bam.org/about/next wave.aspx.

NOVEMBER

Macy's Thanksgiving Day Parade: Nine AM to noon on Thanksgiving Day. Broadway shows are a prominent part of the parade, also known for extravagant floats, marching bands and gigantic balloons shaped like popular cartoon characters. Starts near Central Park, then proceeds down Broadway right through the heart of Times Square, ending up at Macy's store on 34th Street. Free.

DECEMBER

Rockefeller Center Christmas Tree Lighting: First Wednesday in December. A huge crowd gathers at the skating rink in Rockefeller Center to watch a celebrity light the multistory tree. Free.

Gypsy of the Year: Second Monday and Tuesday in December. Culmination of six weeks of fundraising at Broadway, Off-Broadway and touring shows to benefit Broadway Cares/Equity Fights AIDS. One of the most sought-after of these BC/EFA events. Shows compete to raise the most money. The cast and crew of each show write and perform skits and songs—sometimes touching or serious, sometimes bitingly funny parodies of themselves or other shows—to win the title Gypsy of the Year. 1-212-840-0770 Web: www.broadwaycares.org/events/gypsy.html.

Broadway Holiday Tree Lighting: Second Wednesday in December. Actors from Broadway shows, usually led by a star or three, flip the switch on the Broadway Holiday Tree in Times Square and lead the crowd in carols. Free.

New Year's Eve in Times Square: Crowds gather to watch a lighted ball descend to a rooftop at 43rd Street and Broadway precisely at midnight. Crowds stretch from 50th Street to 38th Street along Broadway and Seventh Avenue. Free.

HOW TO ACT AND SOUND LIKE A PRO

"The theatre isn't its successes, though of course they help give it a certain position in polite circles. The theater is its continuum, a living muddle of good and bad that takes its vitality from the equally muddled world about it. It's a hand held out to meandering man as he makes his way through the swamps and over the cloverleafs, now mired, now soaring, always in motion."

—WALTER KERR

There's always one person on the TKTS line who thinks he knows everything there is to know about Broadway. He'll stand there spouting wisdom hard-earned by having seen three shows, one of the them *The Radio City Music Hall Christmas Spectacular*.

But there's more to acting and sounding like an insider than that. And it doesn't take years or a fortune—just a little knowledge. Herewith, a primer on how to talk and act like a Broadway veteran.

TALK THE TALK

Like any specialized world, Broadway has its own terms for many things. If you want to sound like an insider, learn these and use them.

Ad lib—To make things up as you go. When something goes wrong on stage, actors sometimes ad lib to cover it up. Ad libs go over so well with the audience and some comedians and writers sometimes write and rehearse their ad libs in advance, which is a true oxymoron.

Aislesitters—Slang for critics. So named because their seats were traditionally situated on the aisle so they could rush out on opening night to file a review.

Angel—A person who invests money in a Broadway show.

Aside—When characters break the **fourth wall** and say something brief to themselves, meant for only the audience to hear.

Backstage—The part of the theatre the audience doesn't see; the dressing rooms, prop rooms, wings (sides of the stage), fly space (area above the set where stagehands can hoist scenery), etc. Also a term to describe things that happen within the world of a show's cast and crew, as in "backstage gossip."

Book (of a Musical)—A confusing term meaning the basic story of a musical, and the spoken dialog. In operas, the libretto (Italian for "the little book") means "all the words." In a musical there are often two separate people who do this job, one to write the sung lyrics to the songs, and one to write the book, or spoken lines.

Cast Album—A recording of songs from a stage musical. Commonly confused with a "soundtrack," which applies only to a recording of music from a movie (which is drawn from the electronic track that runs alongside the pictures on a strip of film). The surest way to sound like an outsider rube to theatre folk is to call a cast album a soundtrack. An "original cast album" is the cast album from the first production of a show. Cast albums from revivals are sometimes called the "revival cast album."

Cattle Call—Informally, a type of audition for a Broadway show, in which anyone, regardless of union membership, may try out. The name derives from the many, many applicants who turn up. Properly known as an **Open Call**.

Cleanup Act—An act so bad, it drives people out of the theatre. Why would they need such a term? It goes back to vaudeville days when theatres would repeat the lineup three or four or more times a day. To encourage people to leave fast and make room for the next show, management would send in the cleanup act.

Closing—The final performance of a show. In most cases, a closing comes when the show stops making enough money to cover its weekly operating expenses.

Curtain—The cloth drape that separates the audience from the actors. Generally this is closed when the audience arrives, opens when the show begins, and closes when it is over. Other curtains called "travelers: can cover parts of the stage during a performance so a set or costume change can take place on stage. Some productions dispense with a curtain, or leave it open all the time.

Also refers to the beginning or the end of a performance. **Backstage**, the **Production Stage Manager** will alert actors when its "half hour to curtain," meaning the curtain will rise and the show will start in a half hour. "Curtain" is often the last word in a playscript, shorthand for "close the curtain" or "The End."

Curtain Call—Bows at the end of a performance.

Definitive—A performance that is so identified with a role that it becomes very difficult for another actor to play it. For many years Yul Brynner was considered definitive in *The King and I*. Barbra

Streisand was so definitive in *Funny Girl* that the show has never been revived on Broadway.

Diva—A special category of actress: a monster goddess of the theatre, always talented; usually temperamental, eccentric, and demanding; sometimes with a patina of tragedy from a life crisis involving health or romance. Adored and hated, sometimes by the same people.

Doctor—A successful playwright or director called in to cure what's ailing a struggling show out-of-town or in development.

Downstage—The part of the stage closest to the audience.

Drag—Clothing of the opposite sex. Performing "in drag" means performing in the clothing of the opposite sex. Female Impersonators, sometimes derided as Drag Queens, are men who make a career of dressing as women. Julian Eltinge in the early 20th century may be the most famous drag performer, virtually never appearing in man's clothes. He even had a theatre named after him. Contemporary drag performers include Dame Edna Everage (stage name of Barry Humphreys), Lypsinka, Varla Jean Merman, Hedda Lettuce, et al. Contemporary performers who appear in drag often (but by no means always) include Harvey Fierstein, Charles Busch and Lea DeLaria.

Eleven o'clock Number—A big climactic song, generally done by the star, which comes near the end of a musical. Famous eleven o'clock numbers include "Sit Down You're Rocking the Boat" in *Guys and Dolls*, the title song of *Hello, Dolly!*, "Betrayed" in *The Producers*, and "Rose's Turn" in Gypsy. Back in the days when curtain time was 8:30, these songs were indeed often performed around 11 PM. Today they generally land around 10:20 or so.

Flop—A show that fails, sometimes spectacularly. Also known as a Floppola, Floperoo, Bomb, and **Turkey**. In London, however, a Bomb is a success.

Fold—Verb meaning to close a show. "They folded after one performance."

The Fourth Wall—The side of the set that faces the audience, e.g. the fourth wall in the room we're looking into.

Gypsy—A professional dancer, generally in the chorus, who moves from show to show. *A Chorus Line* was the ultimate tribute to gypsies.

Heaven—Not a reward, heavenly or otherwise. Seats metaphorically so far up in the balcony, you could hobnob with St. Peter himself; i.e., really distant seats.

Hit—A success; a show that gets positive reviews; technically, a show that has paid back its investment and turned a profit. A very big hit is called a Smash.

House—The theatre.

House Lights—Chandeliers and other lighting in the part of the theatre where the audience sits. They are dimmed halfway to indicate the performance is about to begin ("house to half"), and blinked at the end of intermission to indicate that the show is about to resume.

House Manager—Person who manages the theatre; who makes sure the heat is on, the lights are working, the bar is stocked, the stage door is guarded, etc.

In One—A song or scene performed all the way downstage in front of a "traveler" curtain, generally to give the stagehands time to make a complicated set change. The most famous "in one" number remains "There's No Business Like Show Business" in *Annie Get Your Gun*, which was written strictly for this utilitarian purpose, but became the show's biggest hit.

"I Want" Song—Song in a musical, usually early in the first act, in which the main character tells the audience what they're seeking (often literally including the phrase "I want . . .") and which forms the impetus for the rest of the show. Famous examples: "Wouldn't It Be Loverly" from *My Fair Lady*, "Before the Parade Passes By" from *Hello, Dolly!*, "Somewhere That's Green" from *Little Shop of Horrors* and "I Want To Be a Producer" from *The Producers*.

Kill, Killed—Words that mean the exact opposite in different contexts. Critics whose reviews are so negative that the show closes are said to have "killed" the show. Shows that get such poisonous reviews are said to have gotten "killed." A producer might say, "The *Post* loved us, but we got killed by the *Times*."

On the other hand, a performer who does a fantastic job and gets a standing ovation is said to have "killed" an audience or "knocked 'em dead." Upon getting offstage, such a performer may remark, "I really killed tonight."

Leading Role (versus the Tony Awards' definition of a **Leading Role**)—The leading role in a play is the part with the most prominence—or simply the most lines. This definition did not work for the Tony Awards, for some reason, which ruled that whoever's name is over the title in posters and other billing is the lead, no matter how many lines they have or don't have. Producers may petition for exceptions to this.

Legitimate or **Legit**—An old-fashioned term meaning full-scale live theatre, originally differentiating it from burlesque, vaudeville, and the movies, but now a shorthand term for Broadway, Off-Broadway, touring and regional theatre.

Legs—A term meaning a show that continues to be popular long after the reviews have been published, or that is popular with ticket buyers regardless of the reviews. A show that "has legs" is one that will run a long time.

Limited Run—A show that is designed to run only for a set number of weeks, either because it's part of a subscription series, or because it's got a big star who is scheduled to do something else afterward. Announcing a "limited run" is a signal to ticket buyers that they'd better come a-runnin' because the show won't be around forever.

Marquee vs. Marquis—The marquee is the protruding, lighted billboard on the front of the theatre, above the doors, which displays the name of the theatre, the title of the show, and, often, quotes from the critics. Marquis is the name of a theatre and hotel on Broadway between 45th and 46th Streets. And, yes, the Marquis has a marquee. Pronounced the same.

Nosebleed Seats—Seats metaphorically so high up in the balcony, the low atmospheric pressure could theoretically cause nosebleed.

Open Call—A type of audition for a Broadway show, in which anyone, regardless of union membership, may try out. Derisively known as a **Cattle Call**.

Open-ended Run—A show designed to run until it stops making money.

Opening Night—The first "official" performance of a Broadway show. It often follows a week or more of **previews**. Originally it was the night the critics saw a show, but now they see the show on designated nights during the final previews, and the opening night has become just a deadline after which critics may post their reviews. There generally is a cast party following this performance, at which the producer either reads the reviews (if they're positive) or pointedly doesn't read the reviews (if they're negative). Cole Porter wrote in *Kiss Me, Kate* that it's the night you "cross your fingers and hold your heart," which is still true.

Previews—The earliest public performances of a show, during which the kinks are (hopefully) worked out in front of a live audience before the reviews appear. These used to be priced lower than regular performances, but no more.

Production Stage Manager, **PSM**, or **Stage Manager**—The person in charge of running the show each night, making sure actors are in their places to go on, lights are switched on and off when they're supposed to be, etc. Generally operates from a desk or rostrum just offstage on the left or right, and stays in radio contact with the technicians throughout the theatre and with the actors in their dressing rooms.

Proscenium—The arch over the sides and top of the stage that outlines the action like a giant picture frame.

Review vs. Revue—A review is a published or broadcast piece of drama criticism, evaluating the quality of the show and performances. A revue is a variety show, a series of songs and skits without a single unifying story. Pronounced the same.

Resumé—For actors, not just a list of a person's credits, but specifically a list of a person's credits attached to the back of a photograph. When you audition, you hand over your resumé so they can see what you look like, in addition to what you've done.

Run vs. **Running Time**—A show's "run" is how many performances it has played since opening night. Its "running time" is how many hours and minutes each performance lasts. The running time of most plays is ninety minutes to two hours (Eugene O'Neill and Robert Wilson plays may go considerably longer); the running time of most musicals is two to three hours.

Shirley MacLaine—An actress who got her start on Broadway and starred in many films, including *Sweet Charity* and *The Apartment*. Also a noun meaning an understudy who goes on for an ailing star and attains stardom herself (or himself), which happened to MacLaine when she was understudying in the original production of *The Pajama Game*. If you have a friend who is an understudy, tell them you hope they "pull a Shirley MacLaine."

Showstopper—A song or other performance that gets such prolonged applause that the show must halt temporarily to acknowledge it.

Stage Door—The entryway for the actors and stage crew. Famous for crusty and colorful Stage Doormen.

Stage Door Johnny—A devoted fan of a show or star who waits by the **stage door** hoping to catch a glimpse of a favored actress (or actor). Also used to describe a fan who has become a star's temporary lover.

Stage Left, Stage Right—Left and right from the actors' point of view. That is, the opposite of the audience's left and right.

Straight Play—A non-musical play. Can mean a comedy or drama.

Suspension of Disbelief—The quality of imagination that enables a theatre patron to pretend that what he or she sees on stage is real.

Turkey—A particularly bad show; a flop. Interesting back-formation: "Oven-stuffer roaster," from an ad campaign for a kind of poultry, but applied here to mean "an especially egregious turkey."

Upstage—The part of the stage farthest from the audience.

Also a verb meaning to do something unexpected that pulls audience attention away from a fellow actor. Generally considered a very hostile act. In one edition of the *Ziegfeld Follies*, comedian Ed Wynn hid under a pool table used by W.C. Fields for his act. Wynn proceeded to upstage Fields by making funny faces. Field famously rewarded him by walloping him with a pool cue.

NAMES YOU SHOULD KNOW

If you spend any kind of time on Broadway, there are a few players whose names you're going to hear all the time, and therefore need to know.

Ben Brantley—First-string critic for *The New York Times*.

Betty Buckley—Texas-born Broadway diva, star of *Cats*, *1776*, *The Mystery of Edwin Drood*, *Carrie*, and *Sunset Boulevard* (replacement). Web fans style themselves "Buckheads."

Barbara Cook—Creamy-voiced chanteuse. Original Marian the Librarian in *The Music Man* and Cunegonde in *Candide*; now a frequent cabaret performer.

The Dodgers (properly, "Dodger Productions")—Not the baseball team, the producing team. Responsible wholly or in part for revivals of *A Funny Thing Happened on the Way to the Forum*, *Guys and Dolls*, *The King and I*, *How to Succeed in Business Without Really Trying*, *Into the Woods*, *42nd Street*, and many other shows.

Equity—Shorthand for Actors' Equity Association, the actors' union.

Hunter Foster—Star of *Urinetown* and *Little Shop of Horrors*, brother of Sutton.

Sutton Foster—Star of *Thoroughly Modern Millie*, sister of Hunter.

IATSE—Shorthand for the International Alliance of Theatrical Stage Employees, the union of stagehands, electricians, etc. Commonly pronounced "eye-AT-see."

Michael Greif—Imaginative director of *Rent* and *Never Gonna Dance*, and former artistic director of the La Jolla Playhouse in California, which hosted many Broadway-bound productions. Last name pronounced to rhyme with "knife."

Jujamcyn—Jujamcyn Theatres, the third-largest theatre-owning company on Broadway. Founded by James H. Binger and Virginia McKnight Binger, and named for their three children, Judith, James and Cynthia. Broadway's Virginia Theatre is named after Mrs. Binger.

Tony Kushner—Pulitzer-winning playwright and liberal political commentator. Plays include *Angels in America*; *Caroline, or Change*; *Homebody/Kabul*.

Michael John LaChiusa—Leading light of the postmodern musical movement. Shows have included *First Lady Suite*, *Hello Again*, *Little Fish*, and two musicals that opened on Broadway just months apart, *The Wild Party* and *Marie Christine*. Alternately lauded and flayed as brilliant and impenetrable. Last name pronounced "la-KYOO-sa."

Nathan Lane—Ubiquitous comedic leading man in *Guys and Dolls*, *The Producers*, *The Frogs*, other shows, and several short-run sitcoms.

Lunt and Fontanne—Alfred Lunt and Lynn Fontanne were a famous husband-and-wife acting team from the 1920s to the 1950s. Also known as "The Lunts," the Lunt-Fontanne Theatre is named for them. Lynn's last name is commonly mispronounced "Fontaine." The correct pronunciation is "fon-TAN."

Patti LuPone—Tough-gal Broadway diva, star of *Evita*, *Les Miserables*, *The Baker's Wife*, *Master Class* (as replacement), and revivals of *Anything Goes* and *Can-Can*. Also, in recent years, a concert performer.

Cameron Mackintosh—British *über*-producer. The most successful stage producer in history. Best known for his four blockbusters, *Cats*, *Phantom of the Opera*, *Les Miserables*, and *Miss Saigon*, but also for nurturing Boublil & Schonberg, and Andrew Lloyd Webber, sponsoring Sondheim in London, and revolutionizing the "road" by making sure his dozens of international touring companies conformed to the same standards of quality as his New York and London shows.

Kathleen Marshall—Busy director, boss of the popular "Encores!" series of musicals in concert. Sister of Rob.

Rob Marshall—Director and Choreographer whose stage work has included *Victor/Victoria* and *Seussical* (uncredited), and 1990s revivals of *Cabaret*, *A Funny Thing Happened on the Way to the Forum*, *Company*, etc. Moved to TV where he directed the award-winning Disney version of *Annie*, then moved to Hollywood where his *Chicago* was named Best Picture. Brother of Kathleen.

Melpomene—The Greek muse of Tragedy, usually represented by a frowning mask.

Thomas Meehan—In-demand librettist. His resume includes scripts for *The Producers*, *Annie*, *Hairspray*, and *Bombay Dreams*.

Brian Stokes Mitchell—Major leading man of the late 1990s and early 2000s. Starring roles included *Ragtime*, *Kiss of the Spider Woman*, *Man of La Mancha*, and *Kiss Me, Kate*. Named one of the "Sexiest Men Alive" by People magazine. Nickname: "Stokes."

The Nederlanders—Nickname for The Nederlander Organization, second-largest theatre-owning company on Broadway.

Antoinette Perry—Pioneering female director, and founder of The American Theatre Wing, which sponsored the Stage Door Canteen during World War II. The Tony Awards—properly The Antoinette Perry Awards—are named for her.

The Polish Tea Room (Nickname of the Café Edison)—Eatery on West 47th Street near Broadway, specializing in East European Jewish fare; famed as a gathering place for theatre folk. Setting of Neil Simon's play, *45 Seconds From Broadway*. More in Chapter Eight.

Frank Rich—Former first-string theatre critic for *The New York Times*, whose tough standards led to the nickname "The Butcher of Broadway." Now a *Times* columnist on general culture and politics, he sometimes still comments on the Broadway scene.

Michael Riedel—Theatre columnist for *The New York Post*, with an appetite for backstage fits, fights, feuds, and egos, especially involving the rich and famous. No printable nickname.

Sardi's—Theatrical restaurant on West 44th Street opposite Shubert Alley. Famed for caricatures of stars on the walls. More in Chapter Eight.

The Shuberts—Nickname of the Shubert Organization, Broadway's largest theatre-owner, and sometimes co-producer of shows that appear on its stages. Founded by the Shubert Brothers, who are now deceased. Chairman Gerald Schoenfeld and President Philip J. Smith are also sometimes called "The Shuberts." In the 1940s, the company was often associated with fluffy operettas packed with pretty chorines. More recent hits: *Cats, Les Misérables, Mamma Mia!* Owner and name-sake of the Shubert Theatre (and many others) and Shubert Alley.

Neil Simon—Prolific playwright who has had more than thirty plays on Broadway, most notably comedies *The Odd Couple, Barefoot in the Park, Brighton Beach Memoirs, The Dinner Party, Plaza Suite*, and Pulitzer-winner *Lost in Yonkers.* Success became elusive, starting in the 1990s. Nicknamed "Doc" for acting as uncredited play "doctor" on musicals and plays having trouble in development.

Stephen Sondheim (a.k.a. "Steve" especially by people who don't know him, but want to pretend they do)—Genius composer of *Sweeney Todd, Into the Woods, A Funny Thing Happened on the Way to the Forum, Company, Follies, A Little Night Music*, and *Passion*, not to mention the lyrics to *West Side Story*, and *Gypsy*. Known for sophisticated music and supremely inventive lyrics. Revered by many as a god, though his work is also considered cold and inaccessible by some.

Susan Stroman—Red-hot director/choreographer whose work includes *The Producers, Contact, The Music Man, Oklahoma!, Big, Steel Pier*, and lots more. Nickname: "Stro."

Jeanine Tesori—Composer of musicals in remarkably divergent musicals styles. Scores include *Thoroughly Modern Millie*, *Violet*, *Twelfth Night*, and *Caroline, or Change*.

Thanos—The Greek muse of Comedy, usually represented by a smiling mask.

Andrew Lloyd Webber—British composer, a onetime colossus of Broadway and the West End, whose scores include *Cats*, *Phantom of the Opera*, *Jesus Christ Superstar*, *Evita*, and *Sunset Boulevard*, but whose last recent new shows have failed to get U.S. productions.

Fran and Barry Weissler (a.k.a. simply "Fran and Barry" or "Barry and Fran")—Tremendously successful husband-wife producing team, responsible for hit revivals, most notably of *Chicago* and *Wonderful Town*. Made an art form of importing unlikely stars from other media for short runs as replacements in their shows. Put Brook Shields in *Grease!*, Reba McEntire in *Annie Get Your Gun*. Also known for thrifty management techniques.

Maury Yeston—Brainy composer of Tony-winners *Nine* and *Titanic*. A former Yale professor.

Jerry Zaks—Popular director of musical comedies, notably *Smokey Joe's Café*, and revivals of *Guys and Dolls*, *A Funny Thing Happened on the Way to the Forum*, *Little Shop of Horrors*, etc.

Florenz Ziegfeld—Legendary early 20th century producer of the *Follies* that bear his name, from the 1900s to the 1930s, as well as groundbreaking musicals like *Show Boat*. A byword for opulent showmanship. Commonly mispronounced "Zig-feeld." Correct pronunciation is ZIG-feld, the second syllable rhyming with "held." A cinema bearing his name stands on West 55th Street.

DATES YOU SHOULD KNOW

The Broadway Calendar

First weekend in January after New Year's—Many of the weakest Broadway shows close.

January and early February—Quietest time of the year at Broadway's box offices. A good time to hunt for bargains.

> ## BROADWAY'S BIGGEST YEAR
>
> Between twenty-five and forty shows open on Broadway each year. Broadway's peak year was 1927–28, when more than two hundred and seventy shows opened, including five on Christmas Day.

February to April—Theatre companies announce their fall seasons. A good time to decide which, if any, troupes to subscribe to.

March and April—The spring rush of Broadway openings.

March 22—Birthday of Stephen Sondheim (1930) and Andrew Lloyd Webber (1948).

Mid April—Pulitzer Prize announced.

Sometime the last week of April or the first week of May—Deadline for eligibility for the Tony Awards.

First or second Monday in May—Tony nominations announced.

May 31—Last Day of each Broadway season.

June 1—First day of the new season.

First Sunday in June—The Tony Awards.

Week after the Tony Awards—Struggling shows that failed to win any Tony Awards announce their closings.

July and August—New York theatre audiences depart on vacation. In their place come tourists, who take over Broadway for the summer.

End of August—New York newspapers and magazines do their fall preview issues. The fall season shapes up.

September—New York theatre audiences return. Subscription seasons begin. First of the fall openings.

October through early December—The fall rush of Broadway openings.

Thanksgiving through New Year's Eve—Broadway does a big chunk of its business. Tourists return to shop, visit Rockefeller Center, and see family-related Broadway shows.

New Year's Eve—Premium-priced tickets makes this night the biggest of the year for Broadway box offices.

FAMOUS SHOWS YOU SHOULD KNOW

Here are thirty famous shows that everyone should know. Not all represent the best that drama has to offer, but all are likely to be referenced in the shows you see and the people you talk to around Broadway.

Angels in America (1993 and 1994)—Tony Kushner's epic drama about war in heaven and plague on earth during the Reagan administration of the 1980s. Presented in two full-length parts: *Millennium Approaches* and *Perestroika*.

Cat on a Hot Tin Roof (1955)—Tennessee Williams' drama about intrigues within a wealthy Southern family as they wait for the patriarch, Big Daddy, to die. Which son will inherit the plantation? Dorky but responsible older brother Gooper? Or the handsome and intelligent—but alcoholic—Brick? Big Daddy wants it to be Brick, but

Brick hasn't produced an heir. Brick's wife, Maggie the Cat, is aching for Brick—and aching to be the new queen of the plantation. But first she has to unravel the mystery of why Brick suddenly turned to drink . . .

Cats (1982 on Broadway)—The longest-running show in Broadway history, this Andrew Lloyd Webber musical is based on T.S. Eliot's "Old Possum's Book of Practical Cats." It tells the story of a pack of semi-magical Jellicle Cats—with names like Rum Tum Tugger, Skimbleshanks, and Mungojerrie—who gather for the Jellicle Ball to tell their personal stories, and to choose one cat who will ascend to the mystical Heavyside Layer. Score includes "Memory."

A Chorus Line (1975)—The ultimate backstage musical takes us inside the life stories of the chorus dancers, known as "gypsies," while dispensing with the leading lady who usually stands in front of them. Seventeen dancers bare their souls as they compete in a daylong audition for eight spots on an unnamed Broadway show. This is the original "American Idol." Music by Marvin Hamlisch, lyrics by Ed Kleban, book by Nicholas Dante and James Kirkwood. Score includes "What I Did for Love."

Death of a Salesman (1949)—Arthur Miller's classic American drama about a salesman who believes that being "well liked" and successful is more important than anything else in the world—but who finds, as he's getting older, that life is looking pretty empty.

The Fantasticks (1960)—This Off-Broadway musical puttered along in Greenwich Village for nearly forty-two years, becoming the longest-musical ever. Based on Edmond Rostand's *Les Romanesques*, it tells the simple story of a boy and the girl next door. Their fathers want them to marry, but pretend to feud on the theory that best way to get children to do something is to forbid it. There's something timeless about the poetic little musical, which uses images of the passing seasons to help tell its tale. The score, by Tom Jones and Harvey Schmidt, includes "Try To Remember," "Soon It's Gonna Rain," and "Metaphor."

Forbidden Broadway (1982)—For more than twenty years, Gerard Alessandrini has been slyly parodying Broadway and its outsize personalities in a series of ever-changing Off-Broadway revues under the *Forbidden Broadway* banner. The successful formula consists of taking current show tunes, keeping the melody but rewriting the lyrics so it pokes fun at itself or anyone else Alessandrini puts in the satirical line of fire.

Godspell (1971)—Long-running Off-Broadway (and for a year, on Broadway) musical that retells the Gospel of St. Matthew in a series of sketches performed with improvisational invention by a clan of clown-like flower children. Stephen Schwartz' score includes "Day by Day," "Turn Back, O Man," and "All for the Best."

Grease (1972)—Originally part of the 1950s-nostalgia craze of the mid-1970s, this musical tells the story of summer love that spills into the school year at a greaser high school. The Warren Casey/Jim Jacobs score includes "Teen Angel," "We Go Together" and "Beauty School Dropout."

Guys and Dolls (1950)—Frank Loesser's "musical fable of Broadway," captures the world of small-time gamblers, thieves, cops and missionary folk in and around a Never-Never-Broadway of the 1930s. The score includes "Sit Down, You're Rocking the Boat" and "Luck Be a Lady."

Gypsy (1959)—This backstage musical by Arthur Laurents, Jule Styne, and Stephen Sondheim had a modest original run, but has exerted a powerful influence on subsequent musicals. Though based on the memoirs of stripper Gypsy Rose Lee, the musical focuses on the mother, Mama Rose, and her bulldog-like determination to make one of her daughters into "a star!" in vaudeville. Or, if not in vaudeville, then as a stripper in burlesque. Each generation since then has gotten its own Mama Rose, starting with Ethel Merman, and continuing to Angela Lansbury, Tyne Daly, and Bernadette Peters. The score includes "Let Me Entertain You," "Rose's Turn," and the song that became Merman's signature, "Everything's Coming Up Roses."

Hamlet—Shakespeare's tragedy about Danish prince Hamlet who seeks revenge on his uncle Claudius for murdering his father, seizing the throne, and marrying his mother. The meaning of life, love, jealousy, lust and murder are explored in its timeless poetry. The role is considered the Mount Everest for actors, nearly all of whom try it at least once in their careers. It serves as the plot outline to the musical *The Lion King*.

Hello, Dolly! (1964)—Matchmaker Dolly Gallagher Levi faces the greatest challenge of her career when she not only has to arrange love matches for three young couples simultaneously—but also one for herself. Jerry Herman's score includes "Before the Parade Passes By," "Put On Your Sunday Clothes," and the classic title song.

Les Misérables (1987 in NY)—As in the Victor Hugo novel, fugitive Jean Valjean is pursued relentlessly across years and over the barricades of a Paris revolution by singleminded policeman Javert. Along the way, Valjean raises an orphan girl entrusted to his care, and even is chosen the mayor of a town, but always he must take to the road again—until a final dramatic confrontation. The Alain Boublil/Claude-Michel Schonberg score includes "Bring Him Home," "One Day More," and "I Dreamed a Dream."

Life with Father (1939)—Howard Lindsay and Russell Crouse wrote the longest-running non-musical in Broadway history, the story of growing up in a Victorian-era American home with a humorously eccentric father. It ran a then-stunning eight years throughout World War II. It's the template for every TV family sitcom.

Macbeth—Shakespeare's tragedy about a Scottish lord who murders the king and seizes the throne while egged on by his wife and the prophecies of a trio of witches. But witch prophecies have a way of turning around and biting you when you least expect it. The drama gets revived frequently, but it is considered strangely disaster-prone and therefore cursed. Certainly the last two Broadway revivals, including a 2002 version with Kelsey Grammer, tend to support that thesis. Actors will not speak the title aloud when inside a theatre, referring to it instead as "The Scottish Play."

A Midsummer Night's Dream—William Shakespeare's magical comedy about a group of supernatural creatures who discover two young couples and an amateur theatre troupe wandering in their woods, and decide to have some nasty fun with them.

The Music Man (1957)—A warmhearted all-American musical about a charming con man who arrives in a small Iowa town in 1912, hoping to sell them on a phony boys' marching band. Instead, he finds he's sold on the garrulous little burg and its pretty librarian. Meredith Willson's score includes "76 Trombones," "Till There Was You," and "Trouble (in River City)."

My Fair Lady (1956)—Alan Jay Lerner and Frederick Loewe ignore George Bernard Shaw and put a happy ending on his play, *Pygmalion* British speech professor Henry Higgins makes a bet that he can pass off flower girl Eliza Doolittle as a princess with just a few weeks of lessons to erase her working-class cockney accent. Score includes "The Rain in Spain" and "I Could Have Danced All Night."

Oh! Calcutta! (1969)—Kenneth Tynan assembled this ragtag revue of playlets (including ones by no less than John Lennon and Sam Shepard) and dance numbers whose selling point was that the actors, at some point in every scene, got nude nude nude! The show became a punchline, but a revival nevertheless ran 5,959 performances—more than seven years. The title is a French pun meaning, "Oh, what a butt you have!"

Oklahoma! (1942)—Singing cowboys (and farmers) are at the heart of Rodgers and Hammerstein's first musical together. Based on *Green Grow the Lilacs* by Lynn Riggs, the show manages to create its own little world of settlers on the verge of declaring their former frontier town a part of civilization. It's amazing that so much meaning can emerge from such a slim plot: Gentlemanly cowman Curley wants to take a local farmgirl, Laurie, to a "box social" party. But she plays hard to get, and winds up going with a wild, scary farmhand, Judd Fry. Which man does she really want? The score includes "Surrey With a Fringe on Top," "People Will Say We're in Love," "I Cain't Say No," and the title song.

On the Town (1944)—Three sailor buddies are on twenty-four-hour leave in Manhattan. They resolve to see all the sights—and fall in love—in their single day before they head back to a war from which they may not return. The Leonard Bernstein/Betty Comden/Adolph Green score includes "New York, New York," "Lonely Town" and "Some Other Time."

The Phantom of the Opera (1988 in NY)—Andrew Lloyd Webber's musical adaptation of the Gaston Leroux novel about a disfigured musical genius who lives in the catacombs beneath the Paris Opera. He haunts and torments the management and the singers until one day he falls in love with a pretty young soprano, Christine Daae, and plots to lure her to his lair and transform her into an opera star. The score, with lyrics by Charles Hart and Richard Stilgoe, includes "Angel of Music" and "All I Ask of You."

The Producers (2001)—Mel Brooks' movie (1968) was a beloved cult favorite for years with theatre folk and businesspeople. Crooked and desperate Broadway producer Max Bialystock teams up with meek and neurotic accountant Leo Bloom to put over a scam Leo accidentally dreamed up. You can sell as many percent of a Broadway show to backers as you like—a thousand, ten thousand, twenty thousand percent—as long as you can be *absolutely certain* the show will be a flop. So no one will ask where the profits went. It took Brooks until the 21st century to turn the film into a stage musical (with the help of Thomas Meehan) that parodies Broadway even more mercilessly. The set-piece in the film—the opening scene from the resulting musical, *Springtime for Hitler*—was expanded and made even funnier with the help of director Susan Stroman. The show won more Tony Awards than any single production in history, twelve, and would have won more if there hadn't been multiple *Producers* people nominated in some categories. Brooks' score includes "The King of Old Broadway," "Betrayed," "I Want To Be a Producer," and "Springtime for Hitler."

Romeo and Juliet—Shakespeare's "star-cross'd" romance about the impossibly sweet but doomed love that is born between a boy and a girl from two families engaged in a murderous feud.

The Sound of Music (1959)—Rodgers and Hammerstein's last musical together is based on the true-life story of the singing Von Trapp family who use their music to escape to freedom after the conquest of their native Austria by the Nazis in World War II. Score includes "Do Re Mi," "Edelweiss," "Climb Ev'ry Mountain" and the title song.

South Pacific (1949)—Rodgers and Hammerstein's musical based on two James Michener stories about how racism affects American seabees and their romances with the natives of the south sea islands during World War II. Score includes "Some Enchanted Evening," "A Wonderful Guy," "Carefully Taught" and "There Is Nothing Like a Dame."

A Streetcar Named Desire (1947)—Tennessee Williams' masterpiece about faded and delicate Southern belle Blanche DuBois who descends into madness as she is confronted by the hard, real world in the person of her crude brother-in-law, Stanley Kowalski.

Sweeney Todd, The Demon Barber of Fleet Street (1979)—Stephen Sondheim's masterpiece that turns a bit of bloody Victorian penny-dreadful melodrama into a tale of self-destructive revenge told in dark poetry. Seeking revenge on a corrupt judge who destroyed his life, Sweeney opens a barbershop where the customers get their throats slit, and wind up as meat pies. Ugly subject for a musical? Sondheim and librettist Hugh Wheeler pull it off. Score includes "Pretty Women," "A Little Priest," "Joanna" and "The Ballad of Sweeney Todd."

West Side Story (1957)—Musical adaptation of Shakespeare's *Romeo and Juliet*, with the action and characters transposed to the world of New York teen gangs—the Montagues and Capulets replaced by the Jets and the Sharks. The Leonard Bernstein/Stephen Sondheim score includes "Tonight," "Maria," "Somewhere," "America."

SUPERSTITIONS

Theatre people are among the most superstitious on earth. Many actors have idiosyncratic private rituals and talismans that they use to ward off mishaps and bring on applause. Here are some general superstitions you should know.

- Never say "good luck" on opening night. It's bad luck. The theatre gremlins always do the opposite of what you say, so you should always say, "Break a leg" to make sure it will not happen. Theatre gremlins are apparently not the brightest lights on the Christmas tree.

- If you really want good luck on opening night, eat a red apple or carry a penny in your pocket.

- If the dress rehearsal is a disaster, the opening night will be brilliant. (And vice-versa.)

- Never put your shoes on any table, especially in your dressing room.

- Never mention the title of Shakespeare's gory tragedy *Macbeth* inside a theatre. The play is widely believed to be cursed, and many strange and horrible things have been known to happen at performances, and to people who mention the title inside any playhouse. If you must refer to it, call it "The Scottish Play." I got nervous just now typing it into this manuscript.

DRESSING FOR THE THEATRE

In years past, it was customary to put on the Ritz—suit, tie, evening gown—when you went to the theatre. It was like going to a dress ball, or to church. Sartorial standards have relaxed throughout American life, and the same holds true for theatregoing. Yes, people still spiff up for opening nights, and Friday and Saturday nights still offer a chance to show off the new eveningwear. But in general, any neat and clean clothes are perfectly acceptable.

You'll see Dockers, jeans, cargo pants, sneakers, t-shirts and Doc Martens, and belly button shirts, especially at matinees and Off-Broadway. And they're fine as long as they are neat and clean and don't have holes. However, ragged clothes like cut-offs, and super informal accessories like flip-flops, are no good. Reserve bathing suits, bare feet and shirtlessness for poolside or the beach. And save cowboy hats for the ranch.

On the other hand, you can get as swank as you like. Theatregoing still counts as an elegant night on the town. So flaunt your threads! Flash your bling!

Is there any sight sweeter than one recently seen at the curb in front of *Hairspray*: a group of girls, obviously celebrating someone's birthday, piling out of a rented limousine, screaming with laughter, tottering on high heels, wearing makeup, grownup clothes and salon hairdos for what looked like the first time. They were young and gorgeous and going to see a big hit Broadway show. It was an unbeatable combination.

As a side note, however, there is still one theatrical event that absolutely commands formalwear. The annual Tony Awards began selling tickets to the public in 1997, and no one is admitted without tux or tails for men and evening gowns for women (and Harvey Fierstein).

WHAT TO EXPECT WHEN YOU GO TO THE THEATRE

- Check the time on your tickets. Arrive a half-hour to twenty minutes before the stated curtain time.

- If you arrive before half-hour, expect to wait in the lobby. Doors to the auditorium generally open thirty minutes before curtain.

- Most theatres have two ticket windows; one for pickup of tickets held at the box office from phone and internet sales, and one for new sales. After a half-hour, box office windows switch over to all pickups.

- An attendant at the door will tear your ticket, give you back half, and direct you either up the stairs to the balcony and mezzanine, or to the proper orchestra row to find your seat.

- If you are carrying a bag, a security person may ask to open and inspect it at this time. There is no consistent policy on this. Polite compliance is the best response.

- Keep the ticket stub handy. It has your seat number on it. Also, if you intend to go outside during intermission, you'll need this stub to get back in.

- If you have a coat and bag, you may wish to check them at this time. You may also take them to your seat. But if they are bulky, checking is best.

- Wait at the head of the aisle. Two or three ushers generally staff each aisle to take people in turn and escort you to your seats.

- It is not necessary to tip the usher.

- Take the seat directed by the usher. Because all seats are reserved, you won't be able to switch seats unless the audience is very sparse.

- If you haven't checked your coat and bag, place them under your seat, or hold them in your lap.

- As you are being seated, the usher will hand you a *Playbill* program. These are free, and contain all credits, Who's Who, song titles and other information about the show, plus photos of cast members and articles about the latest openings and celebrities around Broadway. Larger-format "souvenir programs" have bigger photos and more information about the show, but cost $10 and up.

- If you need to slide past already-seated patrons, face the stage with your back to those seated. Say "excuse me."

- Once seated, you may wish to use the washroom, buy refreshments, or get a laser-listening headset. The headsets are free, but you need to leave a driver's license or other form of ID.

- Women in particular should use this time to visit the restroom. There's always a line at intermission, and never enough stalls.

- Drinks may not be taken to the seats, but candy may. Try to be as quiet with it (especially candy wrappers) as you can.

- Turn off all cell phones, beepers, watch alarms, and any other electronics that may emit sound. A good tip: Even if you are sure your phone is off, **double-check anyway**. There is monetary fine for using cell phones in New York theatres (though I've never heard of it being enforced). Also, actors are known to stop the show and scold people whose phones are ringing. I was at the performance of *Frankie and Johnny in the Claire de Lune* the night Stanley Tucci heard ringing and shouted, "Turn off your f****** phone!" You don't want to be on the receiving end of that sort of message, do you?

- Shortly before the performance begins, the house manager may come on the sound system to remind everyone that the taking of photographs and the use of recording devices is against the law. Flash cameras are distracting for the actors and leave that blue afterimage that may blind them momentarily during an intricate dance number. They could get hurt.

- There is also no smoking.

- Moments before the show begins, the house lights will be dimmed halfway. This is a signal to get in your seat, settle down, and prepare to be entertained.

- Once the overture begins or the curtain rises, it's time to be quiet. Theatre isn't like TV in the living room, or a rock concert. The tradition is complete silence, and theatre folk encourage everyone to join in this tradition. You've paid a lot for these tickets, and deserve to hear every word and musical note.

- If you're having trouble hearing every word, Stephen Sondheim has a tip: Lean forward slightly in your seat. It has the effect of sharpening the senses.

- Immerse yourself in the experience. Forget the proscenium and make believe your seat in the locale of the performance. Good actors will help you suspend your disbelief.

- If you arrive late, the usher may hold you at the back of the theatre until there's a suitable break in the action, so your arrival will inconvenience others in your row as little as possible.

- Applause should be a spontaneous expression of your pleasure in something you've seen. It's polite to applaud at the end of a song, or at the end of a particularly difficult stunt, or as an actor who has done something triumphantly well makes an exit. But it's not required. If you didn't like it, or simply feel ambivalent, clap softly (fingers only) or not at all. If you thought something was really swell, clap hard (a slight cupping of the hands can create a really thunderous effect) and cheer. Some people also like to whistle, though this smacks of the sports stadium. Air horns are n.g.

- Intermission (or "the interval," as it's called in Great Britain) generally lasts fifteen minutes or so. Now is the time to get refreshment, visit the restrooms, or socialize. Show merchandise is also sold at this time, t-shirts, caps and mugs being the most popular. Musicals also sell their cast albums.

- If you go outside for a smoke or to make a phone call, remember to bring your ticket stub. As you return, remember once again to switch off your cell phone.

- The house manager will signal the approaching end of the intermission by sounding three tones on the theatre's sound system, blinking the lights, or making a soft announcement to the effect, "Please return to your seats. The performance will resume in three minutes."

- At musicals there is often a little moment at the start of Act II when the conductor takes the podium. He may acknowledge the audience with a small bow, and he/she will often get a hand.

- If you need to leave your seat during a performance, say, "excuse me," and keep as low a profile as you can. If someone needs to climb out past you, rise slightly in your seat to get your knees out of the way. If the person accidentally steps on your toes, don't curse. Forgive them and re-immerse in the show.

- At the end of the show is the curtain call. Bows are generally taken in the reverse order of billing, meaning the leads and stars come out last. Sometimes the leads will take a bow with the entire company, and then get a separate curtain call of their own. Standing ovations are not required. If you really loved a show or a specific actor, by all means stand. A full-hearted sitting ovation is reward enough. But true audience-wide Standing O's should be reserved for especially magical performances or special occasions, like the final performance of a long-running hit.

- For several weeks each spring and fall Broadway and many Off-Broadway shows participate in fundraising appeals for Broadway Cares/Equity Fights AIDS. These appeals are generally made by the star of the show, backed by the cast, at the conclusion of the curtain call. You are not required to stay for these if you don't wish to. But the cause is a good one. The appeals used to be simple speeches asking people to put money into baskets on the way out. Many have evolved into elaborate mini-shows of their own, with actors auctioning off signed t-shirts, props used in the show, backstage visits with the stars, or even kisses from some of the more comely cast members. You may respond, or not, as your pocketbook allows.

- The final part of the performance of a musical is the "play out," generally three or four minutes of high-energy music from the show to accompany the departure of the audience. Despite its purpose (to clear the house) many people stay to hear every last note. A final round of applause for the orchestra is always appreciated.

ETIQUETTE

Get Me to the Show on Time

Most evening performances start at 8 PM Monday through Saturday, 2 or 3 PM on matinee days and 7 PM Sundays, but there are exceptions. Several shows have begun doing 7 PM performances on Tuesdays. Shows with Sunday matinees usually begin them at 3 PM. Some child-oriented shows, like Disney's *Beauty and the Beast* for many years began evening shows at 6:30 PM So remember to check your tickets.

Most theatres open their doors a half hour before curtain time. If you arrive before that, you may wait in the lobby or under the marquee. Some shows post their best reviews in a glass case in front of the theatre, or on a sandwich board in the lobby for you to read while you're waiting—so you can reflect on what a wise decision you made when you bought the ticket.

If You're Late

If you arrive late, for whatever reason, don't push your way into the theatre or demand to be seated immediately. Most shows post signs saying some variation of, "Latecomers will be seated at an appropriate interval." The ushers and the house manager usually work out when is the next moment when people entering the theatre will cause the least disruption. Usually this is during a scene break or the applause break at the end of a song. Just alert the usher that you have arrived late and ask to be seated. The usher will usually peek into the house, and escort you to your seat when the time is right.

There is a safety issue here, too. Plunging into a darkened theatre could lead to a trip or fall; ushers with flashlights will help you avoid that. If your seat is down near the stage, you also may wish to stand at the back of the theatre until intermission.

Warning: Some shows, especially comedies, will incorporate latecomers into the performance. Stars Nathan Lane and Bill Irwin are notorious for this. During Lane's stint in *A Funny Thing Happened on the Way to the Forum* it almost became a nightly part of the show.

Am I required to applaud when the curtain rises?

No. Applause is always optional, and up to the audience—the reward for a job well done. Audiences often applaud at the rise of the curtain, for a set that is particularly astonishing or pleasing to the eye. Some shows now forego a curtain, so the set is in full view of the audience when they enter.

Are standing ovations required at Broadway shows?

No. In fact, they've become overused in the last fifteen years or so. The act of standing up to applaud is the reward for extraordinary quality in performance or other creative achievement. You should never feel required to stand, even if everyone around you is standing. Generally, the best kind of standing ovations are the ones where you are so moved that you suddenly find yourself on your feet.

Should I applaud when the star makes her/his entrance?

If the star is of sufficient magnitude, such a welcome is polite—but by no means required. As stated above, applause is always at the discretion of the audience.

When is it proper to boo and throw tomatoes?

Hurling rotten fruit at actors was characteristic of wars between 19th century actors' claques (acquiring and packing spoiled fruit does require a certain degree of malicious advance planning, after all). But,

Little Rascals movies notwithstanding, it is completely inappropriate—not to say illegal—today. It's criminal assault.

However, booing is still quite legal, but should be saved for the most egregious unprofessionalism. I once attended a regional production of a famous musical at which the leading actor had not fully memorized his lines, and then made a curtain speech blaming his poor performance on distractions by the allegedly unattractive wheelchair-bound women in the front row. He was heartily and appropriately booed. A tomato in the kisser might actually have done him some good.

Speaking of villains, there is a tradition of hissing the villain in Victorian melodramas. If you see a villain wearing a moustache and twirling it, take this as a cue to hiss. The dastard will likely sneer back in response.

Put 'em away

What to do with electronics? Shut them all off. Period. Turn off cell phones and beepers/pagers during a performance; if you're on call you can always check with your office at intermission. Similarly, make sure that any watch alarm or on-the-hour beeps are turned off. If you have one of those clap-activated car-key locators, turn it off, as well. Don't listen to a Walkman during the performance. If you're trying to follow a sports game at the same time as the show, don't listen to the radio with an earpiece; wait until intermission. Never use a laptop during a performance. (Don't scoff. I've seen people do it!)

Final note on this subject: At a 1999 forum, *Cabaret* star Alan Cumming was asked if he had any regrets in his career. He answered, "Yes. I regret not killing people who leave their cell phones on in the theatre."

Can I bring my own food?

Theatre owners discourage this. Don't bring food with you that's not easy to carry. A small bag of malted milk balls—OK. A huge sack of popcorn—not OK. A pack of M&Ms—OK. Trays of hot food—not OK. I once saw a family try to eat ribs out of plastic trays from a salad bar during a show. The whole mezzanine reeked of barbecue sauce before an usher intervened.

Can I take photos during the show?

No. It's forbidden by law. Audiotape, digital and videotape recording is also forbidden. If you're caught, you'll be asked to leave and your tape/disc/film will be subject to confiscation. Flash photos are actually dangerous to the actors, who may be temporarily dazzled by the flash and step off the stage. Actors will sometimes stop the show if they are photographed. Most Broadway theatres offer illustrated programs and recordings from the show.

Can I smoke during the show?

No. It's forbidden by law. If you light up, you'll be asked to put it out. If you refuse, you'll be asked to leave.

What should I do if my kids get antsy during the show? I mean, they are kids, after all.

Here are some tips for making the experience better for your children, for you—and for those sitting around you. Go over the story ahead of time, preparing the child for any complicated plot twists or obscure references—but don't give away the ending! Play the cast album if the show has one. Explain "The Rules" in advance: Go to the bathroom before the curtain. No talking during the show. No kicking the seat in front of you. Laughing is OK, in reaction to jokes. Wait until the end of songs, then clap and cheer as loud as you want.

Parents should bring something quiet to eat—lollipops are perfect—for children who get restless. Wrap them in plastic-wrap so the cellophane won't crackle. Make sure, however, the lollies are not left stuck to the seats.

Chronically noisy or boisterous children should be taken out of the auditorium for a "time out." It's only fair to those around you.

If a crying child does not respond to fifteen seconds or so of soothing, take the child to the lobby.

On the child's maiden voyage to the theatre, try double-teaming to preserve your investment. One parent or other adult companion goes to see the show with the child while the other parent waits outside. If the child can't make it through and must bail out, the outside parent takes custody while the inside parent remains to see the rest of the show.

Can I talk during the overture and entr'acte?

Preferably not. They're part of the show, too.

What can I do if someone is being loud or annoying— without becoming loud or annoying myself?

Start by turning, facing them directly, and glaring. This is completely silent, and generally alerts 99 percent of offenders that they're being offensive. The next step is a sharp "Shh!" or a sotto voce, "Please be quiet." Do not escalate any further than this yourself. The next step is to alert an usher or the house manager, and let them deal with the offender.

The Zen of meeting celebrities

One of the great things about seeing stars on Broadway is that they are actually there live in the building with you. You may run into them on the street, like any other commuter going to work. And, afterward, they will be coming out the stage door, live and in person.

New Yorkers see so many celebrities all the time, they have developed a kind of cool way of glancing at them without staring. A nod and a smile are OK, too.

If you're forced into close proximity with one—in an elevator, for instance—you may introduce yourself and say something like, "I really admired your work in . . ." and name something specific. But don't drag them into long conversations unless they clearly indicate they are interested. Read their body language. If they look uncomfortable, cut the conversation short.

Staring, shouting, hurling abuse, asking embarrassing personal questions, slobbering and unsolicited hugging are never good form.

And then there's the issue of autographs. Fans are allowed to wait outside the stage door for stars to emerge. At that point you may ask for an autograph. "Miss X, I really love your work. Could you please sign my *Playbill* [or autograph book]?"

If the star says they are in a rush, just accept it. If they rudely brush past you, just accept that, too. Sometimes they are just snobs, but sometimes, too, they have had bad experiences with autograph hounds. Some people get autographs and immediately turn around and sell them on Ebay. The star can't tell if you're a true fan, or just someone who wants to make some money off their fame.

Some stars will stand for forty-five minutes in the snow signing autographs; some just dash for their limos. Respect their choice, even if it's disappointing. At least you got to see them up close. And that's another added advantage to the live stage.

LONG-RUNNING SHOWS

> "On Broadway, boredom is the only
> malady that's fatal."
> —BROOKS ATKINSON

Even though the old high-society social season barely registers with most New Yorkers anymore, the Broadway season still tends to follow it, partly out of habit and tradition, partly out of economic forces that happen to place the two busiest ticket-selling times of year roughly at its beginning and end.

The Broadway season technically begins June 1 of each year and ends May 31 of the following year. The annual Tony Awards have become a major marketing force each year, and are broadcast the first or second Sunday in June, just after the traditional end of the season. However, because the deadline for Tony eligibility lands roughly a month before that, the season now effectively ends by the first week in May.

New Broadway shows tend to open in two rushes each year, one in the fall, roughly October through Christmas; the other in the months leading up to the Tony deadline, roughly March through April. The slowest times of year are the six weeks following New Year, and the middle of the summer. Shows open at other times, too, but most of the openings, and the accompanying reviews can be found during the peaks. The overwhelming majority of them close within a few weeks of opening. If the reviews are poisonous enough, a show will sometimes close on opening night, as happened in fall 2003 with *The Oldest Confederate Widow Tells All*. A few, however, ride (or overcome) reviews to become perennial favorites, running year after year.

Here is a summary of some perennials, and a look at what constitutes their appeal. *Information is subject to change, especially the performance schedules.*

BROADWAY

Beauty and the Beast, Lunt-Fontanne Theatre—Disney knocked one out of the park with its first foray onto Broadway, vintage 1994.. This adaptation of its Oscar-nominated animated film is beautiful, magical and tuneful. It's also a little overblown and a little too long, but, like the huge dinners at Carmine's, you feel like you've gotten your money's worth. And kids like it because it's familiar, yet goes far enough beyond the video to refresh their interest. And it's live, so, yes, the Candlestick lights up, the Cheese Grater dances, the champagne bottles shoot fireworks, and, somehow, the Beast turns back into a prince right before your very eyes. Charming for all ages, offering two early-curtain performances on school nights.

Musical. 205 West 46th St. (between Broadway and Eighth Ave.). Performance times 7 PM Tuesday; 8 PM Thursday to Saturday; 2 PM Wednesday and Saturday; 1 and 6:30 PM Sunday. No performance Monday or Wednesday evening. Official website: www.DisneyonBroadway.com Tickets by phone: 1-212-307-4747 in New York; 1-800-755-4000 elsewhere. Tickets online: www.ticketmaster.com. Tickets: $35–$99.

Chicago, Ambassador Theatre—The film version may have won the Academy Award as Best Picture, but it didn't kill off this 1996 Broadway stage version. That's partly because the stage version is a different animal. Imported from the Encores! series at the New York City Center, it is a stripped-down, streamlined version of the supremely cynical story about an aspiring vaudeville performer who discovers that murdering her husband has catapulted her to fame. There is virtually no scenery; the gorgeous, buff dancers in William Ivey Long's sleek black costumes *are* the scenery. So is the atmospheric score by John Kander and Fred Ebb, who previously wrote *Cabaret*. This is not a musical for kids. The language is rough, the sexual references are blatant and the attitude is as cold and hard as black ice. But the dancing, recreated by Ann Reinking from Bob Fosse's 1975 original, is spectacular.

Musical. 219 West 49th St. (between Broadway and Eighth Ave.). Performance times: 7 PM Tuesday; 8 PM Monday, Thursday, and Friday; 2 and 8 PM Saturday; 2 and 7 PM Sunday. No performance Wednesday. Official website: www.chicagothemusical.com. Tickets by phone: 1-212-239-6200 or 1-800-432-7250. Tickets online: www.telecharge.com. Ticket prices: $43.75–$96.25. Running Time: 2 hours and 30 minutes, with one 15-minute intermission.

42nd Street, Ford Center for the Performing Arts—One of the great backstage legends started as a 1933 film, and in 1980 was transplanted to its natural habitat, Broadway by director/choreographer Gower Champion, whose work has been recreated in this sprawling revival. Peggy Sawyer, an ambitious dancer from Allentown, PA, comes to New York hoping to land a role in a Broadway show. And, gosh, if she doesn't pull it off the very first day. Rivalry with the leading lady works its way through twists and turns until the big opening night when the diva gets injured. Catapulted out of the chorus, Peggy has just a few hours to learn the role and go on in the star part. "You're going out there a chorus kid," the director implores, "but you've got to come back a star!" When Peggy is happy, she tap dances. When she's sad, she also tap dances. In fact, nearly every emotion worth a song also seems to be worth a titanic tap number. Songs include "Shuffle Off to Buffalo," "I Only Have Eyes for You" and "Lullabye of Broadway." Fun (and exhausting) for all ages, but the wisecracking Depression-era humor is pure corn. And, the theatre is easy to find: it's on 42nd Street. Winner of the 2002 Tony Award as Best Revival of a Musical.

Musical. 213 West 42nd St. (between Seventh and Eighth Aves.). Performance times 7 PM Tuesday; 2 & 8 PM Wednesday; 8 PM Thursday and Friday; 2 & 8 PM Saturday; 3 PM Sunday. No performance Monday. Official website: www.42ndStreetBroadway.com Tickets by phone: 1-212-307-4100 in New York; 1-800-755-4000 elsewhere. Tickets online: www.ticketmaster.com. Tickets: $30–$100, plus surcharge.

Hairspray, Neil Simon Theatre—This cheerful and highly energetic musical comedy is based on the campy John Waters film of the same name, set in early 1960s Baltimore. Chubby teen Tracy Turnblad is determined to join the cast of afternoon teen dance TV program "The Corny Collins Show." Along the way, she has to overcome the plus-size prejudices of her mom (played by a man in drag), her rival, and the show's producer. Tracy also mounts a campaign to integrate the show, which formerly limited black teens to one show a month. The show features hilarious early-60s pop music pastiche by Marc Shaiman and Scott Wittman, and nearly non-stop dancing by Jerry Mitchell. Tony Award for Best Musical, 2003.

Musical. 250 West 52nd St. (between Broadway and Eighth Ave.). Performance times: 7 PM Tuesday, 8 PM Wednesday to Friday; 2 and 8 PM Saturday; 3 PM Sunday. No performance Monday. Official website: www.hairsprayonbroadway.com. Tickets by phone: 1-212-307-4100 in New York; 1-800-755-4000 elsewhere. Tickets online: www.ticketmaster.com. Broadway Inner Circle tickets: 1-212-307-4599.

The Lion King, New Amsterdam Theatre—When Disney announced it was adapting its second animated musical to the stage, people at first figured it was going to look like *Beauty and the Beast*, or, more likely, *Cats*, since it was all about a bunch of lions. But Disney, to their credit, surprised everybody by handing the ten-million-dollar extravaganza to Julie Taymor, an Off-Off-Broadway director of avant-garde pieces that relied heavily on masks and puppets. So it was to be a puppet show? Again, no. Taymor tells the story of the film more or less straight. Its plot of a prince disenfranchised by his uncle is borrowed from Hamlet, with a Falstaffian slice of *Henry IV, Part 1*, slipped into the middle for "Hakuna Matata" comic effect. But Taymor takes her cue from the story and reaches back centuries into the old trunk of theatre tricks to fill the New Amsterdam with sunrises, flocks of birds, elephant graveyards, murderous stampedes, and ghostly apparitions from beyond the grave. Everything old is really new in this innovative production, which won the 1997 Tony Award as Best Musical. Great for all ages, though it is lengthy, and has an early curtain only one night a week.

Musical. 214 West 42nd St. (between Seventh and Eighth Aves.). Performance times 8 PM Wednesday to Saturday; 2 PM Wednesday and Saturday; 1 and 6:30 PM Sunday. No performance Monday or Tuesday. Official website: www.DisneyonBroadway.com Tickets by phone: 1-212-307-4747 in New York; 1-800-755-4000 elsewhere. Tickets online: www.ticketmaster.com. Tickets: $35-$100.

Mamma Mia!, Cadillac Winter Garden Theatre—Nostalgia for the 1970s doesn't get any groovier than this musical, which wedges hits like "Dancing Queen" by the disco group ABBA into a story about a young woman who uses her wedding day to discover which of three men is her true father. The leading role in the young woman's mom, a former disco star whose wild youth has led to the present quandary. The show knows its audience perfectly and delivers a steady stream of campy fun. Part of the hoot is the rush of recognition that comes with the initial chords of each song, though those who did not grow up with ABBA may find themselves a little perplexed by it all. If you can hear the title of the songs like "Take a Chance on Me" or "The Winner Takes It All," and the melody instantly pops into your head, this is the show for you.

Musical. 1634 Broadway (between 50th and 51st Sts). Performance times 8 PM Wednesday to Saturday; 2 PM Wednesday and Saturday; 2 and 7 PM Sunday. No performance Monday or Tuesday. Official website: www.mamma-mia.com. Tickets by phone: 1-212-239-6200 in New York; 1-800-432-7250 elsewhere. Tickets online: www.telecharge.com/mamma-mia.

Movin' Out, Richard Rodgers Theatre—The music is all Billy Joel's, but the unique concept and execution are all director/choreographer

Twyla Tharp's. She took Joel standards like "James" and "Just the Way You Are," and strung them together in a way that tells the story of three Long Island buddies in the 1960s who go off to fight in Vietnam, and what happens when only two of them return. The story is told entirely through dance as a great band plays and sings the Joel songs above them. Surprisingly moving, especially in Act II when the surviving friends and their women put their lives back together again. Best for teens and up, but especially for Baby Boomers for whom the music evokes memories.

Dance Musical. 226 West 46th St. (between Broadway and Eighth Ave.). Performance times 8 PM Tuesday through Saturday; 2 PM Wednesday and Saturday; 3 PM Sunday. No performance Monday. Official website: www.movinoutonbroadway.com Tickets by phone: 1-212-307-4100 in New York; 1-800-755-4000 elsewhere. Tickets online: www.ticketmaster.com. Tickets: $40–$100. Inner Circle tickets: 1-212-307-4599.

The Phantom of the Opera, Majestic Theatre—Opened January 26, 1988 at the Majestic Theatre, where it remains more than 6,700 performances later, making it Broadway's lost-running current show. Written by Andrew Lloyd Webber for his first wife, Sarah Brightman, this musical thriller has long outlasted their marriage. Based on the 1910 novel by Gaston Leroux, it's a gothic horror musical about a disfigured musical genius who lives in the catacombs beneath the Paris Opera, and who becomes obsessed with a beautiful young singer name Christine Daae. Appearing to her in a mask, the Phantom hypnotizes her and trains her to become great opera diva, with the idea that she will star in his insane self-written opera and become his queen. Any resistance by the theatre's actual management is dealt with savagely. A falling chandelier provides a dramatic special effect as it plunges over the heads of the audience toward its victim on the stage. It's a big show with a big cast, and a lot of color and costumes and special effects. The music uses operatic voices and orchestrations, but switches over to rock just as easily, as evidenced in the title song. Good for teens and up. Tony Award for Best Musical, 1988.

Musical. 247 West 44th St. (between Eighth Ave. and Broadway). Performance times: 7 PM Tuesday, 8 PM Monday, Wednesday, Thursday, Friday; 2 and 8 PM Saturday. No performance Sunday. Official website: www.thephantomoftheopera.com. Tickets by phone: 1-212-239-6200 in New York; 1-800-432-7250 elsewhere. Tickets online: www.telecharge.com.

The Producers, St. James Theatre—This wildly comic musical is based on the 1968 Mel Brooks cult film comedy of the same title, about a down-and-out Broadway producer who discovers, with the help of a nebbish accountant, a way to make more money with a flop than with a hit. So they set out to produce the biggest flop musical in Broadway history, complete with the worst director, the worst star, the worst choreographer, and the worst story: a lighthearted romantic romp about Adolph Hitler, titled *Springtime for Hitler*. Sounds tasteless? It is! But its tastelessness becomes part of the gag, among lots of other jokes, often at Broadway's expense. Memorable for having won more Tony Awards than any show in history: 13, including Best Musical, 2001. Some strong language. Appropriate for teens and up.

Musical. 246 West 44th St. (between Eighth Ave. and Broadway). Performance times: 7 PM Tuesday; 8 PM Wednesday to Saturday; 2 PM Wednesday and Saturday; 3 PM Sunday. No performance Monday. Official website: www.producersonbroadway.com. Tickets by phone: 1-212-239-5800 in New York; 1-800-432-7250 elsewhere. Tickets online: www.telecharge.com. Broadway Inner Circle tickets: 1-212-563-2929.

Rent, Nederlander Theatre—One of the biggest hits of the 1990s, this landmark musical romance takes the love-among-starving artists story of the opera *La Bohème* (*The Bohemians*) and transposes it to Manhattan's East Village in the 1990s. Aspiring musician Roger, aspiring filmmaker Mark and their friends try all sorts of schemes to scrape together rent money so they can keep living in their broken-down tenement apartments. Roger meets a beautiful neighbor, Mimi, who is dying, not of consumption as in the opera, but of AIDS. They embark on a beautiful but doomed love affair. This show, about the preciousness of love and life, has book, music and lyrics by Jonathan Larson, who, ironically, died of an aortic aneurysm the night before the first public performance, at age 35. *Rent* captures a moment in the history of city when the bohemian neighborhood of the East Village was undergoing gentrification, which was largely accomplished in the years after the show opened. The Nederlander Theatre itself, which stands in the scruffy area just south of 42nd Street, was roughed up and redecorated to suggest the East Village in those days. For mature teens and up. Tony Award for Best Musical, 1996. Pulitzer Prize for Drama, 1996. Just about every other theatre award for which it was eligible.

Musical. 208 West 41st St. (between Seventh and Eighth Aves.). Performance times: 8 PM Monday, Tuesday, Thursday, and Friday; 2 and 8 PM Saturday; 2 and 7 PM Sunday. No performance Wednesday. Official website: www.siteforrent.com. Tickets by phone: 1-212-307-4100 in New York; 1-800-755-4000 elsewhere. Tickets online: www.ticketmaster.com.

Wicked, Gershwin Theatre—*The Wizard of Oz*, first seen on Broadway way back in 1903, has seen many adaptations, variations, sequels and musicalizations. But perhaps none as startling as this prequel, which shows Glinda and Elphaba, a.k.a. the prissy Good Witch of the North and the acid green Wicked Witch of the West, as rival college roommates, and the Wonderful Wizard of Oz, as a scheming dictator. Based on Gregory Maguire's novel of the same title, *Wicked* the musical is spiked with joking references to the classic MGM film and zooms with special effects, but has a completely original score by Stephen Schwartz, composer of *Godspell* and *Pippin*. The Act I finale, "Defying Gravity," in which the Wicked Witch makes her first broomborne flight, is a showstopper, though the show gets complicated and loses some steam by the end of Act II. A great show for kids, and for fans of the film.

Musical. 222 West 51st St. (between Broadway and Eighth Ave.). Performance times: 7 PM Tuesday; 8 PM Wednesday to Friday; 2 and 8 PM Saturday; 3 PM Sunday. No performance Monday. Official website: www.WickedtheMusical.com Tickets by phone: 1-212-307-4100 in New York; 1-800-755-4000 elsewhere. Tickets online: www.ticketmaster.com.

OFF-BROADWAY

Blue Man Group: Tubes, Astor Place Theatre—Similar to *Stomp* in some ways, this strange flower of New Vaudeville consists of three mute men, painted entirely blue, drumming on everything they can get their azure little hands on. That description fails to capture the magical beauty the show sometimes achieves, and which has kept it running since 1990 Off-Broadway and in cities across the U.S. and around the world. Another show with appeal to both kids and non-speakers of English.

Performance piece. 434 Lafayette St. (between 7th and 8th Sts.), Greenwich Village. Performance schedule: 8 PM Tuesday to Thursday; 7 and 10 PM Friday; 4, 7, and 10 PM Saturday; 2, 5, and 8 PM Sunday. No performance Monday. Official website: www.blue-man.com. Tickets by phone: 1-212-254-4370 or 1-800-BLUEMAN or 1-212-307-4100. Tickets online: www.ticketmaster.com/venue/24600. Group sales: 1-212-260-8993. Ticket prices: $55–$65. Running time: 2 hours, no intermission.

Forbidden Broadway, Douglas Fairbanks Theatre—More than twenty years ago, Gerard Alessandrini got the golden idea to take familiar and/or current show tunes and give them new lyrics that parody themselves or other shows and personalities. The show has gone through several editions, including *Forbidden Broadway Strikes Back* and *Forbidden Hollywood*, and has moved to several different New York theatres, but the formula has remained an audience-pleaser. Some of the best include "Season of Hype" poking fun at Rent's "Seasons of Love"; "Somewhat Overindulgent" spoofing Mandy Patinkin's extra-energetic version of "Over the Rainbow"; and "Into the Words," which has fun at the expense of the extra-articulate lyricist Stephen Sondheim. Updated periodically to toast the latest shows, stars and scandals.

Revue. 432 West 43rd St. (between Ninth and Tenth Aves.). Performance times 8:15 PM Monday, Tuesday, Friday, and Saturday; 2:30 Wednesday and Saturday; 3:30 and 7:30 PM Sunday. No performance Thursday. Official website: www.forbiddenbroadway.com. Tickets by phone: 1-212-239-6200 in New York; 1-800-432-7250 elsewhere. Groups: 1-212-840-5564. Tickets online: www.telecharge.com. Ticket prices: $49–$57.

I Love You, You're Perfect, Now Change, Westside Theatre— Off-Broadway musical comedy revue about the agonies and ecstasies of the male-female relationships, from friendship, through dating, to love and marriage. Is this territory familiar? Yes, but songwriters Joe DiPietro and Jimmy Roberts approach it in a witty way, with songs including "Why? Cause I'm a Guy," "The Single Man Drought," "Shouldn't I Be Less in Love With You?" and the title song. It's been running since August 1, 1996, and makes a perfect couples show, although kids under 15 should probably see something else.

Revue. 407 West 43rd St. (between Ninth and Tenth Aves.). Performance times 7 PM Tuesday; 8 PM Monday, Friday, and Saturday; 2:30 Wednesday and Saturday; 3 and 7:30 PM Sunday. No performance Thursday. Official website: www.loveperfectchange.com. Tickets by phone: 1-212-239-6200 in New York; 1-800-432-7250 elsewhere. Groups: 1-212-889-4300. Tickets online: www.telecharge.com. Ticket prices: $65–$75.

DEMOCRACY ON BROADWAY

The 1986 musical *The Mystery of Edwin Drood* was based on an unfinished murder mystery by Charles Dickens. Not knowing how the story was to have turned out, the authors wrote several different endings for the Broadway show, and at each performance the audience would vote on which ending would be played that day.

Gore Vidal's *The Best Man* is about a fictional presidential race. A 2000 revival of the play opened in the midst of that year's real-life campaign. The producers set up a voting booth in the lobby and let the audience members choose between George W. Bush and Al Gore. Gore won—at least on 48th Street.

Perfect Crime!, Duffy Theater—This tiny murder mystery has been running in the since April 18, 1987, and with the same leading lady, Catherine Russell, who plays a pistol-packing psychiatrist who sets out to murder a nosy detective investigating some suspicious deaths around her office. Russell also serves as production manager at the cozy Off-Broadway Duffy Theater (a former strip club) in the heart of Times Square. Warren Manzi's play is the second-longest running Off-Broadway show ever, second only to *The Fantasticks*. Great for mystery lovers from early teens, up.

Drama. 1553 Broadway (between 46th and 47th Sts.). Performance times: 8 PM Monday, Thursday, Friday, and Saturday; 2 PM Wednesday and Saturday. Box Office: 1-212-695-3401. Official website: www.perfect-crime.com. Order tickets online: www.ticketmaster.com/artist/804167. Tickets: $40.

Stomp, Orpheum Theatre—Fulfilling the strange human need to bang on things and make loud, funny noises, the cast of *Stomp* finds percussion everywhere in the world around, it. Brooms, bags, hub-caps, buckets, sink plugs, plungers, sand—even strike-anywhere matches—lend their voices to what's been described as a "percussive symphony." The cast also uses their own bodies to dance and add to the rhythmic sounds. The most successful avant-garde theatre piece ever, *Stomp* has been running since 1994. Because there is virtually no talking, this is a special favorite with non-English speaking theatrego-ers. Also good for kids.

Musical performance piece. 126 Second Ave. (between St. Mark's Place and 7th St.). Performance times: 8 PM Tuesday to Friday; 7 and 10:30 PM Saturday; 3 and 7 PM Sunday. No performance Monday. Box Office: 1-212-477-2477 or 1-212-307-4100. Group Sales: 1-800-677-1164 or 1-212-302-7000. Official website: www.stomponline.com. Tickets online: www.ticketmaster.com. Ticket prices: $35 & $60. Run Time: 1 hour and 45 minutes.

Tony n' Tina's Wedding, St. Luke's Church—The interactive the-atre experience that started the whole movement in 1988, and is still running Off-Broadway. People love weddings, and why not? Great food, lots of dancing, crazy ethnic relatives and the bright hope of the future for a pair of attractive young people. This theatre phenomenon allows you to pay, not only to see the whole thing, but to play the role of one of Tony or Tina's friends. It starts at a real church where you sit in real pews alongside the actors, who play two high-spirited Italian families. The action then moves down the block and across Eighth Avenue to a real restaurant where you eat, dance, and interact with the other audience members, and the actors, who behave like real in-laws. A one-of-a-kind experience, and very popular with groups.

Interactive Play. Wedding: 308 West 46th St. (between Eighth and Ninth Aves.); Reception: Vinny Black's Coliseum at the Edison Hotel, 221 West 46th St. (between Eighth Ave. and Broadway). Performance times: 7 PM Thursday, Friday, and Saturday. No performances Sunday through Wednesday. Box Office (also group sales): 1-718-210-3535. Official website: www.tonylovestina.com. Order tickets online: www.tonylovestina.com/tickets.cfm. Tickets: $85–$125, includes dinner and dancing.

If you're hoping to see one of the following long-running hit shows, sorry, they've all closed in recent years, though revivals are always a possibility: *Les Misérables*, *Cats* (despite its longstanding advertising slogan, "Now and forever!"), *Miss Saigon*, *A Chorus Line*, and *The Fantasticks*.

50 BROADWAY TIPS YOU NEED TO KNOW

1. What's the difference between Broadway and Off-Broadway? Chapter Two, page 15

2. How can I tell if I'll like a show? Chapter Two, page 18

3. How can I tell if my significant other will like it? Chapter Two, page 18

4. Where can I see reviews of shows the morning after they open? Chapter Two, page 20

5. Where can I get feedback from other theatregoers about a show I want to see? Chapter Two, page 23

6. Is there one central place in Times Square where I can buy tickets to all shows? Chapter Two, page 26

7. How do I know when my kids are ready to see a show? Chapter Two, page 28

8. What's the difference between "Orchestra," "Mezzanine" and "Balcony" seats? Chapter Three, page 31

9. What's so great about box seats anyway? Chapter Three, page 31

10. What are the different ways to buy tickets? Chapter Three, page 34

11. What's the best way to buy tickets at the box office? Chapter Three, page 34

12. Is it worthwhile to use a scalper? Chapter Three, page 40

13. What times of year are slow? Chapter Three, page 41

14. How can I get tickets for sold-out shows? Chapter Three, page 42

END OF THE LINE?

New York Shakespeare Festival boss Joseph Papp almost pulled the plug on the project that became *A Chorus Line* because a workshop presentation ran more than five hours long. He was persuaded to give the show a second workshop, where cuts brought the running time down to about two hours and forty minutes, and resulted in a show that won the Tony and the Pulitzer, and became, for a time, the longest running show in Broadway history.

ABOUT THE AUTHOR

Robert Viagas founded the consumer news services for Playbill On-Line and Theatre.com/BroadwayOnline.com. He is co-author of *On the Line: The Creation of "A Chorus Line"* and *The Amazing Story of "The Fantasticks,"* and editor of Louis Botto's *At This Theatre*. He wrote librettos to the musicals *City of Light* and *In a Perfect World*. He is Program Director of Playbill Broadcast (for which he has written more than one hundred scripts broadcast on Sirius Satellite Radio), Editor of Playbill Books, editor of the annual special Playbill for the Tony Awards, and host of the annual webcasts of the Tony Awards. He has spent more than 2,000 nights at the theatre.

Author Robert Viagas in his favorite spot.

INDEX